"This superb guidebook deals with the largely unaddressed topic of helping parents assist their emerging adults into independence. All the issues a parent and their teen/young adults will confront in this transition are here, are well covered, and loaded with sound advice on how to address them. The authors have decades of experience in helping families, teens, and young adults with ADHD through this phase of life and, fortunately they have chosen to share all their wisdom with you here. There is no better book on this topic."

Russell A. Barkley, *Clinical Professor of Psychiatry,*
Virginia Commonwealth University Medical School, USA

"The topics presented in *Successfully Launching into Young Adulthood* are so on target for teens and adults as they enter the real world, which may not always be understanding of their needs. With excellent guidance and practical strategies to help parents support their adolescence as they navigate to transition, this book describes a multitude of postsecondary options and an accurate assessment of the tools a student needs to be successful. I found the honest experience of two parents who have been there, done that, to be exhilarating, encouraging, and most helpful."

Beverly H. Johns, *Learning and Behavior Consultant, Former Public School*
Administrator, Retired Professional Fellow, McMurray College, USA

"Finally, a book for parents who need help guiding our kids as they navigate the transition into adulthood and independence. The authors provide excellent information on next steps after high school graduation, including challenges, solutions, and resources. As mothers of sons with ADHD, Dendy and Hughes speak from their rich personal and professional experiences. The authors give us hope for the future of our kids, and assurances that we can survive the struggle. I highly recommend this book."

Belynda Gauthier, *Past President, CHADD National Board of Directors, Louisiana*
Capital Area CHADD Coordinator, and parent of two young adults with ADHD, USA

T0383603

Successfully Launching into Young Adulthood with ADHD

This new edition of *Successfully Launching into Young Adulthood with ADHD* provides firsthand guidance for both parents and professionals to help teens prepare for a bright future after high school.

The advice and strategies outlined in this book are evidence based and provide much-needed guidance to parents and the professionals who educate, coach and treat these students. This guidance will ensure that teens are ready to meet upcoming challenges and demands after high school graduation. With an always hopeful and personable message, the authors share their own and other parents' insights on avoiding common missteps, the perils of a premature launch to college and finding what works for their unique child. Updated chapters include a discussion around medications and new information on gap year programs, and college accommodations.

This top-notch guide is essential reading for any parent raising a young adult with ADHD and for the professionals who work with them.

Chris A. Zeigler Dendy is a best-selling author, educator, school psychologist and mental health professional with more than 40 years' experience. She is also the mother of three children with ADHD, LD, and executive function deficits. Chris was the lead author for CHADD's *ADHD Educator's Manual* and cofounder of their Teacher to Teacher training program. In 2014, she received CHADD's prestigious Lifetime Achievement Award for her leadership and contributions to the field, and in 2006, she was inducted into CHADD's Hall of Fame.

Ruth Hughes has been a national leader in the field of attention-deficit hyperactivity disorder for many years. During her tenure as the CEO of CHADD, Dr. Hughes advocated with Congress and the federal government to ensure the rights and access to treatment for children and adults with ADHD. She instituted the widely recognized Parent to Parent Training Program, which has helped thousands of parents learn to manage ADHD in the family. Now semiretired, she works with students with disabilities at Howard Community College in Columbia, Maryland.

Successfully Launching into Young Adulthood with ADHD

Firsthand Guidance for Parents and Educators Supporting Children with Neurodevelopmental Differences

Second Edition

Chris A. Zeigler Dendy and Ruth Hughes

Routledge
Taylor & Francis Group

NEW YORK AND LONDON

Second edition published 2024
by Routledge
605 Third Avenue, New York, NY 10158

and by Routledge
4 Park Square, Milton Park, Abingdon, Oxon, OX14 4RN

Routledge is an imprint of the Taylor & Francis Group, an informa business

First edition published by Woodbine House 2021

Library of Congress Cataloging-in-Publication Data
Names: Zeigler Dendy, Chris A., author. | Hughes, Ruth Ann, 1949- author.
Title: Successfully launching into young adulthood with ADHD : firsthand
guidance for parents and educators supporting children with
neurodevelopmental differences / Chris A. Zeigler Dendy, Ruth Hughes.
Other titles: Launching into young adulthood with ADHD
Description: Second edition. | New York, NY : Routledge, 2024. | Includes
bibliographical references and index.
Identifiers: LCCN 2023016447 (print) | LCCN 2023016448 (ebook) | ISBN
9781032427454 (hardback) | ISBN 9781032427430 (paperback) | ISBN
9781003364092 (ebook)
Classification: LCC RC394.A85 Z45 2024 (print) | LCC RC394.A85 (ebook) |
DDC 618.92/8589--dc23/eng/20230527
LC record available at https://lccn.loc.gov/2023016447
LC ebook record available at https://lccn.loc.gov/2023016448

ISBN: 978-1-032-42745-4 (hbk)
ISBN: 978-1-032-42743-0 (pbk)
ISBN: 978-1-003-36409-2 (ebk)

DOI: 10.4324/9781003364092

Typeset in Sabon
by SPi Technologies India Pvt Ltd (Straive)

Contents

Acknowledgments   *ix*

1 A Message of Hope   1

2 Bumps and Challenges That Lie Ahead   12

3 Ensure Success at School   26

4 Nurturing Self-Esteem and Natural Talents   42

5 Getting Along with Others   54

6 Managing Anxiety and Depression   62

7 Navigating the Middle and High School Years   78

8 Exploring Careers Through Firsthand Experiences   89

9 Helping Teens and Young Adults Find Their Passion   96

10 Decisions, Decisions: Options After High School Graduation   108

11 Is College the Right Option for Your Teen (Now)?   116

12 Creating Your Own Personalized Gap Year Plan   126

13 What's the Best College Option for Your Teen?   135

14 Community College: Two-Year Professional and Technical Programs   140

15 Selecting and Applying to a College   148

16 Helping Your Teen Succeed in College   157

17 Helping Your Son or Daughter Launch a Career   167

18 Signs That Trouble May Be Brewing at Work   177

19 Hitting the Speed Bumps of Life   187

20 Our Photo Gallery of Hope   201

    Appendix 1: ADHD Iceberg Form   206
    Appendix 2: Academic and Behavioral Performance Rating Scale   207
    Appendix 3: College Readiness Survey   208
    Appendix 4: Sample Gap Year Plans   212
    Appendix 5: Gap Year Planning Form   217
    Resources   219
    Index   225

Acknowledgments

Special thanks go to our sons, Alex, Christopher and Steven, who have allowed us to tell their stories and share many personal moments.

Thanks to the many parents and young people with ADHD who have participated in our surveys and panel presentations. We are grateful that they were willing to share their stories with us, including the lessons they learned on this journey.

Thank you to CHADD, ADDA and ADDA-SR for supporting and educating us all, plus being there early and often when so little was known about ADHD.

Thank you to the many researchers and clinicians who have shed light on the seriousness of this disorder and the importance of treatment.

Thank you to Dr. Russell Barkley for providing input regarding our parent survey during the early development of our book.

Finally, a special thank-you to our editors, Susan Stokes, Alexis Morgan and Alex Andrews, who understand our message and make our writing so much better.

1   A Message of Hope

It can be hard for any parent to think much about their child's future when they are caught up in the daily routine of getting their kids fed, dressed and off to school, with homework completed and everything they need in their backpacks. When you have a child or teen with ADHD, it's even easier to get caught up in living from day to day. On top of what other parents are dealing with, you also have to closely monitor your child's homework and grades, keep up with doctor visits and medication refills, check to see if your child remembered to take his meds, fight for a Section 504 or IEP educational plan and ensure that the plan is implemented, attend parent-teacher meetings and field an occasional "bad news" phone call from school. Just getting to the end of the week with your sanity intact may feel like a major accomplishment.

When your hands are full just dealing with current problems, you may tell yourself that you will have plenty of time later to plan for the future. But unfortunately, this isn't the case: children grow up much too quickly, and when your child has ADHD, there are crucial transitions on the way to a successful adulthood that you need to plan for ahead of time. If you have an older teen and some of those transitions have not gone as well as you might have hoped, don't despair. There is still plenty you can do to help with the transition to additional education after high school and pursuit of a satisfying career.

Overview of Key Transitions Across the Lifespan

Transitions are often difficult for children with ADHD or learning disabilities beginning in elementary school, continuing through middle and high school and right on into young adulthood. However, the transition from high school to post–high school training or college and then into the adult work world may be by far the most challenging for our teens.

Home to Preschool and Kindergarten: The first transition is from home to preschool or kindergarten. For children with ADHD and late birthdays, pushing kindergarten entry is often a mistake. These children are likely to enter kindergarten at a disadvantage, often struggling to keep up academically with their classmates.

According to a Stanford University study, 79 percent of students with ADHD had impaired school readiness compared with only 13 percent of students without ADHD (Perrin et al., 2019). Children with ADHD showed no impairment in general knowledge and cognitive ability: they knew their letters, numbers and colors. However, they were far more likely to have difficulties related to delays in brain maturity. In particular, they tended to be slower to develop executive function skills such as starting and finishing schoolwork, remembering chores and memorizing math facts. The areas of social and emotional development, language and motor development and physical well-being were also delayed.

DOI: 10.4324/9781003364092-1

Middle School: Next comes the middle school challenge with its increased demands for strong executive skills, such as being on time, getting organized and memorizing rote memorization of information such as math facts or foreign languages. Parents often describe the middle school years as "hitting a brick wall." Because the brain maturity of most children with ADHD is delayed, many of these students are unable to meet increased demands for independently completing their schoolwork without being prompted.

High School: The third key transition is to high school. The same challenges that surface in middle school follow students with ADHD into high school, and there are increased academic demands and increased expectations from adults.

Assuming Adult Responsibilities: Finally, perhaps the most difficult transition is assuming adult responsibilities before your brain is fully ready for the challenge. For too many young people with ADHD, the dramatic increase in expectations coupled with a significant drop in support can feel like falling off a cliff if they're not yet ready for next steps.

We Have Lived This Experience and Our Sons Are Thriving … Finally!

Throughout the book, we may speak to you in the first person because we have struggled through this difficult process ourselves—and we were considered "experts." That's why we've written the book: so you can avoid our mistakes. Both of us are parents of grown children with ADHD who have struggled to find their career path after high school. Plus, we've also faced the daunting challenge of being single parents.

In addition to our lived experience, we both bring extensive professional experience and, more importantly, in-depth knowledge of ADHD science, treatment, research and educational issues. Yet, even with our extensive knowledge and experience, we felt overwhelmed at times during the years when our sons were making the transitions to adulthood just described. Because of the knowledge we gained and the lessons we learned over the last 30 years, we can offer helpful guidance to you as your child or teen makes each of these transitions.

As an added bonus, we have enriched the book with information gathered from a survey of over a hundred veteran parents of grown children with ADHD. The questions we asked gave us greater insights and clarified some key issues that must be addressed. In the parent comments featured throughout the book, these parents offer sage advice regarding what they wished they had known or had done differently when their children were younger.

Two Critical Issues: Two key concerns surfaced repeatedly in our parent survey responses: the importance of *maintaining a strong positive relationship* with your teen despite the ups and downs of these tough transition years (Barkley, 2015); and the significant impact of *not adequately treating anxiety*, which later often becomes a major stumbling block to successfully transitioning to adult life (Denckla, 2019).

We both have long bemoaned the fact that there is little research and limited guidance for parents to help their teens launch successfully into young adulthood. So we co-wrote this book based upon limited available research plus lessons learned from our own family struggles. We hope readers find our information helpful as they guide their own teenagers on this journey to adulthood.

Is It a "Normal Maturation ADHD Process" or a "Failure to Launch"?

Some parents, teens and other family members perceive our children's struggles to reach independence as a "failure to launch." Consequently, both parents and the teen may blame this failure on themselves. Both may feel guilty, disappointed and fearful of the future.

They often don't take into consideration the impact that ADHD has on brain maturation. The fact is, brains mature more slowly in most people with ADHD, and the part of the brain that is most delayed, the prefrontal cortex, is the most crucial in making adult decisions, planning, organizing and anticipating consequences (Shaw et al. 2007).

One young adult, a college graduate who was indecisive about a career choice, said, "I feel like such a failure, because I look at all my friends, and they've moved on to great jobs and are making good money. Meanwhile, I'm stuck working as an office manager and hardly making any money."

Both of us wholeheartedly reject the use of the term *failure to launch* because it inaccurately portrays the significant challenges many of our children must overcome. It's not a failure at all, but rather delayed brain maturity and timing issues. Some young adults take longer to reach adult milestones than others. And forcing these young adults to tackle milestones before they are ready can often lead to disaster. They are our "late bloomers," but they *will* bloom if we help them prepare for next steps and allow them the time to mature.

Late Bloomers: The Power of Patience in a World Obsessed with Early Achievement

Rich Karlgaard, author of the book of the same title, was himself a "late bloomer" and offers encouragement to those who were not "early bloomers":

Late bloomers tend to be more of an explorer type. I do poorly when I'm under competitive pressure. I do much better when I explore my curiosity. It's the difference between feeling being pushed—which I don't like and I think a lot of people don't like—versus being pulled by some vision and dream and higher purpose.

In his discussion of human cognitive development, Karlgaard explains that "in our 30s, 40s, and 50s we began to develop a whole range of skills we didn't have before: executive functioning, management skills, compassion, equanimity. Then wisdom really begins to kick in and our 50s, 60s, and 70s."

(Karlgaard is the publisher of *Forbes* magazine)

Rather than viewing late bloomers with ADHD as experiencing a failure to launch, we suggest reframing your thinking in light of scientific evidence and instead viewing this as a *common maturation process* in those with ADHD (Denckla, 2019). We hear concerns about delays in launching into adulthood far too often from veteran parents with grown children. Truthfully, we both held unrealistic expectations for how quickly our sons would mature and thus faced these same stresses, disappointments and fears for the future that you may be experiencing now. But the most important thing to remember is that our late bloomers do blossom. It may take longer, and for a fraction of our kids, a lot longer. But they do mature and achieve typical adult milestones over time.

Our primary *take-home message* is for parents and educators to learn more about delayed ADHD brain maturity and executive function deficits and then set realistic expectations for their teens. Although it will be difficult, stay positive; keep in mind that ADHD brains continue to mature into the 30s and for some into their 40s (Denckla, 2019). Over time, your teen will develop key skills needed to succeed as an adult. One of the more difficult challenges is to recognize that you'll need to *provide more guidance and support, for longer,* for your teen than for other teens and young adults. This is one of those major lessons that we have learned in hindsight and felt was extremely important to share with readers who are not as far along in this parenting journey.

Reframe Expectations

As mentioned earlier, one of our major challenges will be to *reframe our thinking and expectations* for teens after high school and understand that being a late bloomer is typical of many young people with ADHD. Teens with ADHD are doing exactly what they must do to mature and work through these tough years. So, parents have to make a special effort to reduce the fear and embarrassment each of them feels. Parents must reassure your teen: "Yes, this is a difficult time, but I'll always be here for you. We'll figure this out together." Here are some ways to maintain a positive attitude:

- Read scientifically accurate books on ADHD.
- Attend ADHD seminars, workshops or conferences.
- Watch ADHD-related webinars or podcasts.
- Talk with other parents of children with ADHD.
- Educate your parents, relatives and teachers about ADHD.
- If possible, find an ADHD parent support group.
- Most importantly, really listen to your son or daughter. Often they're trying to tell us what they're ready for in words or actions.

Another important reason to reframe thinking is that if you have unrealistic expectations that are beyond your teen's maturity and capabilities, this can lead to high levels of stress. In turn, stress and anxiety *can actually delay* your son's or daughter's brain maturation and the development of key executive skills such as organization, memory and planning ahead, according to Martha Bridge Denckla, MD, a leading pediatric neuropsychologist and researcher on ADHD and executive functions at the Kennedy Krieger Institute, Johns Hopkins (Denckla, 2019).

Anticipating the Challenges that Lie Ahead

Several potential challenges face our children as they grow up: academic difficulties related to attention and memory deficits, social rejection and the demands of transitioning into young adulthood. As students graduate from high school, the supports of childhood disappear just as the expectations for performance dramatically increase. These years may be punctuated by unsettling ups and downs. Some teens become so demoralized that they get stuck in a paralysis of sorts and hesitate to make any career decisions for fear of making a mistake.

Our late bloomers often don't have the maturity or necessary skills to juggle the demands at this major life transition point. Many parents find it wise to allow a year or two after high school as a midpoint safety net. A formal or personally designed *gap year program* may provide the safety net your teen needs. A gap year allows time for a young adult to mature and develop skills needed to succeed in the work world. Gap year programs are discussed in more detail in later chapters.

Parents and teachers can help teens prepare for these big transitions and make the process easier. A parent's ultimate objective is to see his or her children grow up and become happy, productive adults. Our goal is to give parents and educators the tools to help teens reach these objectives.

PC: During the teen years we parents often worry and worry some more.[1]

Chris's Lessons Learned: Our son, Alex (Figure 1.1) struggled so much in high school, I couldn't help but worry about what the future held for him. He had such difficulty simply meeting the day-to-day responsibilities of handling his schoolwork and chores. How would he ever be successful in life? My husband and I worried: Would he ever graduate from high school? Would he be able to hold a job? Would he be living with us forever? I couldn't begin to tell you how worried we were. In retrospect, we realized that we weren't the only parents who were worried sick about the future. So many of our fellow parents were also worried to death, somewhat baffled, and they didn't always know how to help their children.

Figure 1.1 Chris Dendy and son, Alex Zeigler.

Figure 1.2 Ruth Hughes and son, Christopher.

Ruth's Lessons Learned: My son Christopher (Figure 1.2) languished in community college for four years without passing his math requirements. We both agreed it was time for something different. I wasn't paying any more tuition, and he didn't want to be in community college anyway. He spent six months working with small children in an orphanage in Thailand. This was a life-changing experience for him. It was as if a switch had been turned on. He came home, tackled his classes, transferred to a four-year school and, two years later, graduated magna cum laude in parks and recreation.

I didn't stop to think that maybe I had pushed him into college when he wasn't ready. However, that's exactly what I had done without even realizing it. Nor did I recognize at the time that the extra years, the wonderful experience of working with these orphaned children and living in another country, were all helping him to mature and be ready for the next steps. If I could go back in time, I would be much more supportive of his needs and give him the time to explore and learn about the world before insisting that he go to college and take on adult responsibilities.

PC: *From the late teen years through young adulthood, both of my sons struggled in college. Later, when one son struggled to find a satisfying career path, we were uncertain how to best help him. Finding a balance between how much we should nudge him or whether we should back off was very difficult. Looking back on each of our sons' lives from the early years to adulthood, we both wondered if there was anything we could have done differently to make their launch into adulthood any easier.*

PC: *I wish I had aggressively sought an appropriate education for her at a younger age—say third or fourth grade. I was talked out of getting help sooner by the school. I do think that as a teen grows older and feels less accepted and more out of it, it hurts and has tough repercussions. I think I would have tried to create a more hospitable environment at the school much earlier than ninth grade—by then there was already a lot of trauma.*

PC: *I wish we had gotten an earlier diagnosis. It would have saved lots of tears and frustration.*

PC: *My son got stuck while attending community college for too many years with no direction or idea of what he wanted to do in the world. He was drifting and not moving toward independence and adult roles. What was I doing wrong and how could I help him move on?*

The answer to this last parent's question—whether you can help your teen move on to a successful adulthood—is a resounding YES. Helping a teen with ADHD launch successfully into adulthood is a long-term process that we believe should begin early, ideally in elementary school. *Seeking optimal treatment for ADHD* as soon as possible and *ensuring success in school* are two critical actions parents must take. Obviously, the earlier you are aware of potential challenges, the better.

Distressing Delays and Detours

Many of our late-blooming children will take much longer than usual to mature and launch into adulthood. Throughout your lifetime, your family may face many ups and downs, although thankfully crises will get fewer and farther between as your son or daughter matures. Parenting a teen with ADHD is often an exhausting, lonely job. Many parents feel inadequate, isolated and unsupported by family, friends and even professionals who don't understand the complexities of living with the disorder. Consequently, parents may feel a chronic sense of sorrow and regret that reoccurs in waves throughout the years. You may also go through periods of sadness about how difficult life has been for your teen and experience repeated cycles of self-regret—"if only … I had known this earlier … requested an IEP right away … started medication sooner …"

Marie Paxon, a parent and former CHADD president, shared these words of wisdom:

> Sometimes when our initial reaction is disappointment, fear, regret, or questioning how to move forward, we feel guilty for not being a cheerleader at all times. Which is unrealistic to expect to always be positive and supportive; especially when this journey is so exhausting. Most of us experience an undeniable sadness that our kids' lives are so much harder than others, and it occupies our minds.

Parenting a child or teen with ADHD is not easy for even the most highly trained professionals. An experienced psychiatrist once observed, "I'm so glad I had the opportunity to raise 'an easy child' in addition to my teen with ADHD. Otherwise, I would have always doubted my parenting skills." Obviously, there are no simple parenting or counseling answers. We all struggle to find the best way to help our children. This book provides reassurance that you are not alone, and that there are steps you can take to help your teen succeed.

Chris's and Ruth's Lessons Learned: Expect feelings of self-doubt and emotional ups and downs. At times we both experienced overwhelming self-doubt regarding our parenting approaches. Raising our sons with ADHD was unquestionably the most humbling and challenging experience of our lives. Even with our combined experiences as a veteran teacher, psychologist, mental health counselor and administrator with over 30 years' experience, we often felt inadequate and second-guessed our parenting decisions.

So, we offer this analogy: Parenting children or teens with ADHD is often compared to riding a roller coaster. There are many highs and lows, laughs and tears, and breathtaking and terrifying experiences. These peaks and valleys of emotions may occur at any transition juncture: when moving on to middle school, high school or postsecondary education, and even when starting a job.

Advice for the Road Ahead

You can't always parent "by the book." As treatment professionals, both of us had studied best-practice parenting strategies. These parenting strategies seemed to work well for most of the children and teens with whom we worked. But using these strategies with our boys was often a different story. We both quickly became humbled "experts" and had to scramble to come up with other solutions. Of course, try best-practice parenting first, but if a strategy isn't working, you'll have to come up with a more creative solution.

For example, let's start with the *logic* behind the use of logical consequences: if your teen fails a course, he'll have to attend summer school, and then he'll learn his lesson. Well, guess what? That doesn't work, because most young people with ADHD don't learn from rewards and punishments as easily as other students do (Barkley, 2015).

Here are a couple of basic principles about behavioral strategies (Barkley, 2015): More effective consequences occur immediately. For example, if all weekly homework is not completed, the student can't join his friends for Saturday outings until the work is completed (Denckla, 2019). Punishment does not increase brain neurotransmitters or white matter, or teach needed skills. So having your teen attend summer school a month after failing a class in May isn't an effective strategy to change his academic focus when he starts back to school in the fall. Chris's son had unidentified learning disabilities and deficits in executive functions, so after summer school, he returned to the classroom with good intentions but didn't have the skills to do well academically. Without support, he would again find himself failing classes.

Proven "by-the-book" strategies just don't always work with our teens. So, throughout the book you will find comments about the ideal way that both you and your teen *should* handle a situation—for example, he *should* remember and do his homework, and he *should* complete and submit his college application on his own. After giving by-the-book advice, we'll also sometimes give you a *"Get Real" Tip*.

Keep in mind that different teens with ADHD function with different levels of brain maturity and readiness. Some will be ready to work independently on their own and take on greater personal responsibility, thus making your parenting job easier. But other teens will not be ready and will require greater parental involvement. So, we'll share the approaches we actually had to use that sometimes ran counter to our training.

Prepare to deal with criticism from others who give well-intended parenting advice without any real knowledge of ADHD.

Don't let others guilt-trip you. Never let others make you feel guilty about being supportive and doing whatever your child needs to succeed. Keep in mind that he will need greater support and guidance than his same-age peers, and you'll be guiding him longer than you think you should, and would like. Your comfort level with supporting him as he takes a different path is essential to his self-esteem. If he senses your embarrassment, it will compound his sense of failure.

Our goal for this book is to provide *guidance that is guilt-free*. We all do the very best job that we can to help our children. However, no one gave us a step-by-step instruction manual for parenting our children with ADHD. Raising these children makes some of us feel as though we are walking a tightrope, without a mat or a balance pole, hanging on for dear life. Parenting your son or daughter may well be the toughest but most satisfying job you will ever have.

PC: *Her college performance has really rocked her self-confidence. She needed more structure. I listened to others and let her "do it on her own." I do now believe that a "helicopter mom" is what is needed while we wait for her brain development to catch up with her peers'.*

Ignore derogatory parent labels born of ignorance, such as "helicopter parent," "codependent" and "enabler." Because of lack of ADHD education, your parents and well-meaning friends and teachers may be judgmental and unsupportive of your parenting approach. Some of them may even use these terms to tell you you're doing this all wrong.

Not only are these judgmental words wrong, but they are also hurtful and very difficult to ignore. Derogatory terms simply place blame and shame on parents, induce guilt and, worst of all, are not instructive. Comments like these don't tell parents how to help their teen.

In reality, parents are simply being pragmatic and providing what their teen needs to succeed—*developmentally age-appropriate supervision* (Barkley) 2015). Just remember to trust your gut instincts; you know your teen better than anyone else does. So, give yourself permission to provide your teen the extra supports he or she needs to succeed.

Perhaps the worst consequence of negatively labeling parents is that they hesitate to step in and help their child or teen when it's really needed. Understandably, they fear being judged as a "helicopter parent."

Chris's Lessons Learned: A mom/teacher friend of mine once told me her daughter needed help to pass algebra, but she didn't want to be a "helicopter parent." Her daughter was tackling college algebra again after having failed the class twice. So, I asked the mom, "Did failing the class twice help your daughter pass the class?" Of course, the answer was no. So, I gave her permission to help her daughter—who, by the way, finally passed algebra after they found a creative solution to the problem. The mother took the class with her daughter and was her study partner.

Periodically assess your level of involvement. It's important to continually assess your level of involvement and support, allowing your child or teen to do as much for himself as possible and gradually reducing your support. Ultimately, your goal is to work yourself out of your current parenting job. Otherwise, you deny your teen the opportunity to build confidence in his ability to handle whatever challenges lie ahead. Our children build their self-esteem and brain maturity by assuming increased responsibility.

Of course, the conundrum is to know when the "right time" is to maintain or reduce your involvement. If your child is failing miserably, it's not time to let go. Give yourself permission to provide a loving safety net when needed. Also realize that at times, you may do too little or too much. We parents are always searching for the right balance. Just keep the long-term goal in mind—teaching your young person to function independently.

Chris's Lessons Learned: When my son entered high school, I crossed my fingers and hoped he could be successful on his own. However, I quickly realized this was a mistake. When the consequences of failure are too severe, finding a way to intervene and minimize the damage is critical. For example, when my son was failing five of six classes in his freshman year of high school, I realized that his self-esteem would never survive the consequences of failing all five classes. I knew from experience that he would become extremely depressed, give up, basically shut down and never recover from these failures. Our intervention was to allow him to make up any missed homework assignments and tests. As a result, he failed only one class. As you've already guessed, attending summer school didn't teach the lesson the school hoped for, because consequences that are delayed several months are often ineffective for children with ADHD.

Prepare to make the transition from boss to mentor and partner. Another parenting challenge is to shift their role from telling the child what to do and making decisions for him to discussing issues with him and asking his opinion. Obviously, each young person is unique, so this shift will be done gradually over time and be determined by the teen's level of maturity. As the teen gets older, try providing the information and structure, then encouraging him to make the choices.

"Get Real" Tip: Most people with ADHD need external reminders throughout their lifetimes for important responsibilities such as appointments, college or work assignments and money management. For example, they need emailed alerts to pay bills online or a phone reminder that a term paper is due next Friday. Eventually, as they continue to mature, they'll provide more of their own reminders, but in the meantime, it helps for parents to set up a "safety net reminder system" to address their son's or daughter's deficits in executive skills as they transition through young adulthood. Given the lifelong importance of relying on external reminder systems, parents must introduce their children to these tools and help them practice using them until they become an everyday habit.

Our Message of Hope for Parents

We both bring you a message of hope based upon our parenting experiences. Our sons are grown now, doing work they love, enjoying meaningful relationships, and feeling good about themselves and their accomplishments. Helping our sons reach this level of happiness and success wasn't easy and was fraught with major ups and downs. We wrote this book to share our personal stories and the sometimes-painful lessons we've learned in hopes we can provide other parents with much-needed guidance.

The educational information we offer in this book will help both parents and educators create a solid foundation so the child can succeed in school, launch successfully after high school and develop key skills necessary for making it in the adult world. In addition, we offer strategies to help identify vocational interests and potential career paths before high school graduation. We also provide guidelines to help make the transition years after high school into young adulthood less challenging. Finally, for inspiration, we have scattered photos of some amazing young people with ADHD throughout the book without regard to chapter title and collected even more pictures in a Gallery of Hope at the end of the book.

PC: I would advise parents to see advocating as a lifelong parental job.

Once you are armed with the information in this book, we hope you'll be more confident in providing the extra supports and guidance your child or teen needs as you face each key transition point from middle school to high school graduation and beyond. Although this will be a long and sometimes challenging journey, we wish for you the same results we enjoy as parents today. Our sons have become the happy, productive young adults we always hoped and knew they could be. Best wishes on your journey.

Note

1 Comments shared by parents who completed our survey ("Parent Comments") appear in italics and are preceded by *PC*.

References

Barkley, R.A. (2015). *Attention deficit hyperactivity disorder* (4th ed.). New York: Guilford Press.

Denckla, M.B. (2019). *Understanding learning and related disabilities: Inconvenient brains*. New York: Routledge.

Perrin, H.T., Heller, N.A., & Low, J.M. (2019). School readiness in preschoolers with symptoms of attention-deficit hyperactivity disorder. *Pediatrics*. Published online 2019 August 1.

Shaw, P., Ekstrand, K., Sharp, W., & Rapoport, I.L. (2007, December 4). Attention deficit hyperactivity disorder characterized by a delay in cortical maturation. *Proceedings of the National Academy of Sciences (PNAS)*, 104(49) 19649–19654.

2   Bumps and Challenges That Lie Ahead

Although most of our children will cope successfully with ADHD, we parents worry, and worry some more, about their futures. Our "late-bloomer" children often take longer to mature and "grow up." Consequently, the development of skills critical for success in school, such as control of emotions, organizational skills, the ability to work independently, and plan ahead are delayed as much as 30 percent (Barkley, 2015). In other words, a 14-year-old may act more like someone who is 10 or 11. And an 18-year-old who is getting ready to leave home may actually have the maturity of a typical 15-year-old.

This lag in maturation has enormous implications for parents and educators. Realistically, parents especially must be prepared for the ADHD bumps and challenges that lie ahead and provide support and guidance longer than expected. However, rest assured, our children do grow up, continuing to take on more responsibilities and becoming more independent over time.

Chris's Lessons Learned: Looking back on my son's life from the early years to adulthood, I find myself wondering if there is anything I could have done differently to make his launch into adulthood any easier. From the late teen years through young adulthood, our son struggled to find a satisfying career path, while I stood by helplessly wanting to help but not knowing quite what to do. Having a young adult with ADHD who has struggled to launch into adulthood is a painful experience that many of my most passionate long-time CHADD friends have also shared. We all were worried sick, totally baffled, and didn't know how to help our children.

Parents can indeed do a lot to help their child or young adult be successful. In the following chapters, we'll discuss how parents can help our children surmount those challenges. First, let's review potential challenges for children and teens with ADHD.

What Does Research Tell Us About the Future of Teens with ADHD?

Rather than review each longitudinal research study on ADHD in adulthood, here's a general overview (Barkley, 2015). Roughly 75 to 85 percent of adults cope successfully with their ADHD. A small percentage of this number show little or no symptoms, but most face challenges in everyday living related to family, relationships, or work—for

DOI: 10.4324/9781003364092-2

instance, forgetting to pick up a child at daycare or pay bills, or being late to work and missing deadlines for work completion. Experts tell us that marital conflict in our families is common and results in a higher-than-average divorce rate. However, continued treatment of ADHD with medication, ADHD education, development of coping skills, and use of external supports and counseling if needed can reduce the likelihood of many of these problems.

The good news is that many of our young adults gravitate to careers that they love. Because their skill sets are a good match for their jobs, they are happy and excel at work. Partners who love, accept, and support your son or daughter can be a godsend. Chris's son found and married his soul mate when he was in his 40s. They work together every day and have become a successful real estate team.

A much smaller percentage of adults with ADHD face more serious challenges, such as drug or alcohol use, brushes with the law, or conditions that require psychiatric treatment. The people in this group are often those who never received any treatment as children or adolescents, received ineffective treatment, or have very complex coexisting conditions. Adults who have multiple disorders in combination, such as bipolar disorder, learning disabilities and anxiety, are more difficult to treat effectively and often encounter greater life challenges.

Specific Challenges Facing Young People with ADHD

ADHD is often much more complex than most people realize. Consequently, scientists no longer classify ADHD as a behavioral disorder (American Psychiatric Association, 2013). Rather, ADHD symptoms are classified as a *neurodevelopmental disorder*—in other words, key skills that are controlled by brain maturity, such as learning, memorizing, organizing and controlling emotions are delayed.

ADHD Rarely Occurs Alone

One factor complicating our children's lives is that ADHD seldom occurs alone and typically is accompanied by at least one other coexisting condition (Jensen et al., 1999). Perhaps the best way to visualize the complexities of this condition is through the image of the ADHD Iceberg that Chris and her son, Alex, created over 30 years ago. The ADHD Iceberg and an Iceberg worksheet are free to download from https://www.chrisdendy.com. In addition, free translations of the Iceberg are also available in Spanish, French, Portuguese, Arabic, Vietnamese, Japanese, and Greek.

According to a multiyear study conducted by the National Institutes of Health, over two-thirds of children diagnosed with ADHD (69 percent) have at least one other condition such as anxiety, depression or learning disabilities (Jensen et al.,1999). Another 50 percent may have a third challenge. The ADHD Iceberg identifies potential challenges that may be "hidden beneath the surface."

Our Parent Survey Results: *Eighty-nine percent had at least one coexisting challenge. Nearly 25 percent had two additional challenges.* (That is, children of the parents in our survey sample had a somewhat higher rate of coexisting conditions than found in the NIH study.)

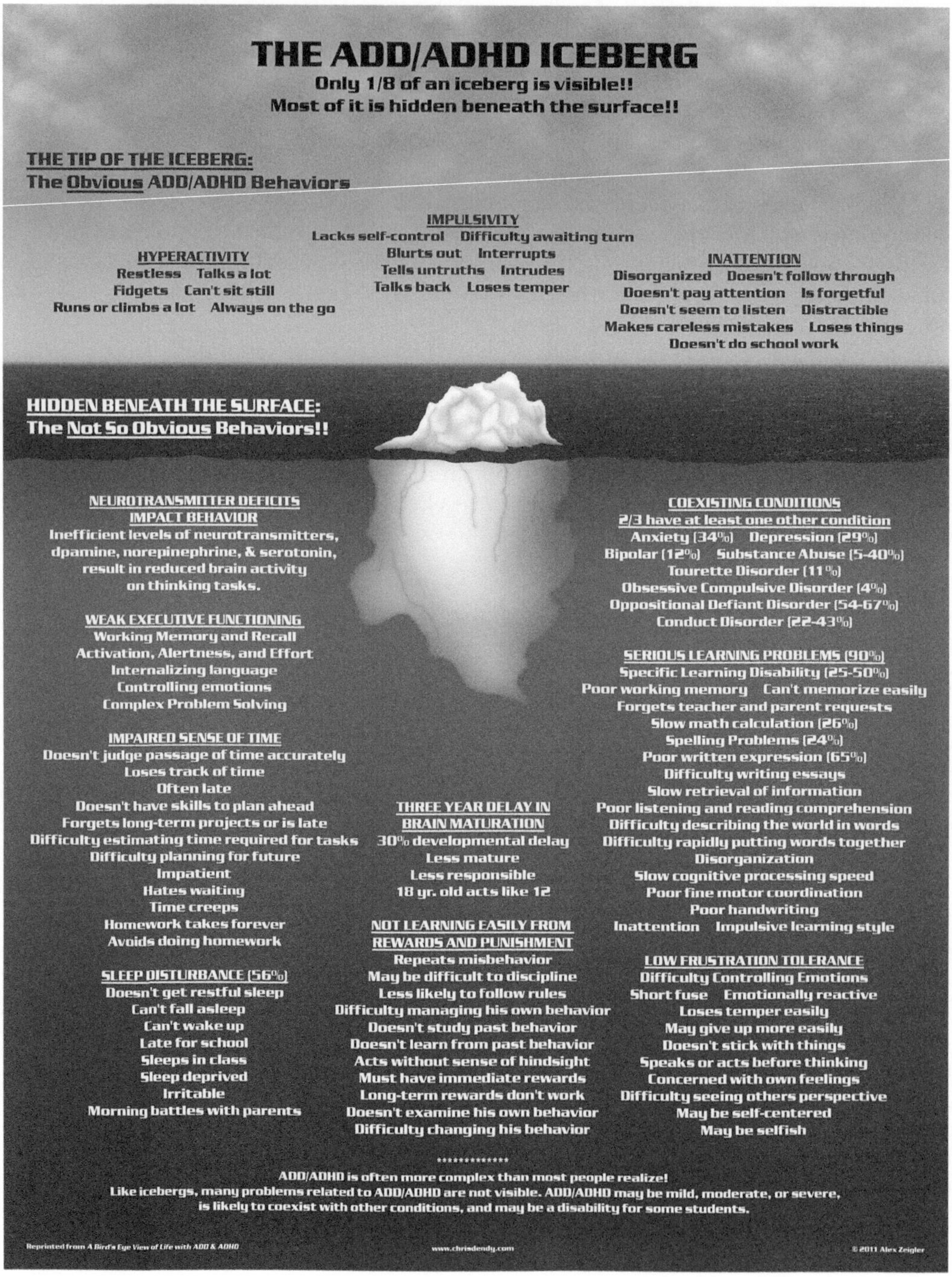

THE ADD/ADHD ICEBERG
Only 1/8 of an iceberg is visible!!
Most of it is hidden beneath the surface!!

THE TIP OF THE ICEBERG:
The Obvious ADD/ADHD Behaviors

IMPULSIVITY
Lacks self-control   Difficulty awaiting turn
Blurts out   Interrupts
Tells untruths   Intrudes
Talks back   Loses temper

HYPERACTIVITY
Restless   Talks a lot
Fidgets   Can't sit still
Runs or climbs a lot   Always on the go

INATTENTION
Disorganized   Doesn't follow through
Doesn't pay attention   Is forgetful
Doesn't seem to listen   Distractible
Makes careless mistakes   Loses things
Doesn't do school work

HIDDEN BENEATH THE SURFACE:
The Not So Obvious Behaviors!!

NEUROTRANSMITTER DEFICITS IMPACT BEHAVIOR
Inefficient levels of neurotransmitters,
dpamine, norepinephrine, & serotonin,
result in reduced brain activity
on thinking tasks.

WEAK EXECUTIVE FUNCTIONING
Working Memory and Recall
Activation, Alertness, and Effort
Internalizing language
Controlling emotions
Complex Problem Solving

IMPAIRED SENSE OF TIME
Doesn't judge passage of time accurately
Loses track of time
Often late
Doesn't have skills to plan ahead
Forgets long-term projects or is late
Difficulty estimating time required for tasks
Difficulty planning for future
Impatient
Hates waiting
Time creeps
Homework takes forever
Avoids doing homework

SLEEP DISTURBANCE (56%)
Doesn't get restful sleep
Can't fall asleep
Can't wake up
Late for school
Sleeps in class
Sleep deprived
Irritable
Morning battles with parents

THREE YEAR DELAY IN BRAIN MATURATION
30% developmental delay
Less mature
Less responsible
18 yr. old acts like 12

NOT LEARNING EASILY FROM REWARDS AND PUNISHMENT
Repeats misbehavior
May be difficult to discipline
Less likely to follow rules
Difficulty managing his own behavior
Doesn't study past behavior
Doesn't learn from past behavior
Acts without sense of hindsight
Must have immediate rewards
Long-term rewards don't work
Doesn't examine his own behavior
Difficulty changing his behavior

COEXISTING CONDITIONS
2/3 have at least one other condition
Anxiety (34%)   Depression (29%)
Bipolar (12%)   Substance Abuse (5-40%)
Tourette Disorder (11%)
Obsessive Compulsive Disorder (4%)
Oppositional Defiant Disorder (54-67%)
Conduct Disorder (22-43%)

SERIOUS LEARNING PROBLEMS (90%)
Specific Learning Disability (25-50%)
Poor working memory   Can't memorize easily
Forgets teacher and parent requests
Slow math calculation (26%)
Spelling Problems (24%)
Poor written expression (65%)
Difficulty writing essays
Slow retrieval of information
Poor listening and reading comprehension
Difficulty describing the world in words
Difficulty rapidly putting words together
Disorganization
Slow cognitive processing speed
Poor fine motor coordination
Poor handwriting
Inattention   Impulsive learning style

LOW FRUSTRATION TOLERANCE
Difficulty Controlling Emotions
Short fuse   Emotionally reactive
Loses temper easily
May give up more easily
Doesn't stick with things
Speaks or acts before thinking
Concerned with own feelings
Difficulty seeing others perspective
May be self-centered
May be selfish

••••••••••••
ADD/ADHD is often more complex than most people realize!
Like icebergs, many problems related to ADD/ADHD are not visible. ADD/ADHD may be mild, moderate, or severe,
is likely to coexist with other conditions, and may be a disability for some students.

Reprinted from *A Bird's Eye View of Life with ADD & ADHD*   www.chrisdendy.com   © 2011 Alex Zeigler

Figure 2.1 ADHD Iceberg.

Untreated coexisting conditions such as *anxiety, depression,* or *learning disabilities* are common among children and teens with ADHD (Jensen et al., 1999; Barkley, 2015). One of the surprising results of our parent survey was learning about the continuing negative impact of anxiety, particularly in young adulthood. Looking back on our own families, we both realized that our sons' anxiety was never adequately treated. If your teen's ADHD is being treated yet she continues to struggle, seek help from a healthcare professional to determine if a coexisting condition is compounding her struggles at school. Anxiety and depression are discussed in more detail in subsequent chapters.

Barkley (2015) states that *nearly half of children with ADHD have learning disabilities and over 90 percent also experience deficits in executive functions.* Consequently, these students often have trouble writing essays, remembering details of what they've read, completing complex, multi-step math (algebra), and, for some, noticeably slower reading, test taking, and homework completion. It's important for parents and educators to understand that deficits in executive functions are a key underlying factor contributing to these learning disabilities. Detailed guidance about these critical ADHD issues is available from the Resources listed at the end of this book.

Brain Maturity Is Delayed

One of the greatest challenges for children with ADHD is often the obvious one—the *delayed brain maturity,* which significantly affects executive skills such as getting started, following through, being on time, and planning ahead (Shaw et al., 2007).

Differences in Brain Maturation and Structure: Children with ADHD have a three- to five-year delay in brain maturation. Plus, a few sections of the brain are a bit smaller than average but are not damaged. Additionally, the ADHD brain shows reduced glucose levels (simple sugars) that are necessary for optimal brain function.

Developmental Delays: Dr. Russell Barkley (2015) explains that because their brains mature more slowly, children with ADHD experience up to a *30 percent developmental delay* in mastering life skills that are expected by a certain age. For example, we expect the average 12-year-old to remember homework assignments and to bring home needed materials. However, many students with ADHD struggle with this seemingly simple task. As shown in Table 2.1, a 12-year-old with ADHD may act more like a 9-year-old when it comes to executive function. Simply stated, *executive functions are like the CEO of the brain.* Executive functions guide a person's academic efforts and behavior.

Catching Up with Peers

Parents often ask, "Will my child ever catch up?" The good news is that young adult brains continue to mature into their 30s and 40s. And according to Martha Denckla, MD, a neuroscientist, and leading expert on executive function at Kennedy Krieger, our young adults reach a point in their 20s when their executive skills *"are good enough for life"* (Denckla, 2019). Unfortunately, the process just occurs much too slowly to suit parents of teenagers.

Table 2.1 A 30 Percent Developmental Delay in Executive Skills

<<30% Developmental Delay in Executive Age						
AGES: Chronological vs. Developmental						
Age in years	8	10	12	14	16	18
Maturation spurt early 20s	↓	↓	↓	↓	↓	↓	Delay impacts organization, independent work, emotions
Executive Age	5.5	7	8.4	9.8	11.2	12.6	Young adults may struggle during transition to work/ college

---

Ruth's Lessons Learned: Information about the developmental delay associated with ADHD has been and continues to be the most important information I ever learned. It helps me respond to my son more appropriately and not stress over little things that will improve over time.

Executive Function Deficits Affect School Performance and Behavior

A major challenge facing students with ADHD is that deficits in executive function skills have a *profound impact* on school performance and behavior, both at home and school. Simply described, the term *executive function* refers to the brain's ability to control our actions and behavior—whether it's remembering or memorizing information, getting started and finishing chores and homework, controlling emotions, or stopping to think before saying or doing things. Our executive functions serve a similar function as the conductor of an orchestra or the CEO of a business. According to Dr. Russell Barkley (2015), most children with ADHD—over 90 percent—have deficits in executive skills.

When it comes to academic performance, executive functions—particularly working memory—is, surprisingly, *a better predictor of school success than an IQ score.* For one family whose son was intellectually gifted, deficits in working memory were the primary reason that he struggled in most of his classes, much more so than the ADHD symptoms. (Working memory is the ability to hold information in mind, manipulate it in your head, and then easily retrieve needed information from memory.) The list of executive functions shown in Table 2.2 is adapted from leading experts on executive functions and ADHD (Barkley, 2015; Brown, 2014; Denckla, 2019; Gioia, 2001).

Our Parent Survey Results: *Forty percent of students struggled with specific learning disabilities. Over 25 percent had failed a grade.* This data is consistent with current research showing that 25–50 percent of students with ADHD have learning disabilities and 25–47 percent have failed a grade.

Ninety percent of students with ADHD struggle academically at some point in their school careers. A critical job for parents is to ensure school success. Parents should work with teachers to identify and address any hidden learning challenges, including deficits in executive skills, learning disabilities (writing essays, reading comprehension, memorization of basic math facts such as multiplication tables), and slow reading and writing (slow processing speed). School officials may not know about the need to evaluate students with ADHD for these difficulties. If needed, parents should consider outside tutoring to ensure their teen's academic skills are on grade level and that she develops good study skills.

Table 2.2 Components of Executive Functions

• Working memory (verbal and nonverbal) and recall • Internalized language; self-talk (verbal working memory) • Holding things in mind, visualizing the big picture, self-management of time (nonverbal working memory) • Initiating tasks, attending, sustaining effort, starting, finishing; processing speed • Analyzing, synthesizing, paraphrasing, summarizing	• Organizing thoughts such as is required when writing an essay, prioritizing, planning, and problem solving • Organizing possessions, notebooks, lockers, room • Emotional control • Inhibiting impulsive acts or words; shifting one thought/activity to another • Self-monitoring • Task monitoring • Task completion

For students who have done well in high school because of parental supports and structure provided at home, be aware that unstructured college life may be much more challenging, and so more support may be needed.

Our Parent Survey Results: *Twenty percent of students with ADHD received no additional supports at school.*

Reminders that your teen can "see or hear" are more effective. Because our children have limited working memory capacity, they need *external reminders*. In other words, the ADHD brain's memory is *unreliable* and doesn't always send messages telling the teen when to start homework or do chores (Barkley, 2015). So, a reminder that can be seen or heard, such as an alarm (on a cell phone, watch, computer, or stove), a Post-it note, or a reminder from a parent is a must.

The drawing in Figure 2.2 may help you visualize the challenge teens with ADHD face in using working memory. Working memory may be compared to "cognitive counter space," according to Claire Wurtzel, faculty member at Bank Street Graduate School, in her presentation at a national LDA conference. The ADHD counter space for memory is much smaller.

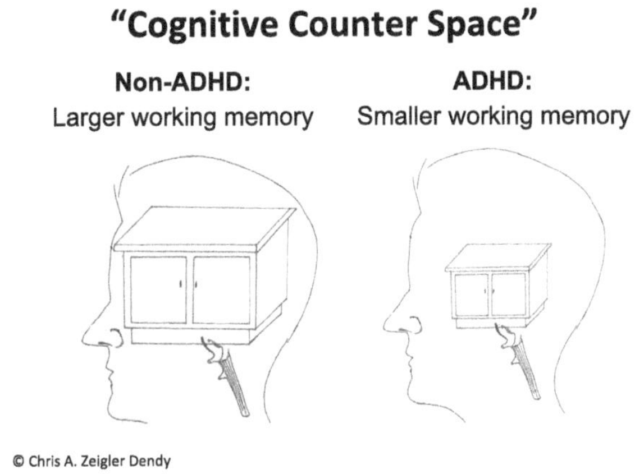

"Cognitive Counter Space"

Non-ADHD:
Larger working memory

ADHD:
Smaller working memory

© Chris A. Zeigler Dendy

Figure 2.2 Working memory skills compared with "cognitive counter space".

For example, children with ADHD typically can remember only two or three instructions at one time, whereas children without ADHD can remember five to nine items.

Consequently, parents and teachers must *reduce demands* on the student's working memory. For instance, if the goal is for students to find the answer to an algebra problem, provide a list of potential formulas so that the student can select the right formula to complete the problem. Tests that rely on *recognition* of the right formula are better indicators of a student's knowledge than tests that require cold memory recall of formulas.

Two categories of executive functions. Dendy (2017) divides executive functions into two categories: (1) *academic challenges* that are easily recognized and addressed by teachers, and (2) *academically related challenges* that appear to be simply choice or laziness, such as difficulty getting started. Informed teachers will put supports and structure in place to address the difficulties students with ADHD have with regard to following directions, being organized, getting started, and completing long-term projects.

Teachers easily recognize some executive function (EF) challenges as learning issues. These academic challenges are shown in Table 2.3. Teachers are generally willing to help students address these difficulties.

However, understanding the executive function challenges shown in Table 2.4 is more difficult because these traits often incorrectly appear to reflect a lack of effort. Chris refers to these traits as *academically related skills*. For many years, teachers have viewed these behaviors as a matter of choice or laziness rather than recognizing that executive skill deficits are the real culprits.

BEWARE of misconceptions! *These behaviors may look like choice or laziness, but they are actually deficits in executive functions.*

Executive functions are discussed in more detail in Dendy's *Teenagers with ADD, ADHD, and Executive Function Deficits* (2017).

PC: I'm embarrassed to think how angry I'd get when my son couldn't get started on his work. Now I realize that "getting started" is an important executive skill.

Table 2.3 Practical Impact of Executive Function Deficits on Academics

Academic Challenges:

- Writing essays or reports
- Completing complex math
- Reading comprehension
- Memorizing letters, numbers, words, multiplication tables, languages
- Completing long-term projects on time

Table 2.4 Practical Impact of EF Deficits on Academically Related Skills

Academically Related EF Challenges:

- Following directions
- Being organized
- Getting started and finishing work
- Remembering chores and assignments
- Analyzing and problem solving
- Planning for the future
- Controlling emotions

Underdiagnosis of ADHD Is Common

ADHD is often underdiagnosed in girls, minorities, intellectually gifted students, and children with other diagnoses such as a learning disability or autism. (Quinn & Madhoo, 2014). So be alert and take a second look at all the children in your family to see if any of them may fall into this category. Chapter 3 contains more detailed information on underdiagnosis of ADHD in girls.

PC: *Get a diagnosis, treatment and support from someone that truly gets it. Many educators and professionals simply don't.*

Lagging Social Skills Can Be a Real Problem

Nearly half of children with ADHD have *difficulty with relationships* (Barkley, 2015; Lavoie, 2005). Specifically, these children may lack basic social skills because they often don't pick up on social cues. As a result, they have trouble making and keeping friends. Classmates may reject them because children with ADHD may be aggressive or bossy, anger easily, complain too often, insist on always being right, or may not realize they're being too loud.

Children with ADHD are often oblivious to the fact that they have said something offensive or have intruded into the personal space of their classmates. Sadly, teachers often view them less positively than other students. Students with ADHD who lack social skills are more susceptible to bullying, more often as the victim but may also later become the bully. Social skills are discussed in more detail in later chapters.

Students with the inattentive form of ADHD are not as impulsive or aggressive as those who are hyperactive, so they may have better social skills and more friends. Predominately inattentive ADHD students are often seen as "daydreamers" and often appear to be listening when in fact they've totally tuned out the teacher. Inattentive ADHD characteristics also include forgetfulness, disorganization and a tendency to lose things, and nearly 30 percent of these students have slow reading, writing and test taking skills. In addition, for some, shyness, anxiety and withdrawal can create a different set of challenging social problems.

PC: *Jeff was so unaware of how others reacted to him. I watched him stand in line for warm-ups at a basketball game. He could never be still. He was in his own world, bumping into other boys. He never saw the dirty looks other boys gave him. He didn't hear their comments to "leave me alone." It hurt me so much to watch this happen. I'd say afterward, "You've got to learn where your space is or people won't want to be around you." He thought I was way off base. He said, "Mom, you don't understand. We boys just got it going on." He didn't even know he was being obnoxious and a pest.*

Sleep Disturbances

Earlier in the chapter, we introduced the ADHD Iceberg. Here we'd like to focus on one of the hidden problems that can lead to major problems at home, school and work: sleep disturbances. Getting good sleep is critical because learning is consolidated in the brain during deep, restful sleep.

More than *half* of children and teens with ADHD are chronically deprived of good-quality sleep because they have significant problems falling asleep and/or waking up each morning and staying alert during the day (Barkley, 2015; Van Der Heijden et al., 2005).

This lack of sleep can exacerbate ADHD symptoms. That's because when people don't get enough sleep, it's harder to focus, remember things, recall information, complete schoolwork and make sound decisions. Ultimately, they may become less patient and more irritable. Many young people with ADHD wake up feeling tired and find it difficult to get out of bed. It's no wonder morning conflicts are common and leave both child and parent feeling frustrated as they leave for school or work.

Here's a brief explanation of how our sleep mechanisms help us concentrate, learn and remember new information:

There are different levels of sleep, with the REM and deep sleep stages being the most critical to learning. *REM (rapid eye movement) sleep* is critical for learning fact-based information (e.g., memorizing math facts), complex and emotionally charged new information, and new motor skills (e.g., riding a bicycle). In fact, increased REM sleep is observed when new information is being learned. *Deep sleep*, also known as restorative or *slow-wave sleep* (SWS), is key for processing and consolidating newly acquired information into memory. Children and young adults need deep sleep so that the next day they can concentrate, organize thoughts and words, have a positive attitude, make sound judgments and retrieve important information from memory. Sleep disturbances make it difficult for working teens and young adults to concentrate, pay attention to detail, maintain good energy levels, get to work on time and complete work in a timely manner.

If a child or young adult is experiencing any sleep problems, it's critical to seek treatment. Helpful medications are available. Additional self-help strategies to use at home are provided in *A Bird's-Eye View of Life with ADHD* in the section entitled "Night Owls and Morning Zombies" (Dendy & Zeigler, 2015).

PC: I wish we'd understood why our son had so much trouble falling asleep and waking up. We assumed it was laziness and a bit of defiance.

There are several reasons that people with ADHD have sleep disturbances. Genetic differences are often the primary culprits causing sleep deprivation. Over half of people with ADHD simply can't fall asleep at a "normal" bedtime due to differences in the *genes that control circadian sleep rhythm.* (Barkley, 2015; Van Der Heijden et al., 2005). These genes control the release of the hormones melatonin and cortisol, which control the sleep-wake cycle. In other words, many teens with ADHD can't fall asleep earlier even if they want to. They actually *need* to sleep later in the morning. Unfortunately, very few schools are delaying school start times for high school students.

In addition, some children and teens who have significant anxiety have trouble falling asleep because they can't stop thinking about the things that worry them. Other young people with ADHD may have sleep-disordered obstructive breathing problems, restless leg syndrome or sleep apnea and wake up struggling to breathe multiple times at night (Barkley, 2015).

ADHD Sleep Facts

- Of all teens with ADHD, 56–64 percent have trouble falling asleep and waking up.
- Of all teens with ADHD, 39 percent wake up frequently at night.
- Teens with ADHD have less REM and deep restorative sleep than usual. Because of this reduction in restful, restorative sleep, they have more trouble remembering

information learned at school, feeling rested each morning and concentrating and retrieving key facts from memory. Night after night, Chris reviewed math facts with her son. And she wondered why Alex couldn't remember his multiplication tables the next day!

- Due to insufficient and fragmented sleep, up to 55 percent of children with ADHD report waking up tired, making it difficult to wake up (Figure 2.3), get dressed and pay attention at school.

Figure 2.3 Cartoon, "Night Owls and Morning Zombies".

Here is how Chris described a typical morning when Alex was a teen in *A Bird's-Eye View of Life with ADHD and EFD* (Dendy & Zeigler, 2015):

My son's alarm would routinely go off. Silence. Sigh ... okay, time for my second stage assault. Next, I turn on his bedroom light, dutifully turn on the TV and call him several times, then keep my fingers crossed. ARGH!&#%!

Next, I call out the big guns. My husband and I would launch all-out war on him ... pulling back the covers, taking his leg or arm, and pulling him toward the side of the bed. But nothing seemed to work very well.

Of course, I'm thinking the worst and my irritation is rising by the minute. "Darn it, he's just so lazy, he's not really trying to wake up. He doesn't care about anyone but himself. It doesn't bother him that he always makes us late and upsets the whole family. He could get up if he'd just go to bed on time."

Other Possible Sleep Disruptors

Sleep Apnea: Some children and teens with ADHD actually have obstructive sleep-disordered breathing problems (Youssef et al., 2011). Chris's son was found to have obstructive sleep apnea (a condition in which breathing stops during sleep because some part of the person's anatomy is blocking airflow into the lungs). During a sleep study, doctors found that Alex's uvula (the fleshy tissue hanging in the back of the throat) was obstructing his breathing, shutting off his oxygen and waking him up. During the sleep study, he had 30 or so "near wakings," which meant that he couldn't drop into a deep, restful, restorative sleep. Although research is limited, roughly 20 to 30 percent of children with ADHD may experience sleep apnea. If parents suspect a sleep disorder, they are encouraged to talk with their doctor as soon as possible.

Restless Leg Syndrome: Another common sleep disrupter, restless leg syndrome, also prevents roughly 35–45 percent of children with ADHD from getting restful sleep (Cortese et al., 2005). This is a nervous system disorder that causes unpleasant sensations in the legs that prompt the person to move her legs. When the sensations occur during sleep, it can lead to a condition called *periodic limb movements of sleep*, which can disrupt sleep repeatedly throughout the night.

Use of Electronics at Night: Another common sleep disrupter is the use of electronic devices such as smartphones and tablet computers at night. These devices emit blue light that can stimulate brain activity; increased brain activity near bedtime prevents people of all ages from calming down into a peaceful state of mind (CDC, 2020). The blue light from a TV, computer, phone or iPad also suppresses the production of melatonin, a hormone essential to allowing a person to fall asleep.

Strategies to Help with Falling and Staying Asleep

What can you do if your child or teen has difficulty falling asleep and/or never seems to get enough restful sleep? Here are several tips:

- *Educate your child or teen about her sleep challenges.* She needs to understand why she has trouble falling asleep and waking up. Otherwise, she may believe she's just lazy and defiant. Explain or have your doctor explain why people with ADHD have trouble getting restful sleep. If she's receptive, give her material to read on ADHD and sleep that also includes strategies to improve the quality of his sleep.
- *Stick with the same sleep schedule.* Go to bed pretty close to the same time during the week and on the weekends.
- *Develop a good sleep routine.* Help your child find something that helps her relax and encourage her to do this every night before bed. Take a nice hot soaking bath, play calming music and maybe drink a glass of milk and eat a cookie near bedtime. Using a relaxing "wind-down" time for an hour or so before bedtime is helpful.
- *Avoid blue light and increased brain activity from electronic devices.* Researchers suggest avoiding bright lights at least an hour or two before bedtime. Those who must work at night can buy blue-light-blocking glasses or use an app that filters blue lights from your screen. As of this writing, research results are mixed as to whether blocking blue light is particularly effective.
- *Spend time outside in bright sunlight,* since sunlight helps regulate circadian sleep cycles.
- *Exercise regularly* earlier in the day, not too close to bedtime.

- Simply *taking deep breaths*, slowly inhaling and exhaling, while concentrating on each breath helps with relaxation.
- *Avoid heavy meals* for three or so hours before bedtime and snacking within 45 minutes of bedtime.
- *Consider downloading sleep apps.* Some apps play relaxing sounds or music (e.g., Relax Melodies: Sleep Sounds). Others (e.g., Sleep Time) also offer soundscapes and white noise, and in addition can track sleep patterns. Older teens or young adults may be interested in monitoring their sleep patterns. Apps offering guided meditation or mindfulness activities may work better for others. (The Breathe app might work well for people who can't stay focused for very long; it includes shorter, five-minute directed sessions.)
- *Avoid caffeine* (coffee, tea, soft drinks, chocolate) for at least six hours before bedtime.
- If your teen is unable to sleep, advise her to *get up and go to another room* until she feels tired. In the interim, she can do something relaxing (listen to music, read a book or magazine, work a crossword puzzle or snuggle with a pet). However, above all else, *don't be tempted to get out a device* ... that will only make things worse.
- A few *over-the-counter medications like melatonin* may be helpful for falling asleep. Combining medication with other strategies in this list will be most effective. Discuss over-the-counter medications with your pharmacist or doctor.
- If the sleep issue continues to be a major problem, schedule a visit to the doctor in order to find out if there's a treatable problem (e.g., a sleep-related disorder or anxiety) that is contributing to the sleep problems.

Strategies to Help with Waking Up

It would be wonderful if children with ADHD could wake up and get dressed without any reminders from parents. However, this is unlikely to occur, unless sleep disorders are treated. Nevertheless, giving your child strategies such as those suggested in this section are often helpful. Obviously, having our teens and young adults wake up on their own is a critical goal to achieve well before they leave home for college, the military, work or other pursuits.

- *Set a wake-up alarm on a cell phone.* It may help to set two alarms, maybe 15 minutes apart. At bedtime, set the phone to night mode with its dimmer light, plus use the "Do Not Disturb" mode or switch to silent and place the phone on a soft surface so sound vibrations are dampened, and the phone is less likely to disturb sleep.
- *Try using a smart speaker as a virtual assistant.* A smart speaker such as Amazon's Echo, Google's Nest, or Apple's HomePod can wake you up to your favorite song, celebrity voice (Amazon), radio station or even a personalized news bulletin. And thanks to Alexa Routines, you can blend music, lights, alarms, and your device for the ultimate alarm clock.
- For a low-tech solution, suggest that your son or daughter *set two radio alarm clocks*, one a little earlier and another five minutes before he or she must get up. Place the later radio alarm across the room so your child has to get up to hit the snooze button or turn it off. Or she could set one alarm to a music station that she hates so she'll want to get up to turn it off.
- *Try a wake-up light alarm.* These clocks gradually emit more light for 30 minutes before the desired wake-up time. Being awakened from a deep sleep with a loud, startling alarm may result in your child or teen starting each day in a bad mood. The slowly emitted

light is designed to wake a person more gently. Although some are quite expensive, several light alarms are available starting around $40. Increasing sunlight in the room by opening blinds can also help your child wake up.

- *Wake early to give meds.* Morning routines are often much easier if parents wake up their child 30 minutes early, give them medication, and let them go back to sleep. When the teen finally gets up, she's more focused and can get ready, get organized, eat breakfast and get out the door on her way to school.

All the challenges discussed in this chapter must be addressed to help teens achieve their full potential. Since so many of the challenges are related to struggles with the demands of school, strategies for dealing with school and learning challenges are discussed in subsequent chapters. Remember that another major challenge that can affect a teen's functioning in all areas of life is her relationship with educators and especially you, the parent or caregiver. So, it will also help a great deal if all the involved adults educate themselves about ADHD and executive function deficits and become the best parent, teacher and advocate they can be.

References

American Psychiatric Association. (2013). *Diagnostic and statistical manual of mental disorders* (5th ed.). Washington, DC: Author.

Barkley, R.A. (2015). *Attention deficit hyperactivity disorder*, 4th ed. New York: Guilford Press.

Brown, T.E. (2014). *Smart but stuck: Emotions in teens and adults with ADHD*. San Francisco, CA: Jossey-Bass.

Centers for Disease Control and Prevention. (2020, April 1). *The color of the light affects the circadian rhythms*. Retrieved January 28, 2023, from https://www.cdc.gov/niosh/emres/longhourstraining/color.html#:~:text=Exposure%20to%20white%20light%20during,or%20orange%20light%20at%20night

Cortese, S., Konofal, E., Lecendreux, M., Arnulf, I., Mouren, M.C., Darra, F., & Dalla, B.B. (2005, August 1). Restless leg syndrome and attention deficit hyperactivity disorder: A review of the literature. *Sleep*, 28(8): 1007–1013.

Denckla, M.B. (2019). *Understanding learning and related disabilities: inconvenient brains*. New York: Routledge.

Dendy, C.A.Z. (2017). *Teenagers with ADD, ADHD, and executive function deficits: A guide for parents and professionals* (3rd ed.). Bethesda, MD: Woodbine House.

Dendy, C.A.Z. & Zeigler, A. (2015). *A birds-eye view of life with ADHD and EFD ... 10 years later* (3rd ed.). Alabama: C.A.Z. Dendy Consulting.

Gioia, G.A., Isquit, P.K., & Guy, S.C. (2001). Assessment of executive functions in children with neurological impairment. In R.J. Simeonsson & S.L. Rosenthal (Eds.), *Psychological and developmental assessment: Children with disabilities and chronic conditions* (pp. 317–356). New York: The Guilford Press.

Jensen, P.S., & MTA Cooperative Group (1999). A 14-month randomized clinical trial of treatment strategies for attention deficit hyperactivity disorder. *Archives of General Psychiatry*, 56, 1073–1086.

Lavoie, R. (2005). *It's so much work to be your friend*. New York: Simon and Schuster.

Quinn, P.O., & Madhoo, M. (2014, October 13). *A review of attention deficit hyperactivity disorder in women and girls: Uncovering this hidden diagnosis*. Primary care companion CNS disorder. Published online, https://doi.org/10.4088%2FPCC.13r01596

Shaw, P., Ekstrand, K., Sharp, W., & Rapoport, I.L. (2007). Attention deficit hyperactivity disorder characterized by a delay in cortical maturation. *Proceedings of the National Academy of Sciences (PNAS)*, 104(49), 19649–19654.

Van Der Heijden, K.B., Smits, M.G., Van Someren, J.W., & Boudewjin Gunning, W.B. (2005). Idiopathic chronic sleep onset insomnia and attention deficit hyperactivity disorder: A circadian rhythm sleep disorder. *Chronobiology International*, 22(3), 559–570.

Youssef, N.A., Ege, M., Angly, S.S., Strauss, J.L., & Marx, C.E. (2011). Is obstructive sleep apnea associated with ADHD? *Annals of Clinical Psychiatry*, 23(3), 213–224.

3   Ensure Success at School

From the very start of the school years, a parent's primary responsibility is to work with educators to ensure school success for his or her children. Children who are successful in school are much more confident in their abilities and decision-making. Sadly, the converse is also true: if they don't succeed in school, then their self-esteem is often damaged—not just for now, but possibly for a lifetime. Children who aren't keeping pace with their classmates—even if they are very bright—will have lower self-esteem as early as second grade. They may spend their entire adult life trying to rebuild their self-image but will still replay hurtful or humiliating criticism from teachers in their minds (e.g., "Your mother may baby you, but I'm not going to").

To reduce the chances that a child will experience school failure and lasting damage to his self-esteem, diagnosis of ADHD no later than the early elementary school years is ideal.

Our Parent Survey Results: *Early diagnosis was delayed for the children in our study; their average age of diagnosis and first treatment of ADHD was 9.2 years of age (third grade).* The average age of ADHD diagnosis reported by National Institute of Mental Health (2022) is between six and seven. Perhaps the later diagnosis in our survey was because the student wasn't hyperactive or a behavior problem, or because deficits in executive functions are often overlooked.

PC: I wish we had gotten an earlier diagnosis. Would have saved lots of tears and frustration.

Conflict at home: Many parents of children with ADHD report that difficulties at school are a source of major conflict at home. If a child or teen faces challenges at school, parents have to learn all they can about ADHD and common learning problems and develop an understanding of your education rights. In addition, parents may have to advocate for him to receive accommodations at school and be more involved in providing extra support and guidance at home. The following sections explore the types of instructional supports and accommodations the school may provide to address your child's academic difficulties.

Quite frankly, deficits in *executive skills are often a greater barrier to school success than the ADHD symptoms*. These deficits may include difficulty being organized, getting started and finishing, remembering homework assignments, memorizing facts and finishing long-term projects on time. In addition to requesting supports at school to help with these difficulties, parents may want to consider tutoring or online programs.

"Teach your teen to …": Mastering new skills is not easy. We both cringe when we hear experts say, "Teach your teen executive skills." This grossly oversimplifies the challenge,

DOI: 10.4324/9781003364092-3

since the implication is that you just need to show the teen how to do something a couple of times and he'll learn the skill. Instead, if you guide your son, daughter, or student to practice a skill repeatedly, it will make positive changes in the brain, enabling the teen to learn the skill or learn to compensate.

Ruth's Lessons Learned: My rule of thumb with my son was practice a hundred times for a skill that children without ADHD might learn with ten practices. Repetition is essential. It is not just about what our children know, but what they actually do. Until your teen masters a skill and regularly does it on his own, you will need to continue to provide opportunities for practice.

How Can Parents and Educators Help Students with School Issues?

Parents may be saying to themselves, "What can I do to help him do well at school? I'm not a teacher." Believe it or not, you can do quite a bit:

1. As recommended earlier, *educate yourself* about ADHD, executive function deficits, and their impact on school performance and behavior. At some point you *will* become the expert on your child or teen and ADHD. Soon you'll be able to identify his specific challenges (Figure 3.1).
2. *Review the challenges listed in the ADHD Iceberg*, identify your son's or daughter's learning challenges, and note them by filling out the blank ADHD Iceberg form in the appendix.
3. *Review the list of major school challenges you identified* from the ADHD Iceberg, figure out which ones are causing the greatest school difficulties, and identify strategies that have been used successfully by previous teachers. Then use these strategies to address each issue, starting with only one or two challenges of greatest concern.
4. *Learn about the federal laws* that ensure that eligible students with ADHD receive extra supports through either an IEP or Section 504 plan. These supports can include *services* such as special instruction or therapies to help students learn new skills, or *accommodations* to help level the playing field for students with disabilities. For example, if your teen forgets to bring his assignments home, an IEP or 504 plan might include the accommodation of having the teacher use the "memory-saving" software app Remind.com, which allows the teacher to send the assignment to the student and parent via a cell phone.
5. *Request an assessment as soon as possible* if you think your child would benefit from an IEP or Section 504 plan. The earlier, the better, but make your request no later than the beginning of senior year in high school. Although IDEA does not apply to college students, Section 504 and the Americans with Disabilities Act (ADA) do apply. Since greater demands are often placed on college students for independent work, most teens will benefit from accommodations in college.
6. *Gather documentation for supportive services that may be needed in college.* Eligibility for extra supports in college will require documentation from several sources. An IEP or 504 plan from high school will be one of the critical documents used to validate the need for supportive services in a technical, community or four-year college. Academic supports such as extended time, a notetaker or early registration are often invaluable for college students with ADHD.

Figure 3.1 Leila, middle school teacher.

Chris's Lessons Learned: As a former mental health counselor, teacher and school psychologist, I firmly believe that *succeeding in school is one of the most therapeutic things that can happen to a teen!* Clearly, ensuring success at school by "doing whatever it takes" is a critical step in building a solid foundation for launching into adulthood.

Would Your Child or Teen Benefit from a 504 Plan or IEP?

Most students with ADHD who are struggling in school are eligible for additional assistance under one of two federal laws: the Individuals with Disabilities Education Act (IDEA), a federal education law; or Section 504 of the Rehabilitation Act, a civil rights law. Students with more difficult challenges should seek special education services under IDEA.

IDEA: IDEA provides the most assistance for struggling students. It is designed to ensure that students with disabilities receive an "appropriate education" that enables them to learn the same material, to the extent possible, that other students are learning. Students who qualify under IDEA are eligible for extra services and accommodations. The school is required to come up with an individualized education program (IEP) for them, a written document that specifies what the school will do to help them succeed in school. This assistance basically levels the playing field by allowing the student to "work around the disability and demonstrate what he has learned" (Wrightslaw.com).

IEP: An IEP (Individualized Education Program) can include services that cost the school extra money—including speech therapy or occupational therapy, instruction provided by a special education teacher, time-limited home schooling, tutoring from an outside consultant or, rarely, placement in a private school (if the public school system can't meet the child's educational needs). The IEP also lists the accommodations the student is to receive in the classroom.

Section 504: In contrast to IDEA, the purpose of Section 504 is to remove barriers that prevent Americans with disabilities from accessing public services, including at school. Students who are found eligible for a 504 plan rather than an IEP are eligible for accommodations but seldom receive services that cost the school system extra money. Typically, this is not a problem since most of the challenges facing students with ADHD can be addressed adequately with regular classroom accommodations. Regardless, the school is legally required to provide accommodations agreed to by parents and school staff. Although the Section 504 plan, unlike an IEP, is not required to be put in writing, the best practice in most schools is to record the plan in writing.

Accommodations: An accommodation is an alteration made to the educational setting, the way information is presented or responded to, the equipment used, or another change that enables a student with a disability to better succeed at school. Accommodations *do not change what students are expected to learn* but make "accommodations" for obstacles their disabilities present in the classroom.

For example, if a student with ADHD has slow processing speed (Kibby et al., 2019) and or writes very slowly, appropriate accommodations might include allowing him extra (extended) time for tests, using a computer rather than pen and paper to write essays, or giving shortened assignments. A student who struggles with math facts might be allowed to use a multiplication fact sheet grid or a calculator. For a student who frequently forgets to write down assignments or turn them in, classroom "row captains" might be assigned to remind students to write down assignments and then take up homework, or the teacher might use a reminder app, as mentioned earlier.

The accommodations that a student receives are decided upon jointly during a planning meeting between parents and school staff and are documented in the written IEP or Section 504 plan.

Determining if Your Child Is Eligible for an IEP or 504 Plan

If your child is struggling in school, you should request an assessment to determine whether he is eligible for services under either IDEA or Section 504. If the school agrees to evaluate your child under IDEA, they will conduct a formal assessment of his intelligence, academic achievement and other factors that might reveal whether he has a qualifying disability. Typically, school staff ask for academic rating scales from parents and teachers, review past report cards and teacher comments, and consider annual academic assessments. In addition, a qualified examiner such as a psychologist will often conduct an IQ test such as the *WISC* and additional academic assessments (such as Woodcock-Johnson or Wechsler) designed to assess how well your child is performing in academic subjects such as reading, math and writing. A letter from your medical doctor documenting that your child has ADHD will be required.

To be eligible for services under IDEA, a student must meet these three criteria:

- The student has a qualifying disability.
- The disability adversely affects educational performance.
- The disability results in the student's inability to progress in the regular education program.

A qualifying disability is one of the 13 eligibility categories such as autism or learning disability listed in the law. Unfortunately, attention deficit disorders per se are not one of the listed eligibility categories. Instead, students with ADHD *should be assessed under the "other health impairment" (OHI)* category, according to guidelines from the USDOE Office of Special Education Programs (OSEP) (Davila et al., 1991).

What exactly is an "other health impairment"? According to IDEA, it means "having limited strength, vitality or alertness, including a heightened alertness to environmental stimuli that results in limited alertness with respect to the educational environment that is due to chronic or acute health problems."

Students with ADHD may also qualify under more than one category, such as a learning disability (LD)—having significant difficulties in one or more academic subjects despite average or above-average intelligence. In addition, a student may be intellectually gifted and still be eligible for services under IDEA.

Beware of the Emotional Disturbance Category

Emotional lability—in other words, greater emotionality—is common among immature children with ADHD and may be mistaken for bipolar disorder or an emotional disturbance (ED), especially in young children. Interpretations of the ED label are easily misunderstood, however, and years after the fact the students' problems may be assumed to be more much more serious than the actual behavior exhibited.

Chris's Lessons Learned: Parents and educators will be wise to follow the old medical advice of "Do no harm." As a parent looking for the appropriate IDEA category, I wouldn't want the baggage of the ED label hung around my child's neck throughout his school career. Start with the OHI category, the least harmful label, and then if behavior warrants it in a few years, consider changing the category.

What if You're Told Your Child Isn't Eligible for an IEP?

If your son or daughter is denied services under IDEA, don't be afraid to ask the school to explain why. For example, what eligibility category were they considering? Ask if they evaluated your child under OHI or Learning Disabilities criteria. Sometimes evaluators inadvertently use the wrong eligibility category criteria to screen students with ADHD. Ultimately, you may be told incorrectly that your child or teen's learning problems are not severe enough to meet strict eligibility requirements for extra supports.

If your child is truly ineligible for an IEP, ask that he be assessed for services under Section 504. If you are worried that your school may not consider your child eligible for a 504 plan, consider hiring an educational consultant who knows federal laws and who will attend the meeting with you. Or ask someone, perhaps a knowledgeable parent who has been to one of these meetings, to support you by taking notes and listening objectively.

Typically, it's easier to qualify for a 504 plan than an IEP. Required documentation varies from school system to school system, but it usually includes teacher and parent reports of struggles, a review of academic records, and documentation of ADHD via a letter from your child's doctor.

PC: School officials told me my son with ADHD wasn't eligible for help under Section 504, but I knew differently because I had attended ADHD education classes with Ms. Dendy. I was angry with myself because I just accepted what the three school officials said. So, after thinking about it, I called the school superintendent's office. Within a week, I had a school meeting to develop a Section 504 plan.

If you disagree with the school's assessment, say so! *Don't sign the evaluation document* saying he's not eligible for services. Instead, restate your child's greatest challenges and the reasons he needs services—for example: "He has already failed a grade and I spend a couple of hours helping him with homework every night." If no compromise is reached, you may be able to resolve the issue informally by requesting help from the director of special education, the superintendent, or the state office of special education.

Failing an informal resolution, you have a right to further discussion through a *mediation process* with a neutral third party. If none of these approaches work, you can notify the superintendent in writing that you are requesting a *due process hearing*. See Chris's *Teaching Teens* book for more details on appeals. You can find this and other helpful publications in the Resources at the back of the book.

Key Facts About Eligibility for Services Under Federal Law

Determining whether a student with ADHD qualifies for supports under either IDEA or Section 504 must be made "without regard to the ameliorative effects of *mitigating measures*." In other words, the fact that a *student* is doing well in school because of medication, informal accommodations or extra parental support at home cannot be used to deny him or her services.

Mitigating measures can include the following:

- Medication and medical supplies.
- Use of assistive technology.
- Reasonable accommodations or auxiliary aids or services.
- Learning, behavioral, or adaptive neurological modifications.

Other key facts were clarified in the 2008 Americans with Disability Act (ADA) amendments and subsequent Office of Civil Rights "Dear Colleague Guidance Letters" (Lhamon, 2016).

- A student *does not have to be failing to be eligible* for an IEP.
- Students with high IQ scores may be eligible.
- A student should not be penalized when seeking a 504 plan because of extra supports provided by parents at home.
- A student with an IEP or 504 plan should never be failing; if he is, revise the plan.
- Students who were denied eligibility in the past may be eligible now.

Potential Obstacles to Service Eligibility: Gender, Race, ADHD Inattentive

Unfortunately, there are several groups of students who are more likely to be underdiagnosed with ADHD and therefore may not be receiving any school supports under IDEA or Section 504. Underdiagnosis is a significant problem among girls, nonwhite students, and boys and girls with ADHD Inattentive type.

Girls with ADHD

Girls with the inattentive type of ADHD often are misdiagnosed initially with anxiety or depression (Quinn & Madhoo, 2014). It's easy to overlook girls who are daydreaming and don't have discipline problems. Many girls are eager to please adults, follow the rules, work harder and hide their academic problems as they suffer in silence. Underachievement in school may be another indicator that you should look more closely at your daughter. Basically, the diagnostic criteria for ADHD identify characteristics typical of boys. However, most girls' symptoms bear little resemblance to those of the boys. Unfortunately, this creates a diagnostic bias against identifying girls.

Diagnostic bias by parents, teachers and doctors also contributes to underdiagnosis of girls. Here's what experts tell us:

- "Pediatricians are more likely to diagnose boys with ADHD than girls, even when problems described by parents are comparable."

  (Slobodin & Davidovitch, 2019)

- "Mothers give more praise and direction to sons, though the boys are less compliant than girls."

  (Befera & Barkley, 1985)

PC: I wish I realized what ADHD looks like in girls and that my daughter was diagnosed earlier.

Key facts about ADHD in girls include the following (Hinshaw et al. 2012; Quinn & Madhoo, 2014; Figure 3.2):

- ADHD is overlooked in girls more than 50 percent of the time.
- Girls are often misdiagnosed with anxiety or depression first (45 percent), and only much later is ADHD identified.

Figure 3.2 This group of girls and women with ADHD has given numerous conference presentations to increase awareness of the underdiagnosis of ADHD in girls and women.

- Disorganized girls who are anxious and eager to please may overcompensate with compulsive actions or frequent list making.
- Nearly half of all teachers have difficulty recognizing ADHD in girls.
- Girls' ADHD symptoms often aren't obvious until middle school, when demands on memory and on executive skills such as organization increase significantly.
- Inattentive girls are often the daydreamers who zone out in class and to all outward appearances seem to be listening. Some of them may be quite shy. Typically, they are not discipline problems.
- Hyperactive girls may talk excessively, be noisy, have low self-esteem, be perfectionistic and/or risk-takers, or be at risk of self-harming behaviors.

PC: If you have a teen with ADHD or have ADHD yourself, take a closer look at your underachieving daughter or inattentive son who may have been misdiagnosed with anxiety or depression.

Students with ADHD Inattentive

As described in Chapter 2, both boys and girls who are inattentive daydreamers are less likely to be diagnosed early with ADHD. Students with the inattentive form of ADHD are forgetful, often disorganized and prone to losing things; plus, nearly 30 percent have slow reading, writing and test-taking skills. Because children with the inattentive type of ADHD do not have hyperactive or impulsive behaviors, they are often less likely to be referred for evaluation.

Chris's Lessons Learned: I was baffled that my gifted son struggled just to make passing grades. Unbeknownst to me, my son had all the challenges often related to ADHD Inattentive: deficits in executive function, slow processing speed, a sleep disturbance and learning deficits in written expression and memorization.

So, what did all this mean in practical terms? He was disorganized, lost things, had difficulty getting started and completing schoolwork, forgot to do chores and homework—and more importantly, to give it to the teacher. He read and wrote more slowly, so homework that took his classmates 30 minutes to complete took him over an hour to finish. When he did read an assignment, he couldn't remember what he read. Homework in the evenings became an emotional battlefield for our family.

Academically, he had great ideas but couldn't remember them long enough to get them written down on paper. His essays were very short, maybe only four sentences long. Memorization of multiplication tables was a nightmare; he'd study them, but by the next day he couldn't remember them.

Nonwhite Students

In the United States, ADHD is more commonly diagnosed in Caucasian students than in students of other races (Coker et al., 2016; Morgan et al., 2013). Currently, about 10.2 percent of Caucasian students have been diagnosed with ADHD compared to 9.5 percent of non-Hispanic black children and 6.5 percent of Hispanic students. Research has shown that nonwhite students who are struggling in school, especially those who act out, may never be screened for ADHD but instead are assumed to be behavior problems.

Gifted Students

Educators may be unaware that intellectually gifted students may also have ADHD or a learning disability (Inahim & Rohde, 2015). In other words, they may be "twice exceptional," also referred to as "2E." Federal education guidelines make it clear that some gifted students struggle because they may have other diagnoses such as ADHD, executive function deficits, anxiety, depression, autism or a learning disability. As discussed earlier in the chapter, they should not be found ineligible for school supports just because they are making good grades.

Here's the Bottom Line

If you have a child or teen who is struggling in school and is considered lazy, a behavior problem or gifted, review the criteria for ADHD and executive function deficits. Consider asking the school for an academic assessment to determine whether your child qualifies for an IEP or 504 plan.

Once the IEP or 504 Plan Is in Place

Parents may breathe a sigh of relief once a plan is in place and the school has made a commitment to help your son or daughter with his or her challenges. But not so fast! Educators often teach multiple classes and have hundreds of students, some with special needs. Unfortunately, there may be a disconnect between the plan and what actually happens in class each day. Section 504 plans are particularly vulnerable to lack of follow-through. It is *crucial that you communicate regularly* with your child's teachers and follow up to find out how your student is progressing.

- *Communicate regularly with teachers.* Ask teachers what the best way is to ask for information about your son's or daughter's progress. Take the initiative and don't expect the teacher to reach out to you. Consider sending an email on Thursday asking if any assignments have not been submitted for the week. Schedule regular communications and always ask what you can do to be of assistance.
- *Convey concern.* Let teachers know you want to work with them to help your child. They will be far more amenable to helping your student if they're not feeling blamed.
- *Work with your child.* Check in with your child regularly about the plan and the supports and accommodations he should be receiving. Help him organize his backpack or notebook.
- *Monitor the plan and advise if problems arise.* If a plan is not being implemented, talk with the teacher respectfully to identify what the challenge is. It may not be the right intervention or may not be practical for the teacher to do, given the classroom dynamics.
- *Monitor the plan for progress.* If the plan is being implemented but not helping your student, talk with the teacher about what changes may need to be made to the plan.
- *Request a planning meeting.* If changes don't resolve the issue, request a new IEP or 504 planning meeting to discuss the problems and develop a more effective plan. Parents have the right to call for another meeting at any time. Don't wait until the end of the grading period to find out that no progress is being made.

Common Misunderstandings About IEP and 504 Responsibilities

When your child's IEP or 504 plan is developed, goals for interventions will be decided upon in each area in which he is having difficulties. Sometimes the intervention objectives are incorrectly written so that they place sole responsibility on the child to achieve the task without any supports. The plan should state what the school staff will do to help your child achieve the goal.

Goal: What the child should achieve. Example: "Complete all homework daily."

Plan: What the school will do to help the student meet the goal. Example: "Assignments will be shortened, and teachers will notify the child and parent of homework assignments via a text from the Remind.com app."

Not This: "John will complete all homework on a daily basis" is an inappropriate objective. It just restates the goal but without any guidance as to the steps that will be taken to help the student achieve the goal.

Then Follow Up Some More

Teachers change, school policies change and your child changes. And every year, the expectations for your child or teen to do more independent work increase. What was appropriate at one stage may well not be the right intervention down the road. You will need to stay in regular communication with your child's teachers until he graduates from high school. All IEPs and most 504 plans are updated yearly. Don't hesitate to ask for changes to the plan whenever your child is experiencing difficulties.

PC: Learn to advocate for your child early on. Don't assume the school will automatically put any effort into helping your child even if there are written contracts. Seek out advocates. Always fight for them and follow your instincts. If something doesn't feel right, then it isn't right for your child.

What if Your Teen Doesn't Have an IEP or Section 504 Plan?

If you haven't asked for supports under these two federal laws, you may want to reconsider your decision, especially when the demands increase significantly in high school and beyond. If you anticipate that your teen will need supports in postsecondary school or college, it's critical to request an evaluation for educational supports under Section 504 or IDEA no later than the year before high school graduation. A copy of the 504 plan or IEP will likely be used to help document the need for accommodations in technical or traditional colleges.

Even if your teen doesn't have an IEP or 504 plan, you could still try some of the strategies for teaching important job skills discussed in Chapter 7. The self-advocacy skills that are included in the federally mandated pre-employment transition program are shown in Table 7.1. You'd be wise to look over the list and ensure that your teen has the opportunity to practice those skills. Later chapters of the book provide guidance on making the transition years after high school into young adulthood less challenging.

Seek the Best Possible Medical Treatment

As mentioned earlier, there are medications that can "ameliorate" some ADHD symptoms, sometimes to the extent that school staff may think a student with ADHD doesn't need supports in the classroom. Some parents and teens choose not to use these medications, but studies have shown that a combination of ADHD education for the whole family, medication, academic supports and behavior interventions offers the best treatment results.

Table 3.1 Impact of Stimulant Medication

Increased	Decreased
Attention	Activity levels
Concentration	Impulsivity
Compliance	Negative behaviors
Effort on tasks	Physical and verbal hostility
Amount and accuracy of schoolwork	
Speed of learning	

Table 3.1 shows some of the typical benefits of using stimulant medications such as Adderall, Ritalin, Concerta or Vyvance. (Swanson et al., 1993).

If you and the teachers don't see these changes, then something is wrong. Perhaps the medication dosage may be too low to allow peak academic performance, or this may not be the most effective medication match. Some children do better on medications similar to Ritalin, and others respond best to Adderall-type meds. Discuss your concerns with your physician.

To determine the correct medications and dosages most effective for your son or daughter, find a physician or other medical professional who specializes in treating ADHD and related conditions. Ask for recommendations of treatment professionals from friends or from members of your local ADHD support group (e.g., CHADD or ADDA-SR).

PC: Get support from a professional who truly gets it. Many educators and treatment professionals simply don't.

Work with Teachers and Your Doctor to Ensure Peak Medication Levels

Getting medication dosage correct is one of the most important jobs that you and your doctor share. Students with ADHD can't do as well in school when peak medication levels are not reached. Medication issues are discussed in detail in *Teenagers with ADD, ADHD, and Executive Function Deficits* (see the Resources section at the end of the book). Here's a brief overview of key points:

Despite being on medication, your child or teen may still struggle in school. If your son or daughter is still spending long hours completing homework, consider asking teachers to complete Dendy's informal Academic and Behavioral Performance Rating Scale in the Appendix. Results will not only identify challenging academic areas but will also give indicators as to whether or not the medication is working effectively. If medication is adjusted, have teachers again fill out the rating scale to see if there has been improvement. Figures 3.3 and 3.4 show the tremendous change in performance brought about by a medication adjustment for one student. If your child doesn't receive ratings of mostly 1s or 2s for each item, share the results with your physician.

1. *Medication dose may be too low.* According to Peter Jensen, MD, lead researcher for the NIMH MTA Cooperative study on ADHD (Jensen & MTA Cooperative Group, 1999) medication levels of children with ADHD are often too low to provide peak academic performance. One reason is that some parents fear the medication and try to keep the levels as low as possible. Unfortunately, that often results in the child continuing to struggle in school. Please work with your physician to find the most effective dosage.

Current Academic and Behavioral Performance
Teacher Rating: (before taking medication)

Student's Name:_____**Date & Class:** ____Feb. 8_____

Completed by: _____**Time of Day Observed:** _____

To identify current academic or behavior challenges, each teacher should answer several key questions. Please circle the answer that best describes the student's behavior and academic performance.

Academic Performance:

When the student is in my class, s/he	Strongly agree	Agree	Neutral	Disagree	Strongly disagree
1. Pays attention	1	②️	3	4	5
2. Completes class and homework	1	2	3	④️	5
3. Does work correctly	1	②️	3	4	5
4. Complies with requests	①️	2	3	4	5
5. Makes passing grades	1	2	③️	4	5

Other Challenges: Are there any other behaviors that are interfering with the student's ability to succeed in school?

The student					
6. Organizes materials/information well	①️	2	3	4	5
7. Gets started easily on work	1	2	3	④️	5
8. Manages time well	1	②️	3	4	5
9. Finishes long-term projects easily	1	2	3	④️	5
10. Remembers information easily	1	②️	3	4	5
11. Thinks carefully before acting or speaking	1	②️	3	4	5
12. Is awake and alert in class	1	2	③️	4	5
13. Is on time to class	①️	2	3	4	5
14. Is on time to school	①️	2	3	4	5

Comments:
_____
_____

© Chris A. Zeigler Dendy

Figure 3.3 Current academic and behavioral performance: Informal teacher rating.

2. *Don't give up on medications too quickly.* Dr. Kathleen Duryea, a physician specializing in treating ADHD, provides helpful guidance about what to expect when first starting meds. If a child starts ADHD medication and appears to be something of a "zombie," the dose may actually be too low, simply reducing the child's hyper behavior. But with a slight increase in medicine, the child may actually focus better on schoolwork.
3. *Some meds work better than others.* How do you decide which medicine will work best for your child or teen? According to the CDC (2022), roughly 70 to 80 percent of all young people respond well to either a Ritalin (methylphenidate) or Adderall (dextroamphetamine) class of medication. However, some children and teens may respond best to only one class of medication. Work with your physician to determine which medication is most effective for your son or daughter.

Current Academic and Behavioral Performance
Teacher Rating: (after taking medication)

Student's Name:_____ **Date & Class:** ___Feb. 14_____

Completed by: _____**Time of Day Observed:** _____

To identify current academic or behavior challenges, each teacher should answer several key questions. Please circle the answer that best describes the student's behavior and academic performance.

Academic Performance:

When the student is in my class, s/he	Strongly agree	Agree	Neutral	Disagree	Strongly disagree
1. Pays attention	①	2	3	4	5
2. Completes class and homework	1	②	3	4	5
3. Does work correctly	1	②	3	4	5
4. Complies with requests	①	2	3	4	5
5. Makes passing grades	1	②	3	4	5

Other Challenges: Are there any other behaviors that are interfering with the student's ability to succeed in school?

The student					
6. Organizes materials/information well	①	2	3	4	5
7. Gets started easily on work	①	2	3	4	5
8. Manages time well	①	2	3	4	5
9. Finishes long-term projects easily	①	2	3	4	5
10. Remembers information easily	①	2	3	4	5
11. Works more slowly than peers	①	2	3	4	5
12. Thinks carefully before acting or speaking	①	2	3	4	5
13. Is awake and alert in class	①	2	3	4	5
14. Is on time to class	①	2	3	4	5
15. Is on time to school	①	2	3	4	5

Comments:

_____

_____

© Chris A. Zeigler Dendy

Figure 3.4 Teacher rating after medication adjustment.

4. *Medication timing is important.* Meds may be taken too close to the start of school. Be aware of the time your child or teen takes medicine each morning. If he takes a long-acting medication (Adderall, Vyvance or Concerta) in the car on the way to school, the medicine typically takes up to an hour to be effective. So, medications may not reach peak effectiveness until the end of first period.
5. *Meds are more effective in the morning.* The effectiveness of medication taken in the morning diminishes in the afternoon and is also affected by your child's rate of metabolism. Request that your child's more difficult classes be scheduled during the morning hours. Talk to your physician about using a different long-acting medication or adding a medication later in the day if that's when he struggles academically.

6. *Consider discussing with your doctor whether or not a short-acting medication might be helpful for homework.* Short-acting medications like Ritalin last only three or four hours, so taking a dose around 4:00 or 5:00 p.m. will improve focus on homework. Otherwise, medication during the school day will have worn off, and your child may be attempting homework without the benefit of medication. Consequently, he'll have difficulty remembering what he studied.

7. *Medication may become less effective over time.* Over time, children and teens may develop a tolerance to a medication so it no longer works as well. This is particularly true around middle school, when preteens typically experience hormonal changes and a growth spurt. Doctors may increase the dosage of present meds or try a new one.

8. *Students who can't take medication.* A few students will be unable to take an ADHD medication because of side effects or other reasons. For example, some teens may refuse to take medication, or parents may object to ADHD meds. Regardless of the reasons, exercise, structure, routine at home, plus identification of learning disabilities and provision of accommodations become even more critical.

PC: I would have started medication and counseling earlier.

In summary, if your son or daughter is on medication yet still struggling at school, talk with your doctor about a possible medication adjustment. Second, work with teachers to determine if your child might have a learning disability or executive function deficits. Ask key teachers to complete Chris's informal Academic and Behavioral Performance Rating Scale in the Appendix. Information from the rating scale will help you and your doctor make a better-informed treatment decision. If the medication and dosage are correct, you and your child's teachers will see immediate improvement in academic performance. If not, go back to the drawing board and work with your doctor to find the right medication and dosage.

See the teacher ratings shown in Figures 3.3 and 3.4 for an example of one student's performance before and after a medication adjustment. The student showed significant improvement in school performance.

In addition to letting you know whether medication is working, the rating scale can also help you identify the most effective intervention strategies and accommodations. For example, the rating scale is a good indicator of whether the teen has working memory or slow processing speed. For students who read and write more slowly than others, extended time for assignments and tests and/or shortened assignments are appropriate accommodations.

Find the Right Level of Involvement

Parenting children with ADHD is often quite challenging. In a sense, parents walk a tightrope without a balance bar. Unfortunately, children with ADHD don't come with an instruction manual, so parents are left to learn on the job and do the best they can. Parents wrestle with how much support to provide at school, especially since other children the same age don't need as much support and guidance.

Sadly, there aren't any easy answers. If you withdraw supports too soon, your son or daughter may fail, and we know that our children don't learn easily from failure and punishment. Failing often doesn't change their behavior because underlying brain chemistry challenges are involved.

On the other hand, if you do everything for them, they may never learn to take charge of their lives. One parent came to an IEP meeting, handed out a list of over 30 possible accommodations from *Teaching Teens with ADD or ADHD* (Dendy, 2011), and said, "I want everything on this list for my teen." Whoa! That's not the way this works.

Address a couple of major challenges first. Select two or three challenges that are most likely causing school failure and focus on them. For example, your child might struggle most with getting started on work, being disorganized and forgetting and not submitting homework or long-term projects. If so, you could work with teachers to practice compensatory strategies or select accommodations that will help him remember assignments (such as using a reminder app like Remind.com) or be more organized (pair with a classmate to organize a required notebook).

It would be wise to avoid aiming for perfect school grades because then the A becomes a grade that the parent earned. If you, the parent, earn the A, your child or teen receives a damaging message to his self-esteem: "You can't do this on your own." Your child builds self-esteem by struggling and learning to handle problems independently.

Monitor your level of involvement across the school years, reducing your assistance if and when your son or daughter masters a specific skill such as using a strategy to remember homework assignments.

Ruth's Lessons Learned: Regularly forgive yourself for the missteps and mistakes. They are unavoidable, and none of us gets it right all the time. And there is the human factor. Even when we know what to do, sometimes we are just too angry or exhausted or stressed to go the extra mile. This is real life, and guilt doesn't help you or your teen. And you can't do everything that everyone suggests. Try to initiate one or two changes at a time. So take a deep breath, go slowly and focus on what you and your child can do today.

Pay attention to your child's or teen's struggles at school and try to pinpoint the source of his problems. For instance, does he have challenges with slow reading and writing, failure to complete and turn in homework, and forgetting long-term projects? Once you identify factors that are contributing to his struggles at school, see if you can figure out possible interventions. If you can't do this alone, consider talking with one of his former teachers who seemed to really understand him and went the extra mile to be helpful. As mentioned earlier, Chris's book *Teaching Teens with ADD, ADHD, and Executive Function Deficits* may help identify helpful intervention strategies. You might also consider hiring an educational consultant who can help you identify effective intervention strategies.

References

Befera, M.S., & Barkley, R. A. (1985). Hyperactive and normal girls and boys: mother-child interaction, parent psychiatric status and child psychopathology. *Journal of Child Psychology and Psychiatry, 26*(3): 439–452.

Slobodin, O., & Davidovitch, M. (2019). Gender differences in objective and subjective measures of ADHD among clinic-referred children. *Frontiers in Human Neuroscience, 13*: 441.

Center for Disease Control and Prevention. (2022, August 9). *Treatment of ADHD*. Retrieved January 28, 2023, from https://www.cdc.gov/ncbddd/adhd/treatment.html

Coker, T.R., Elliott, M.N., Toomey, S.L., Schwebel, D.C., Cuccaro, P., Tortolero Emery, S., & Davies, S.L. (2016). Racial and ethnic disparities in ADHD diagnosis and treatment. *Pediatrics, 138*(3), e20160407.

Davila, R., Williams, M., & MacDonald, J. (1991, September 6). *Clarification to policy to address the needs of children with attention deficit disorders within general and special education.* Washington, DC: US Department of Education, Office of Special Education and Rehabilitative Services.

Dendy, C.A.Z. (2011). *Teaching Teens with ADD, ADHD and Executive Function Deficits.* Bethesda, MD: Woodbine House.

Hinshaw, S.P., Owens, E.B. Zalecki, C., Montenegro-Novado, A.G., Huggins, S.P., Schroedek, E.A., & Swanson, E.N. (2012). Prospective follow-up of girls with attention deficit hyperactivity disorder into early adulthood: continuing impairments includes elevated risk for suicide attempts and self-injury. *Journal of Consulting and Clinical Psychology* (APA), *80*(6): 1041–1051.

Jensen, P.S., & MTA Cooperative Group (1999). A 14-month randomized clinical trial of treatment strategies for attention deficit hyperactivity disorder. *Archives of General Psychiatry, 1999*(56): 1073–1086.

Kibby, M.Y., Vadnais, S.A., & Jager-Rickles, A.C. (2019). Which components of processing speed are affected in adhd subtypes? *Child Neuropsychology, 25*(7), 964–979.

Lhamon, C.E. (2016). *Dear colleague letter and resource guide on students with ADHD.* Washington, DC: US Department of Education, Office of Civil Rights.

Inahim, D., & Rohde, L. (2015). Attention deficit hyperactivity disorder and anomalies. *Brazilian Journal of Psychiatry, 37*(4), 289–295.

Morgan, P.L., Staff, J. Hellemeier, M.M., Farkas, G., & Maczuga, S. (2013). Racial and ethnic disparities in ADHD diagnosis from kindergarten to eighth grade. *Pediatrics, 132*(1), 85–93.

National Institute of Mental Health. (2022, September 22). *Attention-deficit/hyperactivity disorder.* Retrieved January 28, 2023, from https://www.nimh.nih.gov/health/topics/attention-deficit-hyperactivity-disorder-adhd

Quinn, P.O., & Madhoo, M. (2014, October 13). A review of attention-deficit/hyperactivity disorder in women and girls: Uncovering this hidden diagnosis. *The Primary Care Companion for CNS Disorders, 16*(3).

Swanson, J.M., McBurnett, K., Wigal, T., Pfiffner, L.J., Lerner, M.A., Williams, L., Christian, D.L., Tamm, L., Willcutt, E., Crowley, K., Clevenger, W., Khouzam, N., Woo, C., Crinella, F.M., & Fisher, T.D. (1993). Effect of stimulant medication on children with attention deficit disorder: A "review of reviews". *Exceptional Children, 60*, 154–162.

4 Nurturing Self-Esteem and Natural Talents

Children with ADHD who struggle in school receive lots of negative feedback. As a result, their self-esteem is often battered and damaged as early as second grade. Adding insult to injury, parents who don't yet understand ADHD may push their children to work harder to make better grades. This adds another layer of negativity at home. And young adults who struggle with college or jobs are particularly vulnerable to being viewed as failures.

Fortunately, it's never too late for you to nurture your child's self-esteem or help her repair existing damage to her self-image. As a parent, you are uniquely qualified to help your child weather the criticism and extra challenges that ADHD will bring. Since you may need to begin by changing some of your own behavior first, though, we begin the chapter with advice on keeping your relationship with your child positive.

PC: I would advise parents to do whatever they can to make their home a sanctuary and a place of peace for them. They have grief everywhere, so give them a place where they can come and rest, talk or sleep, because life is tough out there.

Chris's Lessons Learned: I must confess I lost my perspective when my son was struggling in high school. At times I found myself thinking that he was lazy and really didn't care. I was always laser-focused on monitoring his homework so he would make better grades, to the point of greeting him when he came home from school by saying, "Did you bring home your books and assignments?" I didn't even bother to ask him how his day went.

When he began avoiding me at the front door and going in through the basement, a light bulb went off in my head. I had lost sight of my most important role as a parent: loving my son, being there for him, building his self-esteem, and not just loving him contingent upon the grades he made. Your job as a loving, supportive parent is to keep the most important things in perspective: nurturing your teen's positive self-esteem and maintaining a strong relationship. Ultimately, your loving relationship with your teenager may one day save his life. I know this from personal experience.

Our Parent Survey Results: *Nearly half of all parents reported that relationships with parents, family and friends were the most important positive influences on transitioning young adults.*

DOI: 10.4324/9781003364092-4

Keep a Positive Relationship with Your Child or Teen

So, what can you do to ensure that you build and keep a positive relationship with your child or teen? Here are some essential tips.

1. *Listen carefully to what your son or daughter says*, and acknowledge his or her perspective. That doesn't mean you have to agree or solve every problem, but let your child or teen know she is heard.
2. *Listen to behavior as well as words.* Often our children speak through their behavior. Younger children may not be able to clearly communicate their feelings. Try saying something like this: "Help me understand why you don't want to take your medicine." You might consider responding to puzzling behavior by asking, "Are you trying to tell me something?" Ruth found that this opened the door for her teenage son to tell her what was bothering him.
3. *Pick your battles carefully.* Not everything we get upset about as parents is worth the conflict and negative fallout from angry discussions. Really think about what things are worth fighting about.
4. *Find opportunities to give praise and do it often.* We need to help our children identify and own their strengths. And they need to feel loved and accepted for who they are.
5. *Be aware of your parental "hot buttons"*—the things that absolutely make you lose your cool. We all have them. Awareness will help you control your temper. During the elementary school years before Chris knew any better, she'd get so frustrated when her son couldn't get started on homework. She didn't know that "getting started" is a key executive skill.
6. *Be willing to walk away.* When you feel the escalation that leads to an angry fight, tell your child or teen you need some time to calm down before any further discussion. Set a time to revisit the issue so she knows you're not ignoring the problem. Ruth's son refined this technique by calling her with bad news so she would calm down by the time he got home—even when that meant leaving home to call her.
7. *Model apologizing after an angry outburst.* We all have our moments when we regret angry words or actions, and an apology after the fact can mend hurt feelings. Better yet, it teaches our children an important skill: to apologize when you're wrong.
8. *Set limits calmly and repeat the message without elaboration.* "No, you may not stay out after ten on a school night." Repeat as necessary with as little emotion as possible.

Ruth's Lessons Learned: For me, the bottom line in picking my battles was to confront my son about any behavior that was dangerous. The switchblade in middle school was absolutely confiscated. Drinking and driving were not tolerated. But opinions, hairstyles, and clothing were not worth the conflict. My son and I would go out to dinner when we needed to have a difficult discussion because we were both reluctant to make a scene in public. Remember—*when yelling starts, communication stops!*

It's absolutely crucial to maintain open communication and a positive relationship with our children. This is especially challenging through the teen years, but the benefits make the hard work worthwhile.

PC: The relationship between you and your child or teen is more important than grades or success in school. If the relationship isn't strong, where else will they go for help and support, especially when they most need it?

Educate Your Child and Yourself About ADHD and Executive Functions

One of the most important things that parents can do is to educate themselves and their child or teen about ADHD and executive functions. In other words, parents must *become experts on their son's or daughter's ADHD.* Here's why this is important. The more you know about ADHD and executive skills, the better you'll understand your child's or teen's behavior and academic challenges. Having realistic expectations for her will make you a more effective parent.

PC: Because I had so little knowledge about ADHD when our son was younger, I was constantly on his case. I was so negative, he ultimately thought of himself as lazy, unmotivated and a failure.

The same is true for your child or teen. The better she understands ADHD behaviors, the better her coping skills will be. So even if problems are mild, find someone—a doctor, counselor, ADHD coach or yourself—to provide education about ADHD. In one or two sessions, a physician or counselor should be able to help your child gain some basic understanding of ADHD and why she faces challenges like forgetting homework and often being late.

Seek educational training opportunities. We urge you to attend ADHD training events in your community and, if possible, attend regional or national ADHD conferences. Ask your friends for suggestions for good books and spend time learning more about ADHD. As discussed in later chapters, a combination of ADHD education for the whole family, medication, academic supports and behavior interventions offers the best treatment results.

Focus on key ADHD facts. Ideally, your child or teen will learn a few important ADHD facts to help her better understand ADHD and her behavior. Simple explanations are best during the early elementary school years and then should become more scientifically exact as your teen progresses through school.

1. *ADHD and executive function basics.* Help your child grasp the basics of ADHD and executive function deficits, how they affect school performance and behavior, and why these challenges make school and other situations so difficult. Students need reassurance that they're not just simply lazy. Initially, a simple explanation may work best. "The medication helps your brain work better and makes it easier to listen to the teacher and do your schoolwork." Describing behaviors rather than giving abstract labels will be more meaningful. Rather than tell your child she has executive function deficits, explain that it's harder for students with ADHD to get started and finish schoolwork and more difficult to remember things to do and to be organized.

2. *Positive ADHD traits.* Make your child aware of ways to use some ADHD traits to her advantage—for example, "You have a unique ability to hyperfocus and think outside the box to come up with creative solutions that no one else has thought of." Our teens often have unique skills. One young adult featured in our Gallery of Hope, Khris Royal, is a gifted musician and played his saxophone at the New Orleans Jazz Festival at age five. Today he has his own band and has produced a popular CD, *Dark Matter II.*

Both of Chris's sons are mechanically inclined and can repair cars or any electronic device. Amelia Hart is a beloved middle school English teacher who also bakes beautiful wedding and birthday cakes. Max Fennel, also featured in the Gallery, is the first professional African American triathlete and founder of Fenn Coffee. So, take a stab at reframing your teen's behavior and skills, as discussed in the next section.

3. *Executive function challenges.* Discuss the challenges of executive function deficits: difficulty getting started and finishing, being disorganized, having trouble memorizing, being forgetful and having an impaired sense of time. Your teen needs to understand that her difficulty with these school tasks is the result of brain chemistry issues and *not* laziness or lack of motivation. The practical impact of ADHD and deficits in executive skills in the classroom are shown in Tables 2.3 and 2.4.

4. *ADHD brain chemistry.* Learn about ADHD brain chemistry issues and how they affect students, the role of neurotransmitters, and how medication helps the brain to work properly. There is helpful, easy-to-read information on this topic in *A Bird's-Eye View of Life* (see the Resources section).

5. *ADHD is challenging.* Acknowledge that *ADHD* is a challenging condition. Assure your teen that you believe in her and that together you'll handle any challenges that may lie ahead.

6. *Key coping skills.* Talk with teachers or counselors to *identify key skills* that will help your child or teen cope with and compensate for ADHD. Discuss and practice those skills with her.

7. *ADHD success.* Ensure that your child or teen is aware that she can cope successfully with ADHD.

See the Resources at the end of the book for suggested videos, books, and other materials that may be especially helpful in educating your child or teen about ADHD and executive functions.

ADHD education for parents must be more comprehensive and will not be achieved overnight. We encourage you to read *Attention* or *ADDitude* magazines, attend conferences, participate in webinars presented by ADHD organizations such as CHADD and ADDA-SR, join a local ADHD parent group, and seek out a knowledgeable treatment professional. Additionally, search for smaller regional ADHD conferences like the one held annually in January at the University of Alabama. Top experts like Dr. Russell Barkley are keynote speakers, and Ruth and Chris have both been featured speakers at this regional conference as well.

Chris's Lessons Learned: I wish I had known back then what I know now. But much of my current knowledge was not even available when my son was younger. I would have understood ADHD better and known how to be a more effective parent. My advice is to educate yourself about ADHD and executive functions. Diagnose and treat ADHD as early as possible. Don't put it off, as I did, thinking that surely things would get better.

Reframe ADHD Behaviors Positively

When students are struggling, it's easy to get caught up in focusing on their problem behaviors. It's extremely important to stop and take time to identify your child's strengths and special talents. Remember that the desirability of specific behaviors changes over time. Characteristics that are not valued in students in school may be valued in many professions.

Table 4.1 Reframe ADHD Behaviors Positively

ADHD Behavior	Reframed Behavior
Bossiness	... leadership (albeit carried too far)
Hyperactive	... energetic, high energy, a great multitasker, works long hours
Strong-willed	... tenacious, goal-oriented
Daydreamer	... creative, innovative, thinks outside the box, coming up with creative solutions
Daring	... risk taker, willing to try new things
Lazy	... laid back, "type B personalities live longer"
Instigator	... initiator, innovative
Manipulative	... delegates, gets others to do the job
Aggressive	... assertive, doesn't let others take advantage of him
Questions authority	... independent, free thinker, makes own decisions
Argumentative	... persuasive, may be attorney material
Poor handwriting	... maybe will be a doctor one day
Impulsive	... decisive, makes decisions quickly, potentially an invaluable skill for an emergency medical technician or physician

As discussed in Chapter 1, it can be very helpful to *reframe* aspects of your child's personality (Dendy, 2017). In other words, put a positive spin on ADHD behavior that isn't valued in school. Perhaps your son's or daughter's characteristics will be valued and considered strengths in the adult work world. For instance, although talking a lot in class may be punished, as an adult it can be invaluable. For example, Lewis Alston, a former DJ in Atlanta, was constantly in trouble at school for talking too much, but now he gets paid to talk (see Chapter 20, "Our ADHD Photo Gallery of Hope").

Review the examples of ADHD behaviors in Table 4.1 so you can identify positive ways of reframing your child's behaviors as strengths. Make it a point of finding appropriate opportunities to praise positively reframed behaviors.

PC: You can't FIX teens with ADHD, but you can really help them become the best they can be. For us, it took a tremendous amount of patience and love. I regret that I maybe wanted my daughter to be "normal" and thereby probably made her feel less than normal. Celebrate your teen!

Find Mentors for Your Child or Teen

Praise and love coming from adults is so important to validate that a child or teen is a good person worthy of love and affection. Chris found that if she praised her son, he'd sometimes dismiss it by saying, "Well, you have to say that ... you're my mom." She therefore looked for other people who really enjoyed her son and were not put off by his inattention and fidgeting, especially in a larger group of children. As a single parent, she was especially interested in finding men who would serve as role model mentors.

Here are some ideas of people who might be willing to mentor your teen, with comments from Chris about how they helped her son Alex:

- *After-school care staff.* We were so lucky that I found an after-school program that employed really loving staff when Alex was in elementary school. They were affectionate and always bragged about him and the things he did well.

- *Youth minister or other personnel at your house of worship.* Our youth minister who served as the after-school program director was a wonderful mentor for my son. Alex's school experiences were negative from first grade forward, so I was overjoyed to find this kind, loving young man who thought my son was as special as I did. Today Alex exhibits compassion, honesty, a willingness to help others, and a loving concern for me … values that I attribute, in part, to his early relationship with the youth minister.
- *Surrogate moms or dads.* Find other mothers or fathers who understand and enjoy your teen—for example, grandparents, aunts, uncles, siblings, or a neighbor. At parent support groups, you may also meet other parents who understand ADHD and can be patient and loving with your son or daughter. An added benefit is that your child may find a new friend and be welcomed to visit.
- *Neighbors.* Our next-door neighbors enjoyed Alex, and he was always welcome in their home. He played well with her two sons.
- *Teachers.* Teachers who understand ADHD can be extraordinary mentors. Alex was lucky; he had several teachers who were very positive and bent over backward to help him. One even honored him by appointing him as the summer custodian of the "school snake"! (Oh, yippee.) He also benefited from being in the school computer club and participating in a low-pressure program for gifted students. By requesting after-school tutoring, he developed a positive relationship with his teachers because they knew he was really trying.
- *Guidance counselors.* Find the "voice of reason" at your school, someone who really likes your child and understands ADHD. Sometimes the school counselor is that person, or perhaps a principal who also has a child with ADHD, or a coach, club sponsor or school custodian.
- *Coaches/friends/scout leaders.* One summer I coached my son's baseball team along with three amazing friends from work who were so patient with the boys. As a single mom, I was so grateful to these men for being such great role models and mentors.
- *Bosses or coworkers at a summer job.* The supervisor at the swimming pool where Alex was a lifeguard always bragged about what a great job he did.
- *Big Brothers Big Sisters clubs or the YMCA.* Having a Big Brother or Big Sister could be especially beneficial for children and teens who are living in a single-parent family.

Identify and Promote Your Child's Special Talents, Skills, and Interests

Exposing your child or teen to a variety of activities is a great idea, even if she loses interest after a short period of time. Engaging in sports increases brain activity and builds new brain cells. Participating in activities of interest such as art, music or singing lessons, science fairs or theater groups (Figure 4.1) will further develop a child's talents and special interests. These activities may also lead to a future career path. At a minimum, discovering strengths outside of school will help your son or daughter realize that excelling in academics is not the only path to success.

As you identify your child's special talents, make positive comments to help her become more aware of her strengths. "You do a wonderful job working with young children." (Give nonverbal praise: smile and pat her on the back.) "Your gifts working on the computer are so amazing. Lucky me—I have my own tech support person."

Practice skills in areas of interest. When your son or daughter participates in activities outside of school, it not only builds confidence but also offers opportunities for interactions with others. So encourage participation in sports, dance, music or computer games.

Figure 4.1 Aidan acting in a school play.

Offer to help her improve her skills by practicing the activity with her at home. For example, kick a soccer ball with her or listen to piano or saxophone practice.

Consider coaching your child or teen's team or activity. If you understand your child's ADHD and could help make her experience more positive, then consider coaching or supervising the activity. If you don't have the time or skills to coach, consider talking privately with the coach to make him or her aware of ADHD behaviors such as zoning out while the coach talks, not listening enough to follow directions, and not paying attention to potentially dangerous surroundings (e.g., walking into the batter's warm-up box and being hit with a bat).

Children's and teens' skills in most sports activities improve when they take medication. However, there are exceptions. For instance, two state champion wrestlers didn't take medicine when wrestling because without it they were able to quickly focus on everything almost simultaneously. In addition, note that young people may be more spontaneous and creative without medication when acting, taking art class or doing similar activities.

If your child is taking medication, there may be no need for you to talk with a coach, teacher or supervisor about your child's ADHD. If you're interested in having your child try the class or activity without medication, talk with your doctor first.

During the teen years, your child will ideally be comfortable advocating for herself in sports or other extracurricular activities. However, if not, ask for her permission before you speak privately to the coach about any major challenges.

Nurturing Alex's Talents and Skills

From Chris's perspective, here are some thoughts on how encouraging outside activities did and did not help her son grow as a person and discover his own unique interests and abilities. Many of these activities were short-lived because Alex quickly lost interest. For example, even though he was the fastest swimmer on the team, he hated the 6:00 a.m. practices, and with his difficulty getting up so early due to his sleep disorder, he soon quit the team. However, he still benefited from each activity in which he was involved.

Computers: Early on I recognized my son's love of gadgets and enthusiasm for new and exciting activities. Intuitively, I knew it was important to give him lots of opportunities to develop skills in his interest area. So I bought us an Apple computer when Alex was eight years old. (This was back when it was relatively uncommon for families to own personal computers.) With his painfully slow and illegible handwriting, he needed to be on a computer as early as possible. His affinity for understanding computers was immediately apparent. Within a very short time, he was teaching me computer skills.

Computers were a lifesaver for Alex. I encouraged development of his computer skills by enrolling him in computer classes at the local college. I realized that successes in working with computers built his self-esteem, and I thought it might open career doors in the future. He was so amazing on computers, but I failed to anticipate that his math difficulties would be a roadblock to a degree in computer science. If you barely passed algebra in high school and college, the required advanced math courses pose a monumental hurdle. Later I also realized that he'd hate sitting at a desk for hours programming information. So, although this initially seemed an ideal profession, later it became clear that computer science was not a good career match. However, his computer talents were invaluable in a variety of other fields.

Swimming: Very early on, I recognized swimming as one of Alex's gifts. He learned to swim as an infant. By age two he was diving off the board, and by four he was water skiing. He was tall, slender, and had long arms and legs—a natural for a swimmer. Swimming provided so many benefits: building new brain cells, siphoning off excess energy, providing structure and self-discipline, and building muscle strength and coordination. Participating in swimming also exposed him to structured group activities that provided leadership experiences and taught him values such as the importance of hard work and persistence. And to this day, he still enjoys boating and water sports (Figure 4.2), both great for staying physically active and spending time outside in the sun.

Baseball: Playing baseball helped Alex build coordination and athletic skills, master basic rules such as taking turns and learn to work with others as part of a team. After the fact, our baseball adventures were also a bit humorous. My son played right field. If you're knowledgeable about the sport, you know you don't put your strongest player in that position. One day I was mortified when I looked up to see him with his back to home plate, taking handfuls of dirt out of his pocket and throwing them into beautiful arcs in the wind.

Taekwondo: Taekwondo was another brief activity of interest (Figure 4.3). I was hoping the training would help Alex become more disciplined, and I'm certain it helped at some level. Probably his greatest joy was simply owning the white uniform and having a sense of accomplishment when he earned a belt.

Scouting: Cub Scouts provided exposure to positive values and gave Alex the opportunity to learn new skills while simultaneously earning badges. Interest in Scouts worked for a short time. However, my son couldn't sit still, stay with a group and pay attention all at the same time. Hmm ... this must sound familiar to you.

Figure 4.2 Alex scuba diving.

Build Resilience

Miraculously, in spite of the struggles our children may face, many develop shields of resilience that enable them to succeed in life. Parents who give their children unconditional love and support will build a level of resilience that will serve their son or daughter well throughout life. Researchers have found that young adults who succeed in life share these common traits and experiences (Katz, 1997):

- An important adult who believed in them.
- A faith in themselves that they can cope.
- A pleasant personality and the ability to relate well to others.

Figure 4.3 Jesse wearing his black belt in taekwondo.

- Experiences taking responsibility for something that is helpful to others.
- Second-chance opportunities such as military, college, a religious experience, marriage, or the birth of a child.

So, the bottom-line message for parents is this: Don't give up hope and remember to keep a lifespan perspective of ADHD.

Be Alert for Coexisting Challenges

Most of our children will face at least one other challenge in addition to their ADHD—for example, anxiety, depression or perhaps a learning disability (Jensen & MTA Cooperative Group, 1999). Since you know your son or daughter best, it's important for you to be on the lookout for any of these additional challenges and discuss them with school officials and your treatment professionals.

As noted earlier, the veteran parents who completed our survey *identified anxiety as a major problem* for their teens both in school and during their transition to adulthood. Because the impact of anxiety on school performance, daily coping and self-esteem is often not recognized, and thus not treated, both self-help and treatment strategies to address anxiety are discussed in a subsequent chapter.

Check out the ADHD Iceberg graphic in Chapter 2 and review the list of potential challenges. Keep these issues in the back of your mind as you monitor your child's self-image and emotional well-being through the school years. Your treatment professional doesn't see your child or teen at school, at home, or in community activities and is less likely to be aware of coexisting conditions unless you bring issues to his or her attention.

Nurture Yourself

Parenting a young person with ADHD who struggles daily with issues at school, at home and in the community can be overwhelming. So, take time out to nurture yourself. Parents can't adequately support their child or teen if they don't take care of themselves. Reach out to understanding friends, and if possible, find a support group either locally or online.

Chris's Lessons Learned: I turned to both friends and support groups for support. I found a mom whose daughter was a year older than my son. When Alex got two speeding tickets in one week, I called her in tears. She laughed and said, "That's nothing. My daughter got a DUI this year. She backed out of a driveway and hit a mailbox. When the policeman asked if she had been drinking, my daughter respectfully replied, 'Yes sir, I have.'" At that point, the tension was broken, as we both broke into laughter. I was relieved to know that I wasn't alone. Obviously, getting the tickets was of serious concern, but I was reminded it didn't mean Alex was a bad person.

Here are some tips for looking after your own mental health:

- *Find a mentor or counselor for yourself.* Parenting a child or teen with ADHD can be a lonely, stressful job, so finding someone who understands, listens and will give you sound advice is an absolute must.
- *Believe in your child and yourself.* It's important to continue to believe in yourself and in the goodness of your son or daughter and to believe that you both will survive the ups and downs of the ADHD parenting roller coaster.
- *Join a local or online support group.* ADHD advocacy organizations like CHADD or ADDA-SR (in Texas) offer onsite parent support groups that provide excellent educational programs and opportunities to talk with other parents who are experiencing the same challenges. If local ADHD groups aren't available, check to see if there is a local Learning Disabilities Association (LDA) group in your area. Talking with other parents about their doctors and counselors may lead you to new, more knowledgeable treatment professionals, and discussing educational issues can lead to helpful advice about working with local schools.

    There are also helpful support groups for ADHD, learning disability and autism on Facebook and other online platforms. However, be aware that the quality and accuracy of information varies greatly from group to group. Look for comments from respected leaders in the field. Otherwise, you run the risk of getting advice from people who know less than you do about ADHD.

Chris's Lessons Learned: My local CHADD group was my lifeline when my son was a preteen and teen. The encouragement from fellow CHADD members who were struggling with similar challenges was invaluable. In talking with other parents, I found a new doctor who was truly an expert on ADHD. Finding someone who really understands ADHD and knows what they're doing is very difficult. In crisis, another CHADD mom and I would call each other and commiserate. Luckily, we never had a crisis on the same day.

PC: Parents MUST make a special effort to find their teen's unique skills and enhance these natural talents even more, thereby building their confidence, self-esteem and resilience. Don't try to change the neurobiology of their brain; build on their strengths and provide supports and accommodations to help them cope with their deficits.

References

Dendy, C.A.Z. (2017). *Teenagers with ADD, ADHD, and executive function deficits: A guide for parents and professionals* (3rd ed.). Bethesda, MD: Woodbine House.

Jensen, P.S., & MTA Cooperative Group (1999). A 14-month randomized clinical trial of treatment strategies for attention deficit hyperactivity disorder. *Archives of General Psychiatry, 1999*(56), 1073–1086.

Katz, M. (1997). *On playing a poor well*. New York: W.W. Norton & Co.

5   Getting Along with Others

Building good relationships is critical for the development of strong self-esteem and a sense of belonging. And in adulthood, building and maintaining good relationships is critical for success at work. No matter how talented or skilled an employee is at his job, if he can't get along with coworkers and bosses, he won't remain employed for long.

Unfortunately, many people with ADHD struggle with the social and life skills needed to get along with others (Barkley, 2015; Cantwell, 1996). From an early age, some children, especially those who are hyperactive, often miss cues from other kids, teachers and coaches; interrupt others; intrude into others' personal space; talk too loudly; emotionally overreact to criticism; and don't recognize how failing to meet others' expectations can cause friction, hard feelings or worse. Once they move on to the world of work, young people with ADHD may miss cues from colleagues and even the boss, often engaging in many of the same behaviors that caused social problems when they were younger.

PC: Her interpersonal skills with other girls (although she is a highly social person) were lacking, and my daughter would internalize her lack of acceptance.

Fortunately, however, these are areas where most children and teens can improve now as they prepare for life after high school. With your guidance, your son or daughter can learn to overcome or compensate for the effects of ADHD on essential social and life skills. The good news is, your child doesn't have to have tons of friends. Experts tell us that having at least one good friend is a protective mental health factor that helps our children cope more successfully with school, life and their ADHD.

Why are social skills so important now and in the future? Ultimately, social skills often determine the level of success adults achieve in the work world. While job competence is always a key factor, *likability is a more important factor* when it comes to who is hired and who other workers prefer as colleagues, according to a study by Harvard Business School (Figure 5.1). Attractiveness, either in appearance or personality, is also an important quality that enhances job success.

Likability

Likable people often have similar personality traits (see Table 5.1). On a positive note, you'll probably be pleased to see that your child has several of these traits. However, young people with ADHD may lack some of these traits due to their immaturity, impulsivity, lack of awareness of how their behavior affects others, tendency to be self-focused and the need to always be right and the center of attention.

DOI: 10.4324/9781003364092-5

Figure 5.1 Mary and Carly, ADHD Ambassadors and friends.

Table 5.1 Common Traits of Likable People

Children with ADHD may exhibit many of these traits. However, if your child is lacking some of these skills, consider finding ways to practice them. Select one or two traits, discuss them, practice, and then praise him. For example, if he has trouble sharing, compliment him or pat him on the back when he is unselfish. This list of likability/friendship traits was adapted from Rick Lavoie's book, *It's So Much Work to Be Your Friend*.

- Upbeat and enthusiastic
- Cheerful
- Friendly
- Happy
- Considerate
- Sense of humor
- Sincere
- Listen
- Understanding
- Honest, truthful
- Unselfish
- Thoughtful
- Kind
- Responsible
- Dependable
- Trustworthy, trusted
- Loyal

ADHD Challenges That Can Interfere with Likability

People who are likable have good communication skills that may be lacking among some people with ADHD. Key skills include the following (Lavoie, 2005):

1. Maintaining *eye contact* and smiling or frowning when appropriate.
2. Building rapport with appropriate *gestures* and body movement (mirroring the emotions of the other person).
3. *Listening* with understanding and empathy (smiling or showing concern, depending upon whether they're happy or sad).

4. *Asking questions* and getting the other person to talk about himself.
5. *Taking turns* and sharing with friends.
6. Being *cooperative* and flexible, not always having to win, be the boss or be right.

Six General Strategies to Enhance Social Skills

What can you do to help teenagers become more likable, make friends and develop the social skills needed for success in school, in adult relationships and on the job? You could set out to explicitly teach him each of the aforementioned communication skills, or perhaps model the desirable likability traits and hope that he picks up on them. However, it's more effective to give the child or teen plenty of opportunities to *practice his relationship skills* by interacting with others. That way he can learn from his mistakes and successes and hopefully find some friends in the process. Since children and teens make friends by doing fun things together, parents can use these strategies to help their son or daughter make friends more easily.

Consider ADHD Medication

First, the most effective intervention to increase likability from the standpoint of classmates, teachers and parents is treatment with ADHD medication (Pfiffner et al., 2000). Students who take ADHD medication are more likely to follow the rules, listen to others, take turns, share, be less argumentative and stop and think before they act or speak. The benefits of medication are discussed in an earlier chapter plus in the books and videos listed in the Resources.

Create Opportunities for Building Friendships

Experts report that social skills training for children in an office setting is often not very effective with regard to carry over into real-life situations (Barkley, 2015). Typically, children with ADHD know what to do but can't automatically use the right skills at the right time. Practicing friendship skills must occur in the moment at home or school during interactions with other children.

Depending on your child's age, he may or may not be receptive to your helping him schedule one-on-one opportunities to interact with prospective friends. And the older he is, the less likely he will probably be to consider your suggestions of kids who might make good friends. Some of the following tips are more appropriate for younger children; try the ones that seem least likely to make your son or daughter roll his or her eyes at you.

- *Place your child or teen in the center of activities* by being the parent who is willing to take a friend along on a special activity such as going to an amusement park, fireworks display or concert, or the lake or beach. Taking one friend along may be best, because otherwise there is a risk that the other two friends may pair off and exclude your son or daughter.
- *Find an activity of interest that allows bonding with other children or teens.* Shared activities give children something in common that they can talk about—for example, playing the online video game *Fortnite*. According to teen development expert Deborah Gilboa, playing *Fortnite* gives children "opportunities for collaboration, communication, problem-solving, perseverance, and other skills that make our kids into the humans we

hope they can be" (Tate, 2020). (Of course, there is always the potential for children and teens to encounter unsavory content or people when on the internet, so discreet monitoring is important.) Other examples of activities that may help build friendships include team sports, theater, chorus, camping trips, youth activities at religious organizations, or skill-building classes for computers or science (e.g., Space Camp).

- *Find one good friend.* Your teen doesn't have to be popular or have tons of friends. Your main goal is to help him find at least one good friend. If your son or daughter is younger, you might be able to identify potential friends while volunteering at school or by asking the teacher or guidance counselor for suggestions.
- *Invite another family* that has children of similar ages to come play table games, horseshoes, cornhole or badminton, or swim. Set the stage before company arrives by sharing just one tip to practice, such as these: "Take turns"; "Share games"; "If you lose, tell your friend 'good game.'"
- *Provide subtle positive feedback after social events.* Give a pat on the back or a smile or wink when good social skills are used. "I was proud of you when you congratulated Andy on winning." Avoid harsh criticism about social skills (e.g., "You're a loudmouth" or "You're so bossy"). Typically, criticism leads to hurt feelings, resentment and damaged self-esteem. Plus, it isn't particularly effective in changing behavior.

Give Tips on Relating to Friends

If your teen or preteen is receptive, you, a teacher or a counselor may give him hints on how to interact successfully with friends. Identify one or two major behaviors that cause trouble in relationships and work on those. Be gentle, subtle and loving. Stay in the background as much as possible when he is interacting with others; don't intervene to solve a problem that the teen can solve.

If your child laughs at a friend for making a mistake, talk with him later. You might say something like this: "I noticed that Danny was really embarrassed when people laughed at him for dropping the baseball. Maybe you could be a good friend and show him how to move in front of the rolling baseball and hold his glove so the ball rolls into it. If you have time, maybe you could practice with him so he can improve his skills?"

Practice Skills Through Role-Playing

If your child or teen is amenable, act out situations where he often has difficulty. Key skills to practice and reinforce include initiating and maintaining conversations, using humor appropriately, dealing with peer teasing and knowing how to join a group.

- Try giving your son or daughter simple "social scripts" and then practice by role-playing. For instance, a script for meeting a potential friend for the first time might include these steps: (1) Look the person in the eye. (2) Introduce yourself by saying, "Hi, I'm [name]. What's your name?" (Or "You're [name], right?") (3) Talk in a clear voice. (4) Give the person a friendly smile.
- Give your child or teen some age-appropriate conversation starters, if he is willing to accept your advice. For example, you might advise him to begin by pointing out *something they have in common.* ("I think we … were in the same soccer league … have history class together … take ballet at the same studio."). Or, "Hey, I see you have a [certain model of smartphone, calculator, etc., or a particular video game or app] too.

Do you know where to get good ringtones [or to do something else]?" He could also *offer a compliment* about something he's observed or heard about someone else (without being creepy or "stalkerish"). For example, "I heard you sing a solo in the last chorus concert; you were awesome!" or "I loved that joke you told in Mrs. Smith's class. Did you make it up yourself?"

• *Ask a question to enter a group.* If the group is playing a game, ask, "Can I play?" Ask one of the more skilled players for tips: "How did you throw the ball like that?" If a group is just talking or eating, smile and walk toward them. If you get a welcome smile in return, ask if you may sit with them while you eat your snack.

Practice Skills in a Particular Interest Area

If your teen wants to join a team that plays a particular sport or hang out with kids who play a particular video game, practice at home to build skills and to ensure your son or daughter knows the rules. If he doesn't want parental help, consider signing him up for a class or program through a local recreational program. Joining a school club or activity can also offer your child opportunities to meet a new friend who shares his interests.

Look for Teachable Moments

If your child or teen complains that he has no friends or that no one likes him, listen while he shares his hurt feelings. Maybe a day or two later, make one suggestion—for example, "I've been thinking about what you said. Sometimes it's harder for kids with ADHD to make and keep friends. Here's one thing you can try …" If he seems interested, offer one or two suggestions about behaviors that may be turning people off: "Listen when someone else is talking, try not to interrupt them." Don't overwhelm him with criticism; make positive statements guiding how he interacts with others.

Challenges with Social Skills and Friendships: The Struggle to Fit In

PC: One of the biggest challenges in school was anxiety in social situations and not being accepted by classmates. She began acting out because of her desire to be accepted and fit in.

Intuitively, parents know that having friends is critically important. But more specifically, researchers have found that friends provide companionship, guidance and support; promote self-validation and emotional security; and serve as reliable allies. So, it's very important to provide interventions aimed at enhancing friendships by practicing when needed.

Unfortunately, nearly *half* of all children with ADHD have poor social skills (Barkley, 2015). To get along with classmates and teachers, children must be attentive, responsible and able to control their impulsivity. However, the biochemical nature of ADHD makes it very difficult for many children and teens to consistently use appropriate social skills.

Due to emotional reactivity, some children with ADHD and/or autism may be louder, bossier or more aggressive than their peers. On top of that, they often miss social cues that let them know they're being too loud, bossy or aggressive. Consequently, they frequently have difficulty making and keeping friends. Girls may have more trouble making and keeping friends than boys, and children with ADHD and hyperactivity may have more problems making friends than children who have ADHD Inattentive.

Emotional Overreaction: Difficulty Controlling Emotions

Children with ADHD who are prone to *overreacting emotionally* are unable to "dial back" the strength of their emotions. In other words, they react more emotionally than a situation should warrant and cannot calm down quickly.

For years, Dr. Russell Barkley (2015), a leading ADHD researcher and author, has argued that difficulty controlling emotions has a major impact on many people with ADHD and should be part of the ADHD diagnostic criteria. Dr. Barkley cites research dating back over 100 years that validates the argument for inclusion of emotional issues. These behaviors are (1) easily frustrated, (2) impatient, (3) quick to anger, (4) overreacting, (5) easily excited, (6) losing temper, (7) easily annoyed. Children with emotional regulation problems may also defy authority and be especially sensitive to rejection. Emotional reactivity is often present in childhood and may persist into adulthood for many people with ADHD.

The longer these emotional issues remain untreated, the more likely children and teens are to become argumentative, talk back, fail to comply with requests, show defiance and resist authority. Obviously, the negative emotions are the most damaging to their relationships and life in general. In extreme cases, their anger may result in arguments or fights throughout their lives with parents, teachers, partners or spouses, bosses or coworkers. Sometimes they may even physically or emotionally abuse family members or have road rage incidents, DUIs or car wrecks.

PC: *My son's major challenges have included unhappy relationships with girls, problems with self-expression, struggles with college academics, drinking in college and breaking up with a girlfriend and not wanting to let her go.*

Helping Children or Teenagers Who Are Emotionally Reactive

Here are some proactive strategies for handling emotional situations that you may want to discuss with your son or daughter:

1. *Identify and avoid* situations that may result in extreme emotional reactions. For example, if you know that being with or near certain people will result in conflict, avoid them. Don't even make eye contact with them.
2. *Modify the situation* by choosing where you sit and whom you sit with or talk to.
3. *Visualize yourself in a calm or happy place.* Picture yourself at the beach or sitting in a swing under your favorite tree at home. If you pass in the hall, look past the person and smile at someone else you may know.
4. Advising someone with ADHD to "stop and think" before they act or speak is a lovely idea—but it seldom works. If the person is taking ADHD medication, he is more likely to stop and think, sometimes. In addition to medication, continuing brain maturity is our greatest hope for reduced impulsivity in acts and words.

The earlier students practice these strategies, the better they'll cope with potentially emotionally charged situations.

For both children and young adults who struggle with intense emotional reactions, Dialectical Behavior Therapy (DBT), a specific type of cognitive behavior therapy, can be very helpful. This strategy focuses on learning to both tolerate and manage emotions more effectively. Learn more about DBT in Chapter 6.

Defiance and Anger: Children diagnosed with ADHD who are defiant and challenge authority during the school years may ultimately be diagnosed with oppositional defiant disorder (ODD) (Barkley, 2015; Jensen, 1999). Factors underlying all this anger often include brain immaturity, delayed development of language needed to express feelings, unrealistic expectations from adults and undiagnosed learning disabilities. Children with ODD may express this anger with temper outbursts, talking back to parents and teachers and defiance of authority figures. Over half of all students with ADHD may develop ODD. Students with ODD are 11 times more likely to be oppositional than their peers.

The good news here is that researchers report that ADHD medication improves ODD symptoms as much as it helps ADHD symptoms. Better yet, according to Barkley, earlier treatment with ADHD medication may actually prevent or even lessen the severity of ODD behaviors.

Our Parent Survey Results: *Roughly half of young adults with ADHD had been suspended from school.*

Sensitivity to Rejection: Some students with ADHD are *highly sensitive to rejection or failure*—more so than their peers—according to Dr. William Dodson (2016), a psychiatrist in Boulder, Colorado. Furthermore, they're prone to ruminating over their negative thoughts and may be unable to move forward because they "get stuck," continually thinking about a failure or negative comments from someone. Consequently, these young people with ADHD are more likely to experience a constant state of anxiety. Self-help strategies and treatment for anxiety are discussed in greater detail in Chapter 6.

Helping Your Child Overcome Shyness

You know your child or teen best, so pay attention to situations where he may be shy or anxious. Perhaps it will help to discuss in advance what to expect and give him some tips on what to do or say. It is a good idea to review the rules or expectations for the game or activity. Another strategy is to suggest that your child or teen bring a friend to events where he knows few people. Also be aware that since children and teens with ADHD are less mature, they may feel more comfortable playing with younger kids.

Does Gender Make a Difference?

It is extremely difficult and perhaps inadvisable to generalize about how a child's gender affects that child's relationships with others—especially now that it is becoming more common for teens and even younger children to openly question traditional ideas of gender identity. So, take the observations that follow with a grain of salt.

In general, the social skills expected of boys and girls are different. Relationships between boys often revolve around activities, especially sports. Girls, on the other hand, frequently view school as the center of their social life. Boys are much less likely than girls to talk about personal or confidential, sensitive topics. Many girls have their most meaningful interactions at school, and many boys have theirs after school and on weekends. Girls often enjoy talking about the lives of other people; boys don't. Girls spend a lot of time talking about the social and academic aspects of school; boys see school as an "interruption" of their social life. Many boys don't require you to be friendly, but many girls do. Girls who pass each other without speaking are often considered "stuck up" or "snobs"; the same is not true for boys. Girls generally need to dress fashionably to be considered "popular," but the same is not true for boys. Being trustworthy and responsible regarding care of property are qualities that both boys and girls greatly respect.

Strategies for Girls vs. Boys: To earn greater acceptance from their peers, children with ADHD can practice strategies based upon what we know about gender-related social skills. For example, it may help your daughter to learn that other girls expect her to smile, make eye contact and greet other girls in social situations. Most girls also try to fit in with their peers when it comes to clothing choices, makeup and hairstyles, but there can be wide latitude in what is considered "acceptable," depending on what groups they tend to associate with (band kids, theater kids, athletes, etc.).

For boys, it may help to learn more about sports and keep up to date on the current won-loss records of sports teams. Computer and video games can also be a great common ground for building relationships among boys. Encouraging both boys and girls to learn more about their friends' favorite topics can also be helpful.

Obviously, there will be girls who prefer so-called male activities and hanging out with the guys. Conversely, some boys will prefer activities that more girls tend to gravitate to. Encourage your child or teen to pursue activities that interest him or her the most and to make connections with others, regardless of gender, who enjoy the same activities.

References

Barkley, R.A. (2015). *Attention deficit hyperactivity disorder* (4th ed.). New York: Guilford Press.

Cantwell, D.P. (1996). Attention deficit disorder: A review of the past 10 years. *American Academy of Child and Adolescent Psychiatry*, 35(8): 978–987.

Dodson, W. (2016, October 16). Emotional regulation. *Attention: Living Well with ADHD*.

Jensen, P.S., & MTA Cooperative Group (1999). A 14-month randomized clinical trial of treatment strategies for attention deficit hyperactivity disorder. *Archives of General Psychiatry*, 1999(56): 1073–1086.

Lavoie, R. (2005). *It's so much work to be your friend*. New York: Simon and Schuster.

Pfiffner, L.J., Calzada, E., & McBurnett, K. (2000, July). Interventions to enhance social competence. *Child and Adolescent Psychiatric Clinics of North America*, 9(3), 689–709. Elsevier.

Tate, A.S. (2020). *Is Fortnite bad for kids?* TODAY Parents. Retrieved April 11, 2023, from https://www.today.com/parents/kids-are-obsessed-fortnite-it-bad-them-t134844

6 Managing Anxiety and Depression

You may as well accept the fact that throughout your teen's lifetime there will be challenges, some large, some small. Your moods may swing from joy to sadness to absolute fear, depending on the situation. At times you may even feel overwhelmed and believe that you have been a complete failure. If you reach this point, do as we did and reach out to others for help: parents, friends and professionals.

The information in this chapter will come in handy at various times during your child's school career and life after graduation. We both found that during the earlier years mini-crises occurred more frequently but gradually tapered off over the years into young adulthood—much to our relief. But we practiced what we preached and made certain that our top priority was maintaining a loving, positive relationship with our sons. And we provided a much-needed safety net when necessary.

Considering all the challenges that children, teens and young adults with ADHD face, it's not surprising that they are often stressed out or even clinically anxious, depressed or both. Parents, too, may become depressed and anxious as they try to help their children cope with life challenges and their worries about the future. In this chapter, we first discuss the impact of anxiety and depression on young people with ADHD, and then the effects on parents.

Sources of Stress on Young People with ADHD

Pressures arise from multiple sources. Sixty-one percent of students in the United States report that *academic pressure* creates the most stress. For example, students may be anxious and fearful of being embarrassed at school. They may worry that they'll be daydreaming and not hear a teacher's question. Those who process information slowly may be afraid they can't think quickly enough to answer questions asked in class. Other pressures include the stress of looking their best, fitting in socially, dealing with social media, bullying (cyberbullying) and not feeling safe in school.

Of course, high-stakes achievement tests add another layer of stress. Teachers are pressured for their students to master often-unrealistic standards, even when ADHD brains are not as mature. Researchers also tell us that some people are biologically inclined to be anxious. And as you may recall, *anxiety, fear and anger all produce cortisol in the brain*, basically blocking the ability to think clearly, concentrate and make wise decisions.

As your teen or young adult transitions to college or into the work world, she will probably hit some rough patches along the way. You may sense that your teen is increasingly anxious or slipping into a depression. Any of these challenges may be overwhelming and impair your teen's ability to think clearly and make wise decisions. So, taking action early is absolutely critical.

DOI: 10.4324/9781003364092-6

Beware: Don't underestimate the power of social media. The American Academy of Pediatrics (AAP) warns about the negative impact of social media on teens and young adults (O'Keefe et al., 2011). These perils can include cyberbullying and "Facebook depression." For young people who are struggling to find their way, greater social media use results in less happiness and satisfaction with life. Our sons' and daughters' sense of disappointment in themselves is often exacerbated when they skim social media postings, comparing their friends' accomplishments with their own. Researchers tell us that taking a break from social media can actually improve a young person's sense of well-being.

A young adult shares her experience:

After college graduation I no longer had the structure of my advanced-level classes, clubs, sports, my sorority and a part-time job. I no longer had a curriculum or guideline for my life and I found myself totally lost. This "lost feeling" was overwhelming by itself.

Layer social media pressure on top of this anxiety, and I was suffocating. I watched social media as my peers from college got amazing jobs, and it made me feel like I was further behind than I probably was. In that place in my life, the pressure from not having an acceptance letter to a master's or doctoral program, job offer from the big company or certification from a specific industry made me feel as if I had no major successes under my belt to post on social media. My peers were posting frequently, and it became such a suffocating feeling of failure it actually completely debilitated me for roughly six months.

Rapid downward spirals are scary. As we know from experience, our children can spiral down quickly when bad things happen. There are high-risk times throughout life, but at no time in life are there as many serious life transitions as during the early years of adulthood. Starting college, leaving home, beginning or ending a serious relationship, starting a new career, passing important academic milestones and so many other stressful and crucial events happen within a few short years.

Stress is a constant companion for most young adults, not just those with ADHD or learning disabilities. It's not a surprise that so many young people have significant personal crises at some point during this period. When a crisis happens, consider the potential impact of these major life changes and seek consultation about treatments for ADHD, anxiety and depression.

PC: Untreated anxiety is a significant factor that makes transitioning into adulthood even more difficult.

Levels of Anxiety and Depression Are Often High

High levels of both anxiety and depression are found among children and adults with ADHD. In our survey of parents of grown children with ADHD, parents reported that 58 percent of their now-adult children struggled with anxiety, and 48 percent struggled with depression. This is slightly higher than the rate of anxiety—33.5 percent—found in a large-scale study conducted at the National Institute of Mental Health (the MTA study) (Jensen & MTA Cooperative Group, 1999). Anxiety and depression occur more frequently in females and in those with the inattentive type of ADHD (Nelson & Liebel, 2018).

Both anxiety and depression can exacerbate the symptoms of ADHD and have a substantial impact on functioning. At their worst, depression and anxiety can lead to suicidal behavior. Young people with ADHD are more at risk for both self-harm behaviors, such as cutting or burns, and suicidal behavior than their peers without ADHD.

Too often there is an assumption that ADHD is the only problem. As a result, anxiety or depression in young people with ADHD is often left untreated. Don't make this mistake.

Based upon our personal experiences and input from the parents who completed our survey, we believe that chances are good that anxiety has already affected or will significantly affect your child's life, even as early as elementary and middle school. We therefore recommend that you take a step back and assess your child's or teen's level of anxiety or depression.

General Strategies to Reduce Anxiety and Depression

Here are several strategies that will benefit your child's or teen's mood and bolster her resilience:

1. *Increase emotional awareness*. The purpose of building awareness and resilience is to help young people recognize emotions, so they'll be aware of their stress, anxiety or deepening sadness. See the "Increase Awareness of Emotions" section of this chapter for steps in building emotional awareness.
2. *Try self-help strategies*. Introduce and practice self-help strategies such as those discussed in the "Depression" section of this chapter to address anxiety or depression. If you intervene early, self-help strategies may be sufficient to enhance your child's skills for coping with anxiety.
3. *Seek counseling for yourself* so you will know how to guide your son or daughter more effectively.
4. *Consider counseling for your child or teen*. Encourage her to talk with a treatment professional or coach to learn better coping strategies.
5. *Adjust medication*. Talk with your physician about trying a medication to address anxiety or depression.

Increase Awareness of Emotions

Making your child or teen more aware of her feelings will help her recognize when she's anxious, angry, scared, or sad and then choose appropriate actions to take. To increase emotional awareness, you can label feelings and empathize with your son or daughter. Here is how that might work: "You seem disappointed (sad). What's going on?" (Listen to her explanation.) "If Mrs. Smith called me lazy in front of the whole class, I'd be angry and upset, too." Begin by helping your child understand and label her own emotions before expecting her to recognize those same emotions in others.

To help your child understand feelings of others, you can make comments about friends and family, interpreting their emotions: "Your friend Belynda is sad because her parents are divorcing." Or, "I can tell that Tom was having a good time because he was smiling and laughing." It may also be helpful to label your own emotions. Chris can remember sitting on the steps with her son and saying, "I'm so scared about having this biopsy. I'm afraid it might be cancer. I'm having trouble sleeping." Alex hugged her, and told her, "It's going to be okay, Mom. We'll get through this together."

Activities involving *emojis* (stylized pictures of people's expressions) can be an easy, nonthreatening way to increase your child's or teen's awareness of her own and others' feelings. If your child or teen has a cell phone or spends time on social networking sites, she undoubtedly has already used emojis as a shorthand method to communicate happiness, sadness, anger, or the like. You might consider using the emojis you send to or receive from your child in messages as a way to encourage more open communication and understanding of feelings. For example, if your teen texts a less-common emoji to you, you could ask her (in person or via a return text) what that emoji means. Or you could make a point of using an usual emoji in a message and then check that your teen knows how you're feeling.

You could also use a physical emoji chart as a quick way to check in with family members about their day or current state of mind.

Chris's Lessons Learned: Just for fun I placed an emoji feeling chart on the refrigerator. All my family members were encouraged to indicate the emoji that reflected how they were currently feeling. If I was having a tough day, I might check the annoyed emoji, or if I was applying for a new job, the next day, I would mark the nervous/anxious emoji. Occasionally I'd ask my son to pick his emoji when he came home from school. This gave me the opportunity to ask him about his day ... and the stresses he was facing.

If you're interested in helping your son or daughter become more aware of his or her feelings, search for "emoji feelings chart" online, print out the chart (or buy one), and try incorporating it into your family's day as described by Chris. Simple emoji charts with fewer faces that show easily recognizable emotions are better.

Another possibility for deepening your child's understanding of emotions is to ask the school counselor if any *social emotional learning (SEL)* classes are being taught. These classes are designed to help students recognize their feelings and develop strategies to cope with them in healthy ways. Availability of SEL classes is expanding nationally in hopes of reducing bullying and school violence.

Try to Reduce Stress

Help Reduce Stress. You can help your son or daughter by reducing as much stress as possible. Rethink your expectations and vision of the future and give your child or teenager the time to mature and grow into adulthood on his or her own timeline, not everyone else's. As we discuss in later chapters, that vision after high school may include participating in a gap year program or taking one class at a local community college. Or if your teenager is more mature and has the necessary skills, she might be ready to attend a vocational college or a traditional four-year college away from home. Regardless of her choice, be sure your teen knows she is loved for who she is.

Minimize Social Media Impact. Discuss the negative impact Facebook may have on your son's or daughter's mental health. Facebook posts often portray an inflated description of accomplishments. Your teen may sink into a "Compare and Despair" situation or "Facebook depression." Encourage your teen to spend less time on Facebook, Instagram, Pinterest, or similar sites when stress is highest, and she is feeling discouraged.

Address Cyberbullying. Here are some key facts about cyberbullying:

1. Roughly 50 percent of all children have experienced cyberbullying, according to the Pew Research Center (Vogel, 2022).

2. Parents or educators are never told about most cyberbullying.
3. Bullying increases the risk of anxiety, depression, difficulty sleeping and academic problems, plus there's a significant link to a risk of suicidal thoughts and actions, according to the CDC.

Indicators that your teen may be being bullied include the following: (1) seeming upset or mad when she is online; (2) becoming withdrawn or anxious or avoiding social situations; or (3) turning off the computer or changing the screen when you come into the room.

Document the bullying by taking a screenshot of the comments, including the website or app name and a picture of the commenter's profile. If the bully attends your child's school, *report it* to school administrators. If they are unresponsive, report it to the school superintendent or, if necessary, the state department of education. You may also report it to the social media site or app where the bullying has occurred.

Is It "Just" Stress, or Is It Anxiety?

Our Parent Survey: *Over half of these young adults struggled with anxiety.*

How do you know if your son or daughter is experiencing anxiety rather than "just" stress? Common symptoms of anxiety include the following:

* Constant worrying.
* Feeling keyed up or on edge.
* Getting tired easily.
* Mind going blank.
* Being irritable.
* Having muscle tension.
* Experiencing sleep problems.

Although sleep issues are common for students with ADHD, anxiety will make sleep problems even worse. For example, a teen may get only three or four hours of sleep each night and then sleep through classes or work the next day. Obviously, all these potential challenges make it difficult to pay attention in class or at work, to think clearly and to answer questions correctly. High levels of anxiety undermine a young person's self-confidence, health, ability to embrace life to the fullest, and willingness to participate in new activities.

PC: My son with slow processing speed was so anxious that he'd rather take a zero in class rather than speak in front of the whole class.

Simple Steps to Reduce Anxiety

When you're anxious, the brain produces "bad" brain chemicals (*cortisol* and *norepinephrine*) that impair memory, increase blood pressure and suppress the immune system. As a result, you can't think clearly since your thoughts are consumed with feelings of anxiety.

The antidote for reducing anxiety is to increase "good" brain chemicals (*dopamine, serotonin, oxytocin,* and *endorphins*) that make a person feel good, increase positive moods and, best of all, decrease cortisol. So, the goal is to "talk to your brain" and take actions that will *increase dopamine* and decrease cortisol.

> Talk to your brain
>   when you're anxious.
>   Do Something to
>   increase dopamine
>   and reduce cortisol.

Simple Activities Can Change Your Brain Chemistry

These strategies can help combat anxiety. Each of these activities actually increases dopamine, serotonin, oxytocin and/or endorphins and reduce cortisol.

1. *Movement*: any movement, such as swinging arms or standing up; not just exercise.
2. *Music*: listen to upbeat music to energize, or calming softer music to relax.
3. *Diet*: increase protein intake, nuts, avocados, bananas, milk, yogurt, dark chocolate, leafy greens.
4. *Sunlight*: take a quick walk outside in the sun.
5. *Novelty*: try something new; change work locations.
6. *Connection*: snuggle with a pet, give hugs, share a meal with friends.
7. *Random acts of kindness*: open a door for someone, give a small thank-you gift; in return you give yourself a "helper's high."
8. *Positive affirmations*: make positive statements about yourself; "My anxiety doesn't control my life."
9. *Gratitude practice*: start the day by listing things for which you're grateful; keep a gratitude journal.

Self-Help Strategies to Address Anxiety

Some teens may be receptive to learning a few self-help strategies to alleviate anxiety; others will not be. If you aren't comfortable teaching such strategies yourself, find a treatment professional who is. Ask your school counselor, coach, psychologist or physician to recommend someone to talk with your teen and introduce a couple of these strategies for her to try.

If your teen is struggling, then chances are parents also are anxious and worried. So these strategies may be helpful to both parents and teens. For clinical anxiety or depression, a combination of medication, counseling and behavioral strategies is the most effective treatment. See the sections later in the chapter for additional suggestions.

Chris's Lessons Learned: I was comfortable introducing some self-help ideas to my son, primarily because of my counseling background and also because I was using them to cope with my own anxiety and stress regarding my cancer treatment.

Here are a few easy stress relievers that you may try out and then suggest that your teen try one or two herself.

1. *Pamper yourself.* Suggest that your son or daughter take a hot, soaking bath or shower. Some may use bath bombs or oils in the bath water.

2. *Play calming, relaxing music without lyrics.* For some, it may be calming classical music for studying, instrumental religious hymns or piano/orchestra recordings. Let your child choose for herself; don't try to impose your own tastes on her.
3. *Use a stress ball.* Your child or teen might want to try squeezing a stress ball while tackling a big project. This will remind her to pause a minute, take a deep breath and let her body relax. Remind your teen that "squeezing the ball will help you relax a little," and hopefully she will begin to associate squeezing the ball with relaxing thoughts.
4. *Make an effort to focus and refocus on positive thoughts.* Your brain can't think two contradictory thoughts simultaneously. So when someone focuses on a positive thought, the negative one is pushed out of the way—but it will continue to "try to sneak back in" to consciousness. So at first it will take more effort to stay focused on the positive thoughts.
5. *Exercise.* Regular exercise is helpful to strengthen muscles and then relax them when the activity is over (Figure 6.1). Plus, moderate exercise like jogging or speed walking has the added benefit of building new brain cells and increasing blood flow to the brain. During stressful homework evenings, suggest that your son or daughter take a "brain break" that may include limited physical activity such as shooting hoops, throwing a Frisbee or ball around for a few minutes, or dancing. Exercise is a great management technique for ADHD and is wonderful for your child or teen's health.
6. *Practice deep breathing.* Have your child or teen take several deep breaths and then gently blow the air out. For a little variety, she can take a deep breath from the belly, then tense her stomach and diaphragm while blowing out all the air until she can no longer

Figure 6.1 Aidan at the gym.

blow out any air. Muscles are tensed and then relaxed, helping her relax her whole body. Relax and take several normal breaths, then repeat the deep breath.

7. *Practice muscle relaxation.* Progressively tensing and relaxing muscle groups throughout the body is an effective strategy to reduce body tension. For example, squeeze each muscle group sequentially, starting with your head, then your face and neck. Next, tense your shoulders, continuing progressively through the arms, then hands, seat, legs, and feet. Calming apps are available that guide you through muscle relaxation activities.

8. *Try guided imagery.* Listening to guided imagery audio recordings of deep breathing, positive affirmations, or other mindfulness exercises may also be helpful. Here are a few examples of positive affirmations your child or teen may say to herself or that you may say to her: "I never give up. I'm more aware of my feelings every day. My courage and bravery continue to grow. I'm feeling less anxious every day. I'm proud of myself today. I have true grit. I recognize when I'm anxious and I know how to handle it." Write a positive affirmation on a slip of paper and give it to her to keep in her pocket and read throughout the day

9. *Try grounding.* This strategy involves breathing through your nose and out through your mouth. Then begin refocusing on things around you rather than your thoughts inside your head. Say aloud:

   - Five things you can see (hair, table, cup, window, bed).
   - Four things you can touch (face, arm, chair, hair).
   - Three things you can hear (fan, music, dog walking).
   - Two things you can smell (coffee, hand soap).
   - One thing you can taste (toothpaste).

10. *Review the daily schedule.* Sometimes better scheduling of your child or teen's time will reduce the stress of meeting last-minute deadlines. Also consider whether she is participating in too many extracurricular activities. If so, discuss the possibility of eliminating one or two.

If you intervene early, self-help strategies may be sufficient to enhance your teen's skills for coping with anxiety.

   "Get Real" Tip from Chris: *My own personal anxiety and fear for my son's future and his life were interfering with my ability to be positive and consistently encourage him. Clearly, my anxiety was palpable to anyone who was around me, especially my son. When I realized my anxiety only compounded his self-doubts, I talked with my doctor and began taking medication to reduce my anxiety. So don't forget to address your own stress and anxiety.*

Managing More Severe Anxiety

If your child or teen's anxiety is more serious, the next step will be to consult a treatment professional such as a psychologist, social worker, licensed counselor or psychiatrist. Look for a professional who has experience treating both ADHD and anxiety. Medication to help reduce anxiety may also be suggested as part of the treatment plan. If you can't find or afford a good therapist, consider which people within your community circle might be of help. For example, you may have a close friend, relative, guidance counselor, physician or minister who relates well to your son or daughter and is knowledgeable about ways to reduce anxiety.

If you're unable to find a treatment professional, your last option will be to educate yourself and do the best you can to provide the needed guidance and support. You'll need to read about anxiety, its underlying causes and possible ways to reduce it. See the Resources section for suggestions. Practicing alongside your child or teen should also be helpful. You'll need to ask her to tell you the things she worries about the most. Since children with ADHD are often unaware of their anxiety, she may have trouble finding the words to tell you what makes her anxious. Fortunately, you probably have a good idea already.

Consider Apps. Start with a simple approach first. Your child or teen might want to try the Stop, Breathe, Think app to help reduce anxiety and body stress. Users begin by rating themselves, both physically and mentally, then add emotions they may feel. For example, if you feel worried, restless and anxious, the app suggests four activities: (1) a body scan for tension; (2) relax, ground and clear tension; (3) mindful breathing; and (4) yoga for stress. The app is user friendly and rated positively by families of children with ADHD.

Another app worth considering is Self-help for Anxiety Management (SAM). This app is a bit more advanced and offers specific self-help strategies. Initially the app gives information about anxiety, then explains how negative, unrealistic fears and thoughts contribute to anxiety. Next, the app offers step-by-step guidance for tackling each situation. Users first list situations that make them anxious, then visualize and practice dealing with the least anxiety-producing situations first. If your teen is receptive, become familiar with the app first, then participate in these activities with her.

PC: We didn't realize how much the anxiety affected his ability to continue working when things got tough. He would just basically shut down.

Depression

Not surprisingly, some young people with ADHD show signs of depression as a result of a combination of challenges: constant struggles at school, poor grades, parental pressure to try harder, rejection by classmates, bullying or breakup of close relationships with close friends, boyfriend/girlfriend or significant others. The same stresses that lead to anxiety also may contribute to depression, and these two conditions often occur together.

Since symptoms of depression are often different for children and teens than for adults, the depression may not be obvious. For example, depression in teens doesn't always involve sadness. Here are a few possible symptoms of depressions in children and teens:

- Loss of interest in favorite activities.
- Withdrawal from friends or family.
- Dropping grades.
- Feelings of hopelessness or worthlessness.
- Sadness.
- Crying spells.
- Difficulty concentrating.
- Changes in weight.
- Fatigue.
- Excessive sleep or insomnia.
- Thoughts of suicide.

Sometimes, irritability or aggression that seems out of character may also be an indicator. Irritability or aggression may actually *mask* underlying depression.

It takes time and support to resolve depression in young people. The most effective interventions involve increasing awareness of emotions, exercise, behavioral therapy and perhaps an antidepressant medication. Addressing school challenges by teaching skills or providing prompts to accommodate difficulties with executive skills may reduce both anxiety and depression.

Our Parent Survey Results: *Nearly half of these young adults struggled with depression.*

Self-Help Strategies to Address Depression

Exercise. Exercise is one of the most effective self-help strategies for dealing with both anxiety and depression. Moderate-intensity exercise such as jogging or power walking releases growth factors that help the brain and body grow new nerve cells. When someone is depressed, it is very hard to get started. But even five minutes of exercise a day will begin to make a difference. Then add five more minutes and keep increasing the time as it becomes a habit. The most important concept is exercising regularly. If your child or teen is reluctant, ask if she will join you on a walk or other simple type of exercise. Or suggest exercising with a friend.

Encourage Outside Activities. Think about activities that interest your son or daughter and that will keep him or her busy. The goal is to help your child or teen focus on something fun, and hopefully it will push negative thoughts away. Possible activities include cooking, chess, video games, dancing, singing, acting or religious activities. Participating in a group that focuses on the activity is often helpful. If a national health crisis requires social distancing, here are a few suggested solo activities to consider: bike riding, walking, archery, kayaking, or tennis with social distancing and liberal use of hand sanitizer. If necessary, consider participating in online meetings on activities of interest.

"Get Real" Tip: Keep in mind that people with depression often feel paralyzed, making it difficult for them to take steps to initiate new activities. If your child or teen expresses an interest in a specific activity, you may have to do the legwork. Call and find out information about the class, start dates and cost, and sign her up. Put a reminder of the start date on both her personal calendar and the family calendar.

Try Mindfulness Meditation. The purpose of mindfulness is to focus your attention on your experience in the present moment. Reported benefits of mindfulness include stress reduction, better self-control, increased concentration, lowered blood pressure and improved sleep (Davis & Hayes, 2011; Gutierrez et al., 2020).

Mindfulness can be particularly useful when a person is consumed by negative thoughts of past problems or anxiety about future events. It involves learning to objectively observe one's thoughts and behaviors in the moment without judgment. When negative thoughts occur, the individual learns to acknowledge them and to realize the thoughts are not accurate reflections of reality and let them pass without getting caught up in a cycle of negative thinking. Several activities that were mentioned in the section on anxiety are good for practicing mindfulness meditation both at home or school, including deep breathing exercises, muscle contraction and relaxation, and the Stop, Breathe, Think app.

Get Peer Support. Some more mature, self-aware young people may be willing to ask for support from others who have experienced depression. Self-help groups may be found both online and in your community. These are not therapy groups, but peers who have dealt with depression and are there to support and help one another. Participants learn that they are not alone. Most groups are free. One word of caution: check periodically to review the quality of comments on any online self-help site since they may not be properly monitored. Bad advice could be extremely damaging.

Use Apps. And of course, there is an app for that. Talk Life connects you with others who are experiencing depression and provides peer support. There is nothing worse than feeling totally alone with your depression and anxiety. And you can participate anonymously if you choose.

Increase Exposure to Light. Artificial light or sunlight can make a difference for those who experience seasonal affective disorder (SAD). We all need sunlight to thrive, but too often we don't get enough sunshine with our sedentary lifestyles. If your child's or teen's depression gets worse in the winter, when daylight is shortened, you may find that more time outdoors or the use of a SAD light (which mimics sunshine) indoors will help her feel better.

Check Vitamin D Levels. Research has shown that some people who are depressed have lower levels of vitamin D. Consider asking your doctor to check your child's vitamin D_3 levels. If levels are low, a vitamin D_3 supplement may help.

Reframe Negative Thinking

It's important for your child or teen to know that her feelings are being "heard." So be careful not to dismiss the feelings she is experiencing. Always let her know you recognize how bad she is feeling. But you can help her change her understanding or reframe these negative thoughts. Treatment often involves helping to change negative self-talk and thoughts. Here are some of the traps we all fall into that make us feel worse.

- *Overgeneralization.* Young people don't have enough life experience to realize that one bad experience is just one bad experience. Help them realize that one breakup doesn't mean they'll never find another boyfriend or girlfriend. One bad grade doesn't mean they'll never graduate. Sharing some of your hard-time stories can help immensely.
- *All-or-nothing thinking.* This sort of thinking results when there is no "gray" or middle ground. Your son or daughter is not a "total loser" because of one bad semester or losing a friend.
- *Replaying a bad situation over and over again.* Help your child or teen learn to interrupt these thoughts. One good way is to wear a rubber band around the wrist, and every time the bad thoughts come back, snap the rubber band. The snap causes the body to release a small amount of adrenaline and trains the brain to stop going down the rabbit hole with negative thoughts.
- *Ignoring the positive and focusing on the negative.* Help your son or daughter identify five good things that happened today. You may have to start small, identifying just one thing and working up to five. If you do this daily, she will learn to be grateful for the positive things in her life.

Several apps based upon cognitive behavior therapy (CBT) help reframe negative thinking by teaching these skills and more. But don't expect an app to make a difference by itself. Doing the exercises together can be a positive experience. Here are some apps to consider:

- Depression CBT is designed specifically to help users change their negative thought patterns and learn better ways to cope with life's stresses. Based upon the interventions used in CBT, the app provides informative articles (and audio) and exercises to learn new skills. There is a "depression" tracking feature to help you monitor your progress.

- What's Up is also based upon the approach used in CBT. It aims to teach the user several coping strategies to cope with depression and negative thinking. And there is a forum for users to connect with each other and offer support.

In the Resources, you will also find a few helpful self-help books that are based on CBT and have been found to be effective in research studies.

Best Treatment Strategies for Anxiety and or Depression

If you are seeing symptoms of anxiety or depression in your son or daughter, the first priority is to seek treatment. Both anxiety and depression should be taken very seriously. The self-help strategies we have outlined in this chapter are best used in conjunction with treatment. Effective treatment for both anxiety and depression usually involves both therapy and medication.

Counseling for Anxiety and/or Depression

Cognitive behavior therapy (CBT) can be effective for those with the combination of ADHD and depression and/or anxiety. If you have difficulty finding a therapist in your area, contact a local university and see if they can help you locate someone trained in these approaches. Don't hesitate to ask a potential therapist if he or she has been trained in CBT or dialectical behavior therapy (DBT). These two approaches are similar, but DBT can be helpful for those who have very intense emotional reactions.

Cognitive Behavioral Therapy: CBT is more likely to be available through a university or in urban areas, but it is growing in availability. It's based upon the premise that our dysfunctional thoughts can affect our behavior and emotions. Rather than explore an individual's past, the therapy focuses on the here and now, teaching practical strategies to deal with difficult situations. The therapist teaches a range of skills to help the person change destructive thoughts and behaviors and to interact with others more effectively. Because it is a skill-based approach, it takes some time to have a major impact. But the skills learned will be beneficial for a lifetime.

Dialectical Behavioral Therapy: DBT is based on the same premise as CBT but also addresses the intense emotional reactions some young people struggle with. The aim of DBT is to help the patient do the following:

- Tolerate distress and negative emotions more effectively.
- Learn to live mindfully in the moment and not obsess about past problems and interactions.
- Learn to communicate and interact effectively with others.
- Learn to better regulate emotions.

DBT is also a skill-based approach, and the therapist will teach dozens of strategies to help achieve these outcomes. It takes time and a willingness to try the new strategies taught by the therapist. But it can make a positive difference in the lives of young people with ADHD.

Medications for Anxiety and Depression

If you are still responsible for making decisions about your child's medical treatment, consult with her pediatrician or psychiatrist about medications that might help with her anxiety and/or depression. If you have an older teen or young adult, encourage her to talk with her doctor to determine which medication may be best for her. Offer to go to the doctor with your son or daughter. Older teens who are depressed or anxious may not be able to explain adequately how they are feeling or how the anxiety or depression is affecting their lives.

What works for one person may not work for your child. Each person's brain chemistry is a bit different, and the doctor will help find both the right medication and the right dosage. Don't give up if your young person doesn't see relief right away. A number of these medications may take as long as four to six weeks to be effective. The most important thing for you to do is to ensure that your son or daughter sees the treating doctor regularly and gives honest feedback about the impact of the medication.

Every Parent's Worst Nightmare

Getting treatment for your son's or daughter's depression is critical. Here's why: *depression is linked to an increased risk of suicide.* As stress increases, if neither anxiety nor depression is treated, the risk of suicide increases. Every parent of a teenager or young adult with ADHD must take this increased risk very seriously. Major issues of concern among young people who are seriously depressed include cutting, biting or burning oneself, suicidal thoughts, developing a plan for committing suicide and actual suicide attempts.

In recent years, suicides among young people 15 to 24 years old have increased, and it's now the second leading cause of death among this age group in the United States, according to the CDC. In 2017, 6,252 young people in the United States committed suicide.

Children and teens with ADHD have a higher risk of attempting suicide than their peers. The greater emotionality, sensitivity to failure, and impulsivity associated with ADHD are major factors in their suicide attempts. Sadly, suicidal thoughts and attempts are more common than we'd like to believe and should be taken very seriously. For example, the long-term Milwaukee study of boys with ADHD reported that 20 of 122 boys (16 percent) attempted suicide in high school (Barkley, 2015). In another study at the University of California, Berkeley, 50 of 228 girls with ADHD (22 percent) attempted suicide (Hinshaw et al., 2012).

Girls tend to use less lethal means then boys during their suicide attempts. Consequently, boys "succeed" in committing suicide more frequently than girls. Note that because the young people in the studies referenced here tended to have more challenging ADHD, *prevalence rates for suicide attempts are probably not as high for teenagers living in a typical community.*

Here are the *warning signs of suicide risk* to look out for:

- Changes in eating or sleeping habits.
- A decline in school performance, grades dropping.
- Withdrawal from family, friends, activities.
- Loss of interest in favorite activities.
- A recent loss: breakup with a girlfriend or boyfriend, death of a family member, moving to a new city, parents divorcing.
- Giving away favorite possessions.
- Giving hints: "I won't be a problem for you much longer"; "Nothing matters"; "It's no use"; "I'm worthless"; "I wish I was dead."
- Talking about unbearable pain, sadness, hopelessness, self-harm.
- Impulsive risk taking.

Suicide is a very difficult, emotional topic to discuss. No parent wants to think that his or her son or daughter might attempt suicide. However, if a loved one is showing several of these warning signs of suicide risk, it's important for you to take action immediately. Suicide risk and intervention strategies are discussed in greater detail in Chris's book, *Teenagers with ADD, ADHD, and Executive Function Deficits* (Dendy, 2017). Here's a summary of steps you may take to prevent your teen from harming herself.

- *Take all suicidal statements seriously.* Any comments your child or teen makes about wanting to commit suicide or kill herself should be taken seriously. "I wish I was dead."
- *Ask about suicidal thoughts.* Although asking the question is often difficult, it provides reassurance that you care and gives your son or daughter an opportunity to talk about sad feelings. "You seem really sad. Are you okay?"
- *Then ask the hard questions.* "Recently you said that you feel worthless, and that life just doesn't seem worth living. Are you thinking about harming yourself?" Or, "Are you thinking about committing suicide?" Or "Have you developed a plan for killing yourself? How were you planning to do it?"

  Don't be afraid to ask these questions for fear that you will plant the idea of suicide in your teen's head. If you're seeing these symptoms, she's already thought about it. In fact, asking the hard questions is more likely to have a positive effect. Once the feelings are shared and she knows help is available, the likelihood of a suicide attempt will be reduced.
- *Seek professional help immediately.* If your son or daughter is showing several warning signs, is talking about suicide, or has a suicide plan, call your treatment professional immediately to discuss the risks and ask for advice.
- *Listening is critical.* Assure your teen that you love her and that together you'll work through this difficult time. Don't argue, criticize or make her feel guilty. Don't say, "Things aren't as bad as you think they are" or "Things could be worse."
- *Show concern and affection.* Hold her hand, pat her on the shoulder or hug her. Tell her you love her and will always be there for her.
- *Take action to reduce depression or anger.* Young people with ADHD often plummet into depression because so many negative life experiences make them feel they have no control over their lives. Talk with your son or daughter to see if a couple of major life stresses can be relieved. For example, if she is failing in school, take steps to help her catch up with her work. If she has just experienced a breakup, it might help for her to talk with her best friend or invite a friend over to play a new video game or attend a concert.
- *Remove weapons and dangerous medications from the home.* The risk of suicide increases significantly when there are guns in the home. Also remove medications that might result in an overdose.
- *Provide close supervision.* Until you develop a plan with your treatment professional, keep your son or daughter busy and provide constant supervision. Enlist the help of family and friends if you need help keeping her occupied.
- *Contact the National Suicide Prevention Lifeline.* If you have concerns but are not sure how to proceed, call the National Suicide Prevention Lifeline at 1-800-273-8255. The person responding will walk you through the next steps.

Chris's Lessons Learned: Maintain a loving relationship with your teen above everything else: your loving relationship may save her life.

PC: Once when my teenaged son was very depressed, I feared a suicide attempt. After he had broken up with his girlfriend and also had his driver's license suspended, we sat together in the garage and talked and cried. He said, "I just want to go to sleep and never wake up. But I would never do that, because I know how much you love me and how much it would hurt you." Through my tears I told him how much I loved him and that I would be devastated if something happened to him.

Suicide is a cry for help. Frequently, teenagers are undecided about living or dying. In some ways it's a form of Russian roulette. They leave it up to fate or others to save them. Asking questions and providing supervision when warning signals are observed could save their lives.

The Roller-Coaster Ride May Be Frightening for Parents

The ups and downs of parenting a teenage son or daughter with ADHD can take a toll on your emotions, too. Especially if ADHD treatment is disrupted during critical life transitions, it can result in increased anxiety and depression not only for young people with ADHD but also for their parents. So one of our important take-home messages is this: *take care of yourself so that you have the energy to provide positive supports for your child.*

Older adults can have the same symptoms of depression as children and teens listed earlier in the chapter. In addition, adults who are depressed may have major memory problems, personality changes, physical aches or pains, extreme fatigue, loss of appetite, loss of interest in sex, and they may withdraw from friends, stay at home, drink more alcohol than usual or have suicidal thoughts.

Chris's Lessons Learned: Parenting a child with ADHD is often very stressful; seek help for yourself as needed. At times I worried so much about my son's academic performance and impulsive behavior that my anxiety caused blood pressure and other health problems. Sometimes I would find myself crying privately and feeling so alone and helpless. At that point I sought help from a counselor in my son's pediatrician's office.

In my talks with the counselor, I learned more about how ADHD affected my son and how I could be a more effective parent for a challenging child. I also talked with my doctor about treating my anxiety. Since anxiety is as palpable as oil in the air, I didn't want my anxiety to trigger my son's already high anxiety. It was important that I be calm and support him in a positive way.

Aside from the doctor and counselor, the only people who really seemed to understand my pain and fears were other moms of teenagers with ADHD that I met through local CHADD meetings. These monthly meetings were so beneficial because we learned new information about ADHD and better parenting strategies. We also helped new members find good doctors who understood how to treat ADHD. By sharing our parenting experiences, we bonded as lifelong friends and knew we weren't alone in this struggle. Finding friends who understood my ADHD life was wonderful since my own misinformed parents didn't understand at all. My parents and some friends believed that if I only disciplined my son more, problem behaviors wouldn't occur.

References

Barkley, R.A. (2015) *Attention deficit hyperactivity disorder*, (4th ed.). New York: Guilford Press.

Davis, D.M. & Hayes, J.A. (2011) What are the benefits of mindfulness? A practice review of psychotherapy related research. *Psychotherapy*, 48(2), 198–208. Washington, DC: American Psychological Association.

Dendy, C.A.Z. (2017). *Teenagers with ADD, ADHD, and executive function deficits: A guide for parents and professionals* (3rd ed.). Bethesda, MD: Woodbine House.

Gutierrez, A., Krachman, S., Scherer, E., West, M., & Gabrieli, J. (2020, October 15). *Mindfulness in the classroom: Learning from a school-based mindfulness intervention through the Boston Charter Research Collaborative*. Transforming Education. Retrieved January 28, 2023, from https://transformingeducation.org/resources/mindfulness-in-the-classroom-learning-from-a-school-based-mindfulness-intervention-through-the-boston-charter-research-collaborative/

Hinshaw, S.P., Owens, E.B. Zalecki, C., Montenegro-Novado, A.G., Huggins, S.P., Schroedek, E.A., & Swanson, E.N. (2012) Prospective follow-up of girls with attention deficit hyperactivity disorder into early adulthood: Continuing impairments includes elevated risk for suicide attempts and self-injury. *Journal of Consulting and Clinical Psychology (APA)*, 80(6), 1041–1051.

Jensen, P.S., & MTA Cooperative Group (1999). A 14-month randomized clinical trial of treatment strategies for attention deficit hyperactivity disorder. *Archives of General Psychiatry*. 1999(56), 1073–1086.

Nelson, J.M. & Liebel, S.W. (2018, February–March) Anxiety and depression among college students with attention deficit hyperactivity disorder. *Journal of American College Health*, 66(2), 123–132.

O'Keefe, G. S., Clarke-Pearson, K., and Council on Communications and Media. (2011). The impact of social media on children, adolescents, and families. *Pediatrics*. 27(4), 800–804.

Vogel, E. (2022, December 15). *Teens and cyberbullying 2022*. Pew Research Center: Internet, Science & Tech. Retrieved January 28, 2023, from https://www.pewresearch.org/internet/2022/12/15/teens-and-cyberbullying-2022/

7 Navigating the Middle and High School Years

If you're reading this book now as your teenager has started middle or high school, please take a few minutes to skim Chapter 3 regarding school success, which covers common difficulties in school and federal laws that can help level the playing field for students with ADHD. Some of the challenges your son or daughter encountered during elementary school may continue to cause difficulties and may actually become worse in middle and high school.

Since major life transitions like those from elementary to middle school and then to high school are often difficult for our children and teens, a few tips are also provided to make these transitions easier and less stressful.

If your teen is struggling in middle and high school, this book will become your best friend. As we have learned from experience, chances are good that if your student is struggling during these years, he will need extra support after high school graduation to make a successful transition to college or vocational training and to move forward into a career.

Chris's Lessons Learned: When my son entered middle school, it was like he hit a brick wall. So many other parents have told me the same thing happened with their children. When Alex's grades dropped, I was mystified because my gifted son was struggling to simply pass his classes.

Demands for executive skills increase significantly during middle and high school (Denckla, 2019). Beginning in middle school and continuing for years to come, the demands for working independently, "being responsible" for keeping up with assignments, starting and finishing work and submitting assignments on time increase significantly. In addition, academic assignments become more complex, and if a learning disability is present, it will become even more obvious now.

Students who have previously been successful in elementary school may struggle and grades may drop. Our children are often successful in elementary school because their teachers provide more structure, support and guidance. In other words, their teachers serve as their "external executive functions" by directing them when to start, finish and turn in their work and by prompting them if they get distracted.

When children with ADHD are suddenly thrust into middle school, they face overwhelming expectations, but they often lack the skills to deal with these increased demands because of their delayed brain maturity. Not surprisingly, parents often say that school issues such as completing homework and long-term projects are the major source of family conflict.

In short, *children with ADHD often aren't developmentally ready to meet the increased expectations and demands* for working independently at the middle and high school levels.

DOI: 10.4324/9781003364092-7

Educational expectations often are not realistic for students with ADHD. Adults frequently fail to take into consideration the ADHD delay in brain maturity. Martha Bridge Denckla, MD, a world-renowned pediatric neurologist and researcher, was the first to identify the significant role that executive functions play in school performance (Denckla, 2019). Here are her words of wisdom based upon decades of research:

> "We have to examine how our educational expectations might be running ahead of what is developmentally appropriate as this may well be an escalation of school stress that can result … in the delayed development of executive function skills." Students should not be labeled as lazy or unmotivated, rather "these children should be understood as needing adult support in terms of modeling, guiding, and scaffolding 'how' and 'when' to accomplish tasks."

In essence, Dr. Denckla is telling us we must recognize the significance of a teen's delayed brain maturity, adjust expectations accordingly and then provide extra supports, accommodations and direct instruction longer than for other children. To be clear, students with ADHD can master academic content if they receive the type of supports discussed throughout this book and in the resources we've recommended. So give yourself permission to provide supplemental "external executive function skills" for your son or daughter—for example, by providing structure, reminders and supervision.

Chris's Lessons Learned: Difficulties in school foreshadowed my son's struggles in life and in finding his way into a career path. Although intellectually gifted, he struggled all through middle and high school, and into college.

Get a "Tune-Up" During the Transition to Middle or High School

Just as you may have a 20,000-mile checkup for your car, you'll need to do periodic checkups on your child's progress as he enters middle school and then high school. Students who struggle in school may have more difficulty launching into adulthood. So one of your most important jobs is to address any problematic school issues that may arise in the preteen and teen years. At a minimum, reassess both medication effectiveness and school performance halfway into the first grading period in middle school and then later after your teen starts high school.

Medication adjustments are of particular importance around the middle school years due to the changes in growth and hormonal levels typical in preteens. Medications and dosages that worked previously may become less effective. In addition, some children build up a tolerance to their medication, and the dosage must be adjusted, or the medication changed to a new one.

Also in middle school, teacher expectations for students to work independently will increase. That means most students with ADHD will require more support and guidance from parents or a tutor than other students will need.

Chris's Lessons Learned: As a mental health professional, I felt very guilty about my involvement in my son's academic life. All through high school, I kept trying to find someone else to be his academic coach but never found anyone to replace me. Although my son was bright, high school was a terrible struggle for him. If I had totally stopped providing extra supports at home, I don't think he would have graduated.

Review Academic Performance

If you are concerned about how your teen will adjust to the demands in middle or high school, subtly monitor his homework and any graded papers during the first few weeks of school. Attend the Open House to meet his teachers, ask if they assign long-term projects in this class and ask to be notified of the start and due dates of projects. If the school doesn't use an online system for keeping students and parents updated on work completion and grades, periodically check in with teachers to see if he is completing his assignments—are grades passing, or are they dropping?

If your son or daughter has an IEP or 504 plan, you need to ensure that the educational plan is being implemented correctly and that your child is receiving the accommodations, services and supports in the plan. Make sure you have a copy of the plan plus the daily school schedule each quarter or semester. Students should be involved in selecting their classes as much as possible.

Explore Vocational Training Opportunities

Depending on your son's or daughter's interests and skills, we encourage you to check out what career exploration and training might be of interest or beneficial to your teen now. See Chapters 8 and 9 for guidance on exploring possible vocational interests. Don't wait until your teen's senior year.

Two different federal laws—IDEA and Section 504 of the Rehabilitation Act—mandate that schools provide services to help young people with disabilities to launch into the work world (see the next section). Consider taking advantage of the career exploration and training offered by each of these laws if your child is eligible. Students who have qualified for an IEP or Section 504 plan may request these services. It's essential to know what your teen is entitled to under the law. Federal laws, accommodations for common learning challenges, and tips on developing an IEP or Section 504 plan are discussed in greater detail in Chris's book *Teaching Teens with ADD, ADHD and Executive Function Deficits*, Summaries 42–49.

Transition Service Planning

For students with either an IEP or 504 plan, transition service planning is mandated. Action steps *must* be included in an IEP or a Section 504 plan by age 16 to help students explore future careers. Eligible students *may* request services as early as age 14. Here's an explanation of what this means at age 14 and then later at 16, according to a Wrightslaw position paper on transition (Bateman, 2022).

1. *A statement of transition service needs at age 14.* If appropriate, parents meet with teachers and other members of the IEP or 504 plan team when the teen is 14 to discuss possible career paths and courses or training the student may need. A plan is developed, and the teen may or may not receive any additional services, but the team will ensure he is taking the right classes for any potential future career interests.
2. *A statement of service needs and specific classes needed.* Starting at age 16, a written list of classes and transition services the teen needs and a scheduled plan for implementing them must be developed. The teen must be invited to the meeting.

Table 7.1 Pre-Employment Transition Services for Students with Disabilities

1. *Job exploration counseling*

   • Jobs in demand, interest inventories, job shadowing, field trips.

2. *Work-based learning experiences*

   • Work tours, internships, apprenticeships, job training, volunteer work.

3. *Counseling for transition and postsecondary education*

   • Discuss careers with educational requirements.
   • Identify interests, learning style, helpful technology, accommodations.
   • Assist with college and financial aid applications.
   • Review disability support services available at schools.
   • Arrange tours for tech schools/college.

4. *Workplace readiness training*

   • Job-seeking skills, good hygiene/dress.
   • Communication/interpersonal skills/social skills.
   • Money management.
   • Positive attitude/body language/teamwork.
   • Decision-making.
   • Employer expectations/conflict resolution.
   • Accessing community services.

5. *Instruction on Self-Advocacy*

   • Peer mentoring.
   • Understand legal rights/responsibilities.
   • Use or request accommodations, goal setting.
   • Participate in youth leadership activities.
   • Seeking "student support services" in technical or traditional colleges.

Pre-Employment Training Services: In 2015 Congress passed the Workforce Innovation and Opportunity Act (WIOA). One part of that act requires that 15 percent of each state's vocational rehabilitation budget be spent on *pre-employment transition services* for students with disabilities who are transitioning from middle and high school to postsecondary education programs. This program offers wonderful opportunities for teenagers with ADHD who are eligible. In some states, though, this service is available only for students with the most severe disabilities, or there may be a long waiting list for services. If your teen has an IEP or Section 504 plan, ask about this program. Your teen could receive these services prior to age 16, and as early as 14; but at age 14, the student's parents *must ask for services*.

Pre-employment training services are administered by the Department of Labor and funded under each state's Rehabilitation Services Department (Vocational Rehabilitation). Examples of services are listed in Table 7.1.

Transition Planning Meetings

Request a transition planning meeting if your school does not incorporate transition planning into a regular IEP meeting. When you attend the meeting, come prepared to ask questions.

Find out in advance who will be invited to the meeting. Ideally, this will include parents, the teen at age 16, the guidance counselor, someone from the school district's high school vocational school and, for students with more complex challenges, perhaps a staff member from the Department of Rehabilitation Services, sometimes known as Vocational Rehabilitation. Before the meeting, parents and teens should have discussions regarding possible careers of interest to the child.

PACER's National Parent Center on Transition and Employment has suggested addressing these questions at transition planning meetings (PACER Center, 2015). PACER is a highly respected national advocacy center for children and young adults with disabilities.

1. What are the outcomes that the youth and parents want?
2. What are the programs, services, accommodations, or modifications the young person wants or needs?
3. What kinds of accommodations will students need when they go on to higher education or employment?
4. Who will be responsible for each part of the transition plan in the IEP?
5. Should the educational and transition programs emphasize practical or academic goals?
6. How do young people develop self-advocacy skills?
7. What are the community-based vocational training opportunities the school provides?
8. If a student plans on going to college, is he or she taking the courses needed to meet college entrance requirements?
9. When will the young person graduate? What kind of diploma option is the best choice?
10. Are work experience classes appropriate to reach employment goals?

Vocational Interest Inventories

Consider requesting a vocational interest inventory for your teen. Several inventories (online or paper-and-pencil series of questions) are available that can help young people clarify their future educational and career areas of interest. The Armed Services Battery (ASVAB) is free. The MAPP may be taken online. Your son or daughter may want to ask their guidance counselor about these tests. Additional details on these career interest inventories are discussed in Chapter 9 regarding finding their career passion.

The primary benefit of an interest survey is that it offers a picture of potential careers and, perhaps for the first time, shifts the teen's mindset to "What do I want to do when I grow up?" Clearly, these inventories are for general guidance. Even if a student gets a high or a low score in a particular occupation, that doesn't necessarily mean that he should rule in or out a career in that field. For example, even if he scored low for teaching, he still might be an excellent teacher, although he might need help keeping up with the written reports and other paperwork involved. (Ah, the dreaded "homework" can continue to haunt some of our grown children.)

Chris's Lessons Learned: My son and I found the Strong Interest Inventory helpful. He answered questions regarding his likes and dislikes related to careers and interests, and then his answers were compared to those of adults in hundreds of professions.

My son's best scores were found in the Realistic and Investigative occupational themes. He scored very high on the Basic Interest Scales for Adventure and average on Nature,

Figure 7.1 Ryan working on his computer.

Agriculture, Military Activities, Mechanical Activities, Medical Science, and Medical Service. Vocations in which he scored similarly to successful people currently working in the field included emergency medical technician, radiological technologist, veterinarian, electrician, computer programmer (Figure 7.1), farmer, police officer, enlisted military personnel, geologist, optometrist, bus driver and photographer.

He received a very low score on the Conventional Occupational theme of the Office Practices scale. Specific occupations in which he received lower scores and probably would not be well suited were accountant, business education teacher, public administrator, foreign languages teacher, minister, social worker, elected public official and, not surprisingly, school administrator.

This test turned out to be a helpful guide regarding his special talents and interests. Six years later, he graduated with a forensics degree and a minor in computers. He was also a licensed private investigator.

Tips for Transitions to Middle and High School

The transitions to both middle and high school are difficult for many preteens and teens with ADHD, primarily because of the increased demands for executive skills. As discussed previously, because of their delayed brain maturity, our children often have trouble meeting the expectations of their teachers. In other words, these students struggle to complete work independently without prompts from adults, to start and finish work, to remember books and homework assignments, to take work back to school and to remember long-term assignments.

If you have concerns about class scheduling for a new school year, set up a meeting the spring before your son or daughter enters middle or high school to explain the need to schedule the main courses during the mornings when medication is at peak performance. Depending on your relationship with the school, you might also try requesting specific teachers. ("My son does better with teachers like Mrs. Smith, who understands students with ADHD and academic struggles.") Here are a few more suggestions from Chris's book, *Teenagers with ADD, ADHD, and Executive Deficits Disorders.*

Schedule a School Conference. At the beginning of the transition school year, meet with teachers and counselors to notify them about your teen's diagnosis. Try to schedule the meeting before school begins, or as soon as possible after school starts. Don't wait until midterm when you're notified of failing grades. As one parent explains, "Be proactive, not reactive."

Document ADHD with School Officials. If your teen needs extra help, it's critical to have ADHD documented in writing in school records and/or in an Individualized Education Program (IEP) or Section 504 plan. Otherwise, you could end up in an unexpected crisis, and the principal will look at you and say, "We have no record that your son [or daughter] has ADHD." It's difficult to get special consideration in the midst of a major crisis.

If ADHD hasn't already been documented with school officials, ask your physician or psychologist for a letter confirming the diagnosis and take it to the meeting with you. The letter should include the diagnosis of ADHD, academic or intelligence test results, identification of any learning problems and suggestions for classroom accommodations. Once the ADHD has been documented at school, you have more options available:

1. If your teen has *occasional minor problems* at school, just dropping by his classrooms at the first open house may be enough. Discreetly advise the teachers of your teenager's ADHD and assure them that he wants to do well in school. Ask the teachers to call or email if there are any problems.
2. If your adolescent *needs extra help* but has no major problems at school, informally ask the teacher for needed classroom supports or accommodations.
3. If he's *experiencing significant difficulty* (in danger of failing classes without accommodations or suspension/expulsion because of behavioral problems) or you *anticipate serious problems* in making the transition to middle or high school, consider requesting services under an IEP or Section 504 plan as described in federal laws.
4. If your teen is already *eligible for special education*, ask for additional accommodations in his regular classes if he is struggling; rarely, the school may recommend participation in a resource class one or two periods a day.

Continue to Identify and Affirm Special Talents and Skills. Encourage your teenager to participate in clubs, sports and other activities that will help build skills and expose him to potential career opportunities. Encourage him to continue activities he's previously enjoyed, such as art, music, sports, debate and theater, and to explore new opportunities according to his interests (Figure 7.2).

Figure 7.2 Perry, former debate coach.

Here are a few examples of extracurricular activities often available to middle and high school students:

- Subject Area Clubs or Teams
  - Photography, film, math, history, drama, improv, foreign language, art, yearbook, science fairs.
- Hobby Clubs
  - Chess, video games, religious, book club, creative writing, manga, robotics, quiz bowl.
- Sports Teams
  - Varsity, junior varsity, or intramural baseball, basketball, football, wrestling, hockey, lacrosse, gymnastics, etc.
  - Cheerleading or pep squad.
  - Team management or score keeping.
- Performing Groups
  - Musical ensembles (pep band, a capella groups, orchestra, etc.).
  - Poetry slams.
  - Theater (acting, set design, stage crew, lighting and sound design).
- Skill and Leadership Clubs
  - Student government, holding an office in any club, speech and debate team.
- Community Service Groups or Volunteer Opportunities
  - Habitat for Humanity, Key Club.
  - Environmental clubs, community or school clean-ups or landscaping, recycling
  - Tutoring, mentoring a younger student, peer mediator, befriending other students at school ("no one sits alone").

- Career Interest Clubs
  - Future Business Leaders, future scientists/STEM, Future Farmers of America (FFA), mock trials, Entrepreneur/DECA, investments.
  - Technology: computers, coding, game design.
  - Home and fashion: modeling, participating in home economics classes.
  - Community service.

Begin Thinking About Your Teen's Future After High School. Since young people with ADHD have delayed brain maturity and executive skills, they're unlikely to initiate planning for the future. So you may have to partner with your teenager and provide "external executive function" supports and help him plan ahead. For example, if you suspect that he will not be ready or mature enough to tackle college courses right after high school, read more about gap year programs in Chapter 12.

If your teenager has his heart set on attending college, you'll need to review admission deadlines and the requirements for obtaining extra supports and accommodations in college. Information on required documentation for admissions, Section 504 eligibility and helpful accommodations is provided in Chapter 15 regarding applying for college.

Model Self-Advocacy Skills. Two of my longtime friends and respected colleagues, Jill Murphy (ADHD coach and special educator) and Judy Bandy (founder of ADHD Life Tools), emphasize the importance of teaching and practicing self-advocacy skills with their clients. By the middle school years, parents should follow their wise advice and talk with their teen about self-advocacy, especially during his IEP or 504 plan meetings. Encourage him to speak up and ask for needed supports that have been identified in the educational plan.

One mom who was a special educator trained her son so that by his high school years, he actually chaired his IEP meeting. As a high school senior, he was able to explain to the group which supports he still needed and identify supports that were no longer necessary. Today, that young man is a college graduate and the assistant director of an ICU hospital unit.

In advance of the school meeting, tell teachers and administrators that your teen will be attending and outline your hopes for the meeting: (1) discussions will include your teen as a respected partner, (2) the teen's strengths will be discussed, (3) challenging areas will be identified and accommodations suggested and (4) most importantly, there will be no shaming or bashing the teen for his shortcomings related to his ADHD and executive function deficits.

Suggested self-advocacy skills for your teen to practice include the following:

1. Understanding and identifying his learning challenges: seeking peer mentoring; studying with a friend; requesting tutoring if needed; attending a study skills class.
2. Understanding legal rights/responsibilities and which accommodations may be most helpful.
3. Building leaderships skills by participating in leadership activities: being willing to ask for help when needed; requesting accommodations; practicing setting goals; using strategies such as entering due dates in a computer calendar; knowing when his brain works best for studying; using timers or alarms as a prompt to start working.
4. If teachers are not providing the services ensured by IDEA or Section 504, then suggest that your teenager ask the high school or college counselor for guidance about the best way to remind teachers of his educational rights.

5. When your teen enters technical or traditional college, seek "student support services" under Section 504.

Review the ADHD Iceberg with Your Teen. Jill Murphy discusses the complexities of ADHD by reviewing the iceberg with her student clients prior to IEP or 504 meetings (Dendy & Zeigler, 2015). You may want to do the same thing. Have your son or daughter either put a checkmark by the behaviors that cause the greatest difficulty at school or actually fill out the blank iceberg as he or she identifies key challenges. Then discuss potential accommodations for these challenges. The goal is for your teenager to be more involved, speak up and play an active role at meetings, and become more confident in taking charge of his life.

If you know the issues and accommodations that will be suggested at the meeting, discuss them with your teen in advance. Help him figure out what to say and then practice with him. For example, your son or daughter might say: "I know I have trouble remembering my homework assignments. Last year the teacher sent the assignment to me via the Remind. com phone app, and that really helped a lot." Or "Last year, I took a picture with my phone of the homework assignment on the board." He can take a copy of the iceberg to the planning meeting to help him remember what to say.

Do Whatever It Takes to Help Your Teen Succeed. We encourage parents to give themselves permission to provide *developmentally appropriate support* when it is needed. In other words, your teen will need your guidance and support longer than classmates without ADHD. As he takes on increasing levels of responsibility and independence, you may be able to reduce your level of support. However, during times of high stress with deadlines looming, you may have to step in and be more involved.

Trust the science about delayed ADHD brain maturity. Don't be swayed by uneducated adults who say, "You're too involved in your teen's life. Let him fail and he'll learn." The truth is, no; our children don't learn easily from negative consequences because ADHD brains may be delayed in maturation by three to five years. Children with ADHD will need more support longer than their peers because of their delayed maturity.

Ruth's Lessons Learned: Be sure to also teach your teen the importance of using good social skills along with self-advocacy. In middle school, one of my son Christopher's teachers mentioned his disability (confidential information) in front of the other students. Christopher, who was a bit of a troublemaker but knew his rights, immediately went to the guidance counselor to complain. When the guidance counselor suggested he forget it, he then went to the principal, who was not happy to receive this complaint. Christopher stormed out of her office saying he would be back in the morning with his mother, who was a professional advocate. By the next morning, the school was prepared for a lawsuit and the teacher had been instructed to not talk with me. The principal had a list of all of Christopher's infractions and was ready to do battle. My job was to calm everyone down and model advocating without antagonizing everyone. Christopher was absolutely correct that his rights had been violated but had not yet learned how to get the message across without alienating everyone. It was an important teachable moment.

References

Bateman, B. (2022). *Transition—legal requirements for transition components of the IEP.* Wrightslaw. Retrieved January 28, 2023, from https://www.wrightslaw.com/info/trans.legal.bateman.htm
Denckla, M.B. (2019). *Understanding learning and related disabilities: Inconvenient brains.* New York: Routledge.
Dendy, C.A.Z., & Zeigler, A. (2015) *A birds-eye view of life with ADHD and EFD… 10 years later* (3rd ed.). Alabama: C.A.Z. Dendy Consulting.
PACER Center. (2015). *Parent tips for transition planning.* NPC-34.pdf. Retrieved January 29, 2023, from https://www.pacer.org/transition/resource-library/publications/NPC-34.pdf

8   Exploring Careers Through Firsthand Experiences

Although at times it may seem as if your teenager will never be finished with school, the reality is that she will likely spend much of her lifetime working. For any child, but especially for teens with ADHD, it is crucial to start thinking ahead to possible careers well before high school graduation. Unfortunately, since students with ADHD seldom plan for the future, they will need support and guidance from parents and educators to begin exploring potential careers. Otherwise, some may graduate from college with no clue as to a career path or job prospects. Roughly 40 percent of all recent college graduates are underemployed, with low pay and few career advancement opportunities (Statista, 2022). Clearly, identifying job interests and planning ahead for a career is critical.

For students who struggle with academics, just thinking about being free from school and in a job they enjoy can be highly motivating. And your teen is much more likely to exit school with a plan for the next steps in life if she has at least a general idea of what sorts of careers she might be interested in.

In addition, there are many important values and skills you will want your son or daughter to carry into his or her life and career. It's important to start early to build such skills as being organized, being on time, meeting deadlines and keeping commitments, traits that will be of value to your teen as he or she reaches adulthood.

In this chapter, we examine a variety of options for exploring careers while still in high school. You may want to read this chapter in conjunction with Chapter 8 on helping your teen find her passion, since working in a field that someone is passionate about can often lead to a career with high job satisfaction.

STEM Programs in High School

To address the lack of skilled workers, a nationwide push for the development of STEM-related (*S*cience, *T*echnology, *E*ngineering, *M*athematics) programs at the elementary through high school levels has emerged. In the southern United States, for example, Georgia and Texas are strong leaders, with 72 and 93 STEM programs, respectively. Dr. Billie Abney, a teacher at Northwest Georgia College and Career Academy, in Dalton, Georgia, reports a significant increase in parents wanting to enroll their children in the academy. Ask if your school system has STEM programs. Attendance at these schools is optional, and there are generally limited openings, so students must apply to attend. Note that specialized STEM programs may be housed within typical high schools in your school district or in buildings with specialized "academies."

Funding for STEM programs in public high schools is sometimes provided, in part, by local or nationwide businesses, and these companies may offer students significant inducements to

DOI: 10.4324/9781003364092-8

participate. For example, Pratt & Whitney, an aerospace manufacturer in Columbus, Georgia, not only contributes hundreds of thousands of dollars to support STEM labs in schools but also has scholarship and internship programs. And students who attend the Taft Information Technology High School in Cincinnati, Ohio, are eligible for paid summer internships with Cincinnati Bell.

STEM careers are not just for boys. Encourage your daughters to check into STEM careers in manufacturing and other professions. In the United States, women are still woefully underrepresented in most science, technology and engineering fields. For example, only about 20 percent of undergraduate engineering degrees were awarded to women in 2017, and only 8 percent of female college students overall consider STEM-related degree programs.

College and Career Academies

If your teen is lucky, she might be able to explore career fields right in her high school. A growing trend nationally is the addition of college and career academies to traditional high school systems. Your school system might offer academies in several broad career fields such as health, sciences, arts and entertainment, finance and business, technology engineering, construction or public service. Typically, students who choose to enroll in a career academy rather than pursue the usual high school course of study take three or four core academic classes that are required for graduation and one or two career technical classes each year. They might also have the opportunity to leave campus to complete internships or apprenticeships related to the academy's field of concentration.

Check to see whether your school system has any career academies. If your neighborhood school does not have one, it might be possible for your teen to attend one within your school system.

Northwest Georgia College and Career Academy (NGCCA) is an example of a stand-alone public high school whose students take classes focused on science, technology, engineering and mathematics (STEM). NGCCA offers specialized training in the following career paths: Automotive Technology, Foundations of Mechatronics (electrical and mechanical engineering), IT Computer Science, Healthcare, and Law and Justice. Students take math and science courses at NGCCA and return to their home schools for language arts and social studies. For students with IEPs or 504 plans, basic accommodations are still applicable. Since participation is voluntary, any student in the school system may apply. If the student doesn't like the specialized course of study, she may transfer back to a regular high school at the end of a school year.

In contrast to NGCCA, some career academies are housed within high schools that also serve students who are pursuing the typical general course of studies. In these schools, academy students usually take their core graduation requirements in classes with the regular student body and their specialized classes with other academy students. Career academies are available in many states and in a variety of fields.

Volunteer Opportunities, Apprenticeships or Internships

Many school systems require their students to spend a certain number of hours performing community service in order to graduate. Typically, students can volunteer on weekends or in the summer doing menial labor such as cleaning up ponds, digging up weeds in a park or picking up trash along roads. However, they can also volunteer in positions that give them a taste of particular career fields—for example, by volunteering in a school, hospital, recreation program, nonprofit organization, etc. If volunteer opportunities are carefully selected, they can give your teen insights into a variety of work settings and careers.

If your school system doesn't require community service hours for graduation, you can seek out opportunities on your own. If your teenager loves to talk, perhaps the teacher will allow her to read a story to younger children. Volunteering to help with an after-school enrichment program for younger students or setting up for a sports event may teach your teen how to organize and get ready for special events ahead of time. Helping deliver gifts or food to needy families during the holidays or volunteering at a food pantry is another possible idea.

In contrast to volunteering, apprenticeships and internships generally require more of a commitment and usually have specific eligibility requirements. Students who seek apprenticeship may have an idea of which career path they want. The student trains for a specific job while also taking high school coursework that provides related skills. Students who are successful may move directly into a job after graduation. Some apprenticeships are paid; others are not. Shaw Industries in Dalton, Georgia, pays high school juniors with an apprenticeship $12 to $15 an hour; a second-year apprentice who is a senior could be paid $20 to $25 an hour. The apprenticeship may well lead to a job with the company, which is a subsidiary of Berkshire Hathaway and one of the world's largest flooring and carpet manufacturers.

Like apprenticeships, internships involve doing real work in a specific field. But, especially at the high school level, internships are generally meant more to give the student a taste of what a specific career involves than to lead to a job with that organization. In addition, student interns generally don't learn all or even most of the skills required to do a particular job and may often be asked to do relatively menial work to assist employees, such as word processing, filing or answering phones.

Examples of Internship and Volunteer Opportunities

The earlier discussion of "finding their passion" will help you and your teen pinpoint interests and skills that she might want to develop further in a future career. Once you are aware of these interests and skills, spend some time searching the internet for internships, apprenticeships or volunteer opportunities that are a good fit for your teen. Some of these placements are free, but others may be very costly. Do a thorough check on a potential internship to make certain it will be a positive experience; look for online ratings by previous interns.

Here are a few examples of programs open to high school students from across the country.

- The *Hutton Junior Fisheries Biology Program* is a paid summer internship and mentoring program for high school sophomores, juniors and seniors from the United States, Canada and Mexico interested in pursuing science disciplines associated with natural resource and environmental management. Scholarships are available at various locations across the country.
- The *Bank of America Student Leaders program* offers paid internships to work at local nonprofit organizations like Boys and Girls Clubs and Habitat for Humanity.
- The *Research & Engineering Apprenticeship Program (REAP)* of the US Army is a summer STEM program that places talented high school students from groups historically underrepresented and underserved in STEM in research apprenticeships at area colleges

and universities. The program was developed by the Army Education Outreach Program to strengthen the army, the Department of Defense and the nation's workforce.

- The Centers for Disease Control (CDC) Museum, *Disease Detective Camp*, is an academically demanding educational program open to rising juniors and seniors with an interest in public health topics. The program is held at the CDC's headquarters in Atlanta.
- The *Junior Volunteer Program* is available at hospitals around the country for high school students with an interest in healthcare careers. Positions are unpaid and the length of the program varies; contact your local hospitals for information on eligibility.

And here are a few examples of regional and local programs for high school students:

- *BRAINYAC* is a program offered through Zuckerman Institute's Brain Research Apprenticeships at Columbia University and connects high school students from New York City with scientists for intensive summer lab internships, including hands-on experience.
- *Business Partners in Education* is a nonprofit organization that helps place student volunteers and interns with businesses in Santa Barbara County, California.
- *Plymouth Whitemarsh High School* in Conshohocken, Pennsylvania, offers an internship with local business Proud Pouch to learn dog grooming.
- The *Medical Immersion Summer Academy (MISA)* is a program for high school students in the San Francisco Bay area that offers hands-on skills training for young people interested in careers in healthcare; current cost is about $900.
- The *Microsoft Summer High School internship* is a boot camp encouraging students who live within 50 miles of Redmond, Washington, to become involved in STEM programs.
- *NASA internships* are available for high school and college students at four of its regional campuses: Greenbelt, Maryland; Wallops Island, Virginia; New York City (Goddard Institute); and Fairmont, West Virginia. Students must have at least a 3.0 GPA and be US citizens.
- *STEM/STEAM educational partnership with Northwest Georgia College and Career Academy (NGCCA)*. NGCCA collaborates with Shaw Industries to provide academic and technical content, together with work readiness skills and a paid apprenticeship opportunity. Notably, a couple of their programs were established to enhance math and science skills in girls. These programs are located within a 50-mile radius of their Dalton, Georgia, headquarters.
- The *TAG-Ed Summer Internship Program* was created to give students real-world STEM experience at companies around Atlanta and the state of Georgia. Students must be able to find and pay for their own housing and transportation.

Check apprentice and internship opportunities in your surrounding areas. You can do an internet search of similar programs in your region of the country. For example, a quick search of the Houston, Texas, area came up with nearly 40 apprentice/internships for high school students, including programs specifically for low-income families and those focused on nuclear power, manufacturing and gas infrastructure.

Websites Listing Internships: The following are several websites that post internships for both high school and college students.

- *Internships.com* (www.internships.com/high-school): The largest student-focused internship marketplace has a direct link to high school internships.

- *Idealist* (www.idealist.org/en/?type=INTERNSHIP): This is a well-known site for volunteer opportunities, internships, and nonprofit jobs.
- *LinkedIn* (www.linkedin.com/job/high-school-internship-jobs/): The popular professional networking site has many internship listings.
- *Indeed* (www.indeed.com): This prominent search engine aggregates job listings, including internships.
- *Glassdoor* (www.glassdoor.com): The career community website includes internship listings.
- *YouTern* (https://www.youtern.com/cm/candidate/search_jobs): This site is dedicated to connecting people with internships.

Summer and After-School Jobs

Most high school students aren't going to be able to find part-time work in a field that they want to work in long term. But any kind of paid employment can help teens learn critical "soft" job skills such as punctuality and getting along with colleagues and bosses. It can also help them learn what sorts of jobs they would *not* like to have long term.

Some jobs available to teenagers let them explore career fields in a general way. For instance, if your teen is considering a career involving teaching or working with children, she might find work as a camp counselor, a lifeguard at a local pool or a swim or dance instructor. Likewise, if she is interested in a career in cooking or business, a job in a restaurant or store can expose her to some aspects of those types of jobs.

Students who are struggling academically may not be able to keep up with schoolwork and also juggle an after-school job. For these students, getting a summer job would be the better option.

Summer Classes and Camps

Not all career exploration has to involve actual work or traditional classroom learning. Learning about a topic of interest in a relaxed environment outside of school can also be a good way for young people to figure out their possible vocational interests.

Traditional Sleep-Away or Day Camps: Especially for preteens and younger teens, a general camp can give your son or daughter an opportunity to sample a variety of activities, such as nature studies, boating, horseback riding and care, arts and crafts, sports and music.

Specialty Camps and Clubs: To help your son or daughter determine if a hobby interest might become a career interest, it might be worthwhile to try a specialty camp in robotics, theater, archeology, art or the like. For example, she could explore interests in engineering, science and medicine at Space Academy at Huntsville, Alabama, or attend a sleep-away camp where talented young musicians study conducting, performance or composition with professional musicians.

Hands-on Classes: Check out classes geared for middle school or high school students at your local community college. Look for courses that are more hands-on (e.g., in robotics, coding, art, etc.) and that don't involve aspects of school your teen struggles with.

Religious Classes or Service Projects: The religious institution of your choice may offer classes geared to teens that teach valuable principles of honesty, integrity and kindness to others, especially those less fortunate, and may offer opportunities for leadership and building skills such as public speaking. Your teen might also be interested in participating in community service projects such as food drives, fundraising and home repair, or perhaps social justice programs.

PC: Sunday evening classes at our church allowed our son to speak in front of his class-mates. At first, he read a section of the lesson, and then he was able to just describe it in his own words. We recognized that public speaking was one of his strengths.

Informal Discussions of Careers and the Future

Informally talk about various careers and make comments about your teen's strengths. Use teachable moments—for example, if you're watching a program on the National Geographic channel, you could point out what a geologist's job might entail (studying landslides, earthquakes, floods and volcanic eruptions).

Make positive statements about your teen's strengths and tie them to potential future career paths. Periodically make comments about your own job or the careers of family friends and relatives. These chats can occur even when you're watching TV shows.

For example, if you see interest in or a flair for specific skills, you might say, "You really like the *NCIS* TV program. I do, too. That would be an interesting career." Or you might comment, "You're so patient with younger children and they adore you. You seem like a natural-born teacher." Or, "Your computer skills are really amazing. Computer skills will be invaluable in any career you choose."

Take Your Teen to Work

By middle school, occasions may arise, especially during the summer or during holidays, to take your teen to work with you. If possible and allowed, consider finding a few tasks she may be able to do for you. Over time and in short increments, explain what your job entails. Afterward, engage her in a discussion about the pros and cons of your job. You might say, "I really love my job, especially when I ..." Or ask, "Did you enjoy coming to the office today?" Just leave the topic hanging and see if she says anything else. Of course, if your teen has slow processing, she may not say anything. But that's okay; you've still planted a seed regarding the future.

If you have a job that you know would not appeal to your son or daughter, or work in a setting where it's inappropriate to bring a child, check with family members or friends. Perhaps they would be willing to have your teen "shadow" them at work.

The Bottom Line

Find opportunities early and often to introduce your teen to career opportunities. In earlier generations, college was often viewed as a time to explore different areas of interest and decide upon a career. But this often doesn't happen today, particularly on larger college campuses. The number of students who graduate from college without a clear career path is astounding, and they often end up with entry-level jobs with little hope of turning it into a career. Furthermore, many students with ADHD may not enroll in college or other post-secondary programs, and if they do, they may not graduate. If so, they may have even less time to think about and explore careers that would be a good fit.

For young adults who have ADHD, finding a career that is interesting and engaging is extremely important. They are unlikely to succeed in a position that is boring or doesn't engage them. But they can be highly successful in jobs that they love. See Chapter 9 for more suggestions on helping them find their passion! Afterward, you can help your son or daughter understand what kind of training or background is needed to pursue a career in that field.

References

Statista Research Department. (2022, November 15). *Underemployment recent college graduates U.S. 2022*. Statista. Retrieved January 28, 2023, from https://www.statista.com/statistics/642037/share-of-recent-us-college-graduates-underemployed/

9 Helping Teens and Young Adults Find Their Passion

If your teen or young adult hasn't discovered his passion in life, then he is like most young people. But now is exactly the time to help him explore possible careers that he can be passionate about. Expecting this process to happen naturally often leads to years of underemployment and thousands of dollars spent on college or training that doesn't lead to a career. All teenagers live in the moment, and this is even truer for young people who have ADHD. Thinking about long-term goals doesn't come naturally to them, so identifying a career can be all the more challenging. As a parent, you can help your son or daughter begin to explore possible careers now and save much angst later.

PC: I should have worked harder to help her find her passion when she was younger. She is still searching.

Why Is It So Important to Identify Potential Careers Now?

Today's colleges and universities invest little time or money in making sure their students have clearly identified career paths, and many do little to ensure their graduates get jobs in the career of their choice. There are thousands of psychology, history and English graduates who can't find a job outside of teaching or are employed in low-paying positions that don't require a degree.

The result is massive underemployment in the United States. In 2022, 40.6 percent of recent college graduates were underemployed (Federal Reserve Bank of New York, 2022). So, even though the unemployment rate was low at this time, many young adults were not seeing the benefits. While this percentage is scary, it's probably worse for young adults with disabilities. In 2022, they had an unemployment rate about twice what the rate was for people without disabilities—10.1 percent versus 5.1 percent (Bureau of Labor Statistics, 2022).

By getting a head start on career exploration and helping your young person focus on a career area, you can help him avoid the pitfalls, the expense, and the stress that is so often associated with starting a career.

Helping Your Son or Daughter Identify Possible Careers

While young adults must ultimately make their own career choice, parents and other mentors can help start the process and provide the structure and resources needed to explore and learn. There are many ways to begin this exploration. The previous chapter reviewed general strategies to acquaint your child with a wide variety of jobs. Here we will focus on three strategies that are especially helpful for older teens and young adults with ADHD. One way

DOI: 10.4324/9781003364092-9

is to explore careers that are ADHD-friendly—many people with ADHD and executive function deficits have found success in these jobs. Another path is to invest the time in some vocational testing and find out what jobs your young person would be well suited for. And the last path is simply diving in and exploring areas of interest to your son or daughter.

Careers That Work with ADHD

Some of the symptoms of ADHD are likely to follow young people into the workplace and throughout life. Finding a career that's a good fit with the particular executive function challenges experienced by your son or daughter is therefore important. So what kinds of jobs are typically good for people with ADHD and/or executive function deficits? Look for careers that have a lot of external structure but also a lot of variety and flexibility. These may sound like two contradictory statements, but many careers have both characteristics. For example, teaching is a profession with both structure and lots of variety every day (Figure 9.1). It is usually wise to avoid careers that require lots of detailed work, are repetitive, are physically inactive, or have rigid expectations.

ADHD-Friendly Jobs: Here is a list of characteristics of jobs that may create an ADHD-friendly environment:

- Hands-on work.
- Builds on the strengths of the worker.
- Short-term deadlines.
- Not detail-oriented or boring.
- Less paperwork.
- Intellectually or physically active.
- Clear job expectations.
- Good external structure/supports.
- Changing environment.
- Supervisor who is flexible and willing to guide when needed.

Figure 9.1 Mary, a pre-K teacher.

Possible Careers for People with ADHD: Here are some examples of careers that often work well for people with ADHD:

- *Chef or Cook.* The timelines are tight, the work is fast and the feedback is immediate.
- *Parks and Recreation.* Time at a desk is balanced with lots of time outdoors. Each day there are clear expectations for tasks to be done, but no two days are exactly alike. The work includes lots of physical exercise and lots of time working with children and adults.
- *Jobs in construction, manufacturing, and specialized professions.* Jobs as electricians, plumbers, carpenters, offset printing operators, flexographic printing operators, die cutter operators and skilled construction and manufacturing workers combine variety with very specific tasks and tight schedules. In today's world, a highly skilled construction or manufacturing worker can make a good salary. And a paid apprenticeship is a great way to be trained.
- *Sales.* If your son or daughter loves people and is a great talker, this can be a wonderful area of work. Think corporate or real estate sales, not retail.
- *First responders.* People with ADHD rise to the occasion when things are exciting. Careers as a police officer, firefighter and emergency medical technician can be great jobs for those who can hyperfocus in an emergency.
- *Nurse/ER doctor/physician's assistant.* There is nothing like emergency medicine to get the adrenaline pumping. Of course, first the young adult must be able to pass a rigorous academic program in college requiring lots of memorization.
- *Entrepreneur/business owner.* The flexibility and excitement of forging your own business can be a great path for someone with ADHD. And you can create your own external supports tailored to your needs, such as by working with an executive assistant for the details while you are the innovator.
- *Teacher.* Teachers have stimulating and ever-changing jobs. For young people who aren't turned off by school, this is a great way to pursue a passion, such as history or English, that otherwise may have few job options.
- *Coach/Physical Trainer.* Not only are sports and exercise great activities for anyone, but this is also a great career area for those who need some variety and excitement in a job.
- *Arts/Actor/Musician.* These build on the creativity and out-of-the box thinking that often come with ADHD. Music, drama and art are all possible career paths for someone who needs to work differently. And think of the ancillary careers in management of the arts, dealers, costume design, etc.
- *Child care or elder care worker.* Kids are never boring, and each day is different. As the baby boomers are aging and retiring, demands for in-home support have increased significantly. This group of retirees may need help with everyday tasks such as yard maintenance, food preparation, grocery shopping or driving to doctors' appointments.
- *Communications.* Although vacancies are often limited, jobs as TV or newspaper reporters, radio DJs or "crowd entertainers" for events are a perfect match for some young people with ADHD.
- *Journalist/blogger/social media influencer.* If your son or daughter loves to write, this is a career with short-term deadlines that involves researching potentially exciting stories.
- *IT innovator/software developer.* Your son or daughter may not be great at cleaning up code, but if he or she loves programming, the need for innovators in the IT world is only going to grow. Website development and maintenance is another option in this field.

Ruth's Lessons Learned: Many nontraditional careers can be a perfect fit for those with a different learning style and out-of-the box thinking. One of my son's friends loved to sew, and she ended up with a job sewing shoe prototypes for one of the major sports apparel companies. Today she is making custom shoes for celebrities. Don't rule out the unusual. There can be real opportunities there.

Chris's Lessons Learned: One young man earned MS and PhD degrees in plant pathology and nematology and now consults with the superintendents of golf courses. He is an expert on grasses, weeds and common problems affecting golf courses. Initially, paperwork (homework) was a nightmare. Today he has developed strategies for coping with paperwork demands: using templates for reports, alternating "fun" visits to golf courses and then returning to write up observations and chemical treatment needs, studying lab specimens and completing reports, taking breaks and sipping sugary drinks like Gatorade to enhance brain functioning.

What About Vocational Testing?

If your teenager feels clueless about potential careers, you might want to consider a vocational test to jump-start the process. Several good tests have been designed by analyzing the characteristics of thousands of people and the careers they have chosen.

One of the major benefits of having test results to review is that it's a conversation starter and a springboard for discussion with your teenager regarding the future and life after high school. Otherwise, teens and young adults with ADHD are less likely to discuss career directions or even think about the topic.

The parent's role here is to lead the discussion by asking questions and restating their son's or daughter's opinions. You might ask, "What do you think about the results? Does this description sound like you?" Or, "So do you think the results do a pretty good job of describing you?"

Parents should encourage their teen to contact the guidance counselor to request one of these test batteries as early as the freshman or sophomore year in high school and then repeating the procedure in a couple of years to assess your teen's most current interests.

Here are a few of the standard assessments, but these are by no means the only valid tests available:

- *Armed Services Vocational Aptitude Battery (ASVAB).* This is the test the US military uses to identify the best jobs for potential recruits. You don't have to be interested in the military to take the exam, and the results can be helpful in thinking about possible careers. The results are geared toward military careers, but that includes an amazing range of careers (ASVAB, 2023).
- *Strong Vocational Interest Inventory.* The Strong is a multiple-choice test that asks you to choose between preferred and less-preferred activities. With 80 years of research behind it, the test is based upon the responses of the many thousands of people who have taken the test and gone on to develop careers. After taking the test, a detailed report is generated that tells you what careers people like you have found to be rewarding. It is available online for a fee (The Myers Briggs Company, 2022).

- *Motivational Appraisal of Personal Potential (MAPP)*. This test asks questions to identify your personality, your skills and your motivations and matches the results with specific career areas. With over eight million users to date, this is one of the most frequently used tests. A summary of test results is available free online. However, there is a fee for a more detailed report. (Assessment.com, 2022).
- *Focus 2*. Many career centers and colleges are using the Focus 2 to help students pinpoint potential careers. Find out if your local community college offers testing and career counseling and if your young adult is eligible to use these services. Focus 2 is also available online for a nominal fee (Career Dimensions, 2023).

Consider Taking the DISC Personality Assessment

The DISC assessment offers insights into an individual's personality at school or work by measuring four basic behavior traits. Again, a major benefit of taking this short test may be as a conversation starter with your teen. It can also confirm what your teen already knows subconsciously about himself and how he communicates, relates to others and approaches tasks. Being aware of how he comes across in the work setting may also help reduce conflicts at work (Personality Profile Solutions, 2022).

The DISC short test summary is available free online. The following four traits are assessed:

- *Dominance*: direct, strong-willed and forceful.
- *Influence*: sociable, talkative and lively.
- *Steadiness*: gentle, accommodating and soft-hearted.
- *Conscientiousness*: private, analytical and logical.

Typically, the test results represent a blend of traits. For example, Chris Dendy's recent test results reflect an equal blend of SCD: Supportive, Cautious, and Dominant traits such as being helpful, kind, results-oriented and getting things done right.

Chris's granddaughter Ashley found out she has high "D" traits, indicating that she likes to be the boss. Knowing this tendency, she is more aware of the need to rein in impulsive comments that may make her appear bossy. She also took the Strong Inventory and noted that combining the results of the two tests was more helpful to her. For example, one of her top suggested jobs on the Strong Inventory was customer service. Because she scored High D on the DISC, she might want to consider a management position in retail.

Where Are These Tests Available?

If your teenager's high school doesn't offer these surveys, he can take some of them independently online. If he is in college, he can ask career service staff about signing up to take one of the inventories.

- *High school and college counseling or student services*. Most schools offer some form of vocational testing. Many high schools offer the Armed Services Vocational Aptitude Battery (ASVAB, 2023) for free. Find out what your student's school offers and take advantage of it. Ruth's community college offers the Focus 2 for free for any resident of the county.

- *Psychologist/career counselor.* Many psychologists and career counselors will provide a comprehensive vocational assessment for a fee. This often includes a more in-depth assessment, including executive function deficits, intelligence, academic functioning, and personality in addition to vocational testing. Your teen should receive a comprehensive and detailed written report as well as counseling about the results.
- *State vocational rehabilitation agency.* All states are required to have a vocational program for students with significant disabilities who are transitioning from high school (ages 14 to 22). The services will usually include an assessment, vocational counseling and work readiness training. For young people who are ready to go to work, services can include job placement and support. And for people who are older than 22 but have a severe disability that has affected their job prospects, vocational rehabilitation agencies can provide a wide range of employment supports. Note that in many states there may be a long waiting list for vocational rehabilitation services, and that young people with the most severe disabilities are usually served first.
- *Online.* Several vocational interest tests are available via the internet. Some are free, and others require a modest fee. If there is a fee involved, you should expect a comprehensive report. Some services also include a phone consultation after the testing is complete. Be sure it is a legitimate test and not just a ploy to get your teen to sign up for job placement services.
- *O*NET Online* (www.onetonline.org). The Department of Labor has created a wonderful, free resource that helps you identify careers that are a good fit and gives you a wealth of useful additional information. Your young adult can complete a quick survey that results in both general guidance and possible careers. But that's just the beginning. O*NET describes the knowledge base, the skills, the personality characteristics and the level of training or education needed. And you can see what salary ranges are in your local area. O*NET also gives you information about the projected future growth (or decline) of a career. And you can discover where local training or education is offered to move you into a specific career—all for free! (O*NET online, n.d.).

Diving into the Exploration Process

Your son or daughter can start by making a list of jobs he or she thinks would be good possibilities. Ask young people to make a list of several careers that they think they might like. Once your teen has a list of ten or more careers he might be interested in pursuing, it's time to find out more. Work with him to select the areas of the most interest. The internet is a great tool for finding out more about a career. Talking to people in the field of interest is even better. And once the list is narrowed down, getting some real-life experience is the true test. As your teenager learns more about possible careers, encourage him to pinpoint the ones with a sweet spot where passion, skills and earning a living come together. Those are the careers to pursue.

Key Questions to Answer

The investigation process conducted by your son or daughter needs to answer some key questions.

- *What are my strengths? What are the things I'm not good at or hate doing?* This list can help sort out potential successful careers. Challenges and dislikes are as important as strengths. If sitting still all day is difficult, then an office job may not be for you.

If you always hated babysitting, then a teaching or childcare career is an unlikely fit. If focus and detail aren't your strength, then an accounting job is probably not in your future. If you love to talk and like meeting new people, then sales, being a part-time clown, or a job in the entertainment field such as a DJ or crowd entertainer might be a great fit (Figure 9.2).

- *Is this something I am passionate about? Can I see myself doing this for decades to come?* Too many of us work at jobs we don't enjoy. For a person with executive function deficits and difficulties with attention, this can be the kiss of death. For many of our young adults, a job must be engaging enough to keep them focused and to get them over the rough patches that are inevitable with any job. Liking what you do is a key factor in eventual success.
- *Will I be good at this job?* Having a job that you love but aren't good at is a recipe for heartbreak. This question is designed to help your young adult evaluate his strengths and weaker skills compared to the expectations for a career. It will help him weed out those fantasies of being a professional basketball player (at five-foot-seven) or being an engineering or computer science major if he hates math.
- *What training or education is required?* A bachelor's degree from college is not a blanket entry into all jobs. Many careers don't require a college degree but do entail some professional training such as an apprenticeship or a specific training program. A traditional four-year college degree won't help. And some careers require an advanced degree—think lawyer, physician, scientist or psychologist. Does your teen have access to the training required and funds to pay for it? Is he willing to undergo the years of training or education required?

Figure 9.2 Lewis, former DJ.

- *Will there be a job for me?* Nothing is more frustrating than training for a career with few positions in a highly competitive job market or an industry that is shrinking. In today's world the job market is changing rapidly and dramatically. Retail sales positions have shrunk severely over the last decade as sales have moved to the internet. Automation and the internet are affecting every field. Jobs are disappearing in newspaper publishing and journalism, mortgage lending, and libraries, for example.

  But jobs are increasing in fields related to the internet, software, healthcare and alternative energy sources. Software development, graphic design and cybersecurity are all growing areas. A major shortage in highly skilled workers in specialized professions such as nurse, electrician, plumber, welder and certain manufacturing positions has led to wide-open opportunities in these fields.

  In health care, anything related to elder care is booming. Jobs as physical therapists, occupational therapists, nurse practitioners, and physician assistants are all increasing. There is a real need for truck drivers in today's world but anticipate changes when autonomous vehicles become the norm. The goal is to find a career where there will be a job over the long term.

- *Will I earn enough money to support myself?* This question forces teens to think about the lifestyle they anticipate and what kind of income is needed. Some wonderful jobs don't pay a steady or living wage. Some careers are so competitive (actor, musician) that only the very best succeed. Other careers require advanced degrees. For example, an undergraduate degree in psychology, social work or speech-language pathology only qualifies you for low-paying jobs. Advanced degrees will be required if your young adult wants to work as a therapist and be able to bill clients. This is not to say that young people shouldn't follow their passions. But they should do it with their eyes wide open to the eventual financial consequences.

- *Are there restrictions for people with ADHD or other disabilities?* Some jobs have medical requirements that make it difficult for someone with a disability or chronic medical condition to make it a career. For instance, the military has restrictions for recruits who have been treated for ADHD and many other disorders (Department of Defense, 2022). Find out early in the vocational search process. The Federal Aviation Administration requires a medical evaluation and may deny a commercial pilot's license for ADHD (Federal Aviation Administration, 2022). To proceed down the path for a career that you love only to find that the door is shut is devastating. It's better to be forewarned.

Ruth's Lessons Learned: Sometimes short-term sacrifices are required. My son became a park ranger by first working as a part-time seasonal ranger at a low rate of pay, a typical entry process for his chosen profession. He supplemented this by working as a plumber's assistant for a HVAC company and moved back home to keep costs down. A little over a year later, he was promoted to a full-time position in his dream job.

PC: I would advise others to actively listen to their adult child. As they talk to us parents, they're figuring it all out in their minds, and communication helps them do that. Always do your best to be patient and remember they are still learning (as we all are). Tell them you love them and that you're proud of them daily! Positivity helps in a world that often doesn't give of that freely. Be your teen's biggest fan!

Getting Your Teenager Engaged in Career Exploration

For some young people with ADHD, this may be a gentle dance, with your teen leading the way. You want to be certain that this process doesn't become a chore or, worse, result in family conflict. Your job is to ask the questions and listen as your young adult grapples with the answers.

For other young people, especially those with executive function deficits or ADHD Inattentive, more support and direct guidance will be needed. As we know, these teenagers are often content to live in the here and now and often don't plan ahead. So parents may help by making observations of their teen's strengths and careers that might be a good fit for them. Here are examples of types of comments you might make:

- "You amaze me that you can stay so calm during a crisis. You would make a great EMT."
- "You're always helping your friends repair their cars or install stereos. Hmm, maybe after you graduate, you might sign up for classes in automotive technology."
- "You were one of the best debaters on your team. Do you think you would be interested in learning more about what lawyers do on a daily basis?"
- "Your robotics team won your regional championship this year. After you graduate, you might enjoy taking courses in electrical and mechanical engineering. We should check out the high school STEM program, and if you're interested, put your name on their waiting list."

PC: *Our daughter loves riding horses, grooming horses, cleaning tack, all things horses. She works part-time at several stables, helps groom and feed the horses and teaches lessons to younger riders—all the things she loves. My husband and I are college graduates, and to be honest, at first, we saw this as simply a hobby.*

However, supporting her interest in horses was the smartest thing we've ever done. Suddenly, more doors opened. A woman who owns off-track retired thoroughbred racehorses invited our daughter to accompany her to competitions that are held in the Kentucky Horse Park in Lexington, Kentucky. She now owns and trains a retired thoroughbred racehorse affectionately known as "Ice" (Figure 9.3) and has won several ribbons competing in equestrian events. Her riding successes have given her an incredible gift: unshakeable self-confidence.

In addition to her work with horses, she is also taking college courses as part of her gap year plan. Kendal has decided that ultimately, she wants to become a speech therapist so she can help others.

Once They Have Ideas About Potential Careers

While all of this exploration is a great starting point, it's only the beginning. Help your young adult think about ways to actually get some real-life exposure to the career areas they are considering. Here are some ways they can make that happen:

- Interview a person in the profession.
- Do a follow-along (job shadow) for a day, a week, or longer.
- Look for volunteer opportunities in the field.
- Is there an internship opportunity available?
- Get a part-time, entry-level job in the profession.

Figure 9.3 Kendal with her horse "Ice".

Ruth's Lessons Learned: Real-life experience can be a game changer. Ruth's son Christopher thought he wanted to be a teacher. He loved working as a camp counselor and was passionate about his time volunteering in an orphanage for children with disabilities. His next step was an internship in a middle school. He found he disliked school no matter which side of the teacher's desk he sat on. This is also not a linear process and there may be many career steps along the way. Christopher considered being a policeman, a fireman and a camp director, and eventually he became a park ranger. Today he feels he won the job lottery.

Helpful Ground Rules

Take one step at a time. Big questions about the future can be overwhelming to teens and young adults, particularly for those who have been the recipients of criticism and negative messages from others along the way. Go slowly and break this down into small steps. Tackle one thing at a time. Base your timing on your teen's progress, with some gentle nudging if necessary. You have more time than you think. Don't feel pressured to have all the answers because your son or daughter will soon be 18. Finding the right career is a journey that takes time.

Work together or with a trusted mentor. Make this a joint project and share the work. Let your teen assign you tasks that he would like help with completing. Get him to do as much as possible on his own. Some teenagers may be overwhelmed by the task and will require greater support and involvement from you. If you're not the best person to do this with your son or daughter, enlist the help of a friend or relative who is well liked and trusted by your teen.

Have fun along the way. Whatever your teen's interests, there will be ways to have fun and bond together. If your daughter thinks she wants to be a chef, consider taking a cooking class together. And if she is a better cook than you, more power to her. If your son is interested in being a park ranger, you could plan a trip together to national parks he would like to visit. Let your teenager teach you new skills. Share stories about your own mistakes and bumps in finding a career.

There are no bad ideas. You may (and probably will) consider some of the career goals proposed by your child as unreasonable or not achievable. But that is ultimately not up to you. No judgments, please.

Ruth's Lessons Learned: I found this was one of the most challenging lessons of parenting a young adult. I could see the problems and risks ahead that I thought my son did not have the life experience to know. And I was often wrong. Keep your opinions to yourself unless asked, and otherwise let your child take the lead. If your daughter wants to be a professional clown, then help her find out about training for clowns. If your son is certain he will be a rock star, help him learn more. You will see risks ahead, but keep an open mind and discuss the pros and potential challenges ahead. Your job is to realistically encourage, not discourage.

Communicate your confidence in your child frequently. Most teens with ADHD have received lots of criticism over the years, resulting in a lack of confidence in their abilities. Your belief in your child is crucial if he is to take the risks that are part and parcel of growing up. And belief in him is even more important when he hits some rough waters.

Problems in life are real. Also help your young adult understand that every life is full of problems and challenges. As a parent, you will always be there to listen and help your son or daughter sort out how to tackle these challenges. Share some of your growing-up challenges and how you eventually got through the tough times.

Expect twists and turns. Finding a career usually entails trying on many ideas until the right one clicks. At various times during his young adult years, Ruth's son wanted to be a soldier, a teacher, a policeman, a firefighter, a camp director and, finally, a park ranger. He tried each career on for size and learned more about himself every time.

Listen, listen, and then listen some more. This is by far the most important thing you can do. Ask questions and then really pay attention to what your teen has to say. Let him know that he has your full attention and that you are seriously considering his thoughts. Pay attention to what is not said as well. What does your teenager's behavior tell you about what he is thinking? For instance, if he avoids pursuing an area he has expressed interest in, it may convey anxiety and fear of failure. Or it could mean he has changed his mind and doesn't want to disappoint you.

References

Assessment.com. (2022). *Take the MAPP career test and find your new career*. Assessment.com – Home of the MAPP Assessment – Assessment.com. Retrieved January 17, 2023, from https://www.assessment.com/

ASVAB. (2023, January 9). *Official site of the ASVAB Enlistment Training Program*. Armed Services Vocational Aptitude Battery. Retrieved January 17, 2023, from https://www.officialasvab.com/

Bureau of Labor Statistics. (2022, February 24). *Persons with a disability: Labor force characteristics—2021*. Retrieved January 18, 2023, from https://www.bls.gov/news.release/pdf/disabl.pdf

Career Dimensions. (2023). *Focus 2 Career*. Career Dimensions ®Career & Education Planning Systems. Retrieved January 17, 2023, from https://www.focus2career.com/

Department of Defense. (2022, June 6). *DOD Directives Division*. Medical standards for military service: Retention. Retrieved January 18, 2023, from https://www.esd.whs.mil/dd/

Federal Aviation Administration. (2022, July 18). *Guide for aviation medical examiners*. Retrieved January 23, 2023, from https://www.faa.gov/ame_guide/dec_cons/disease_prot/adhd

Federal Reserve Bank of New York. (2022, November 4). *The labor market for recent college graduates*. Retrieved January 17, 2023, from https://www.newyorkfed.org/research/college-labor-market/index.html#/underemployment

The Myers Briggs Company. (2022). *Strong interest inventory* [Career test]. Retrieved January 17, 2023, from https://www.themyersbriggs.com/en-US/Products-and-Services/Strong

O*NET online. (n.d.). *O*NET online*. Retrieved January 28, 2023, from https://www.onetonline.org/

Personality Profile Solutions. (2022). *What is the disc assessment?* Discprofile.com. Retrieved January 17, 2023, from https://www.discprofile.com/what-is-disc

10 Decisions, Decisions

Options After High School Graduation

In the United States today, societal expectations are high that teens will attend a traditional college immediately after high school graduation—assuming they can afford it. Many of our teens also are burdened with the self-imposed expectation that they must earn a college degree. Parents, grandparents and teachers also subtly promote this idea. After all, parents often want their children to be more successful than they were and to make the family proud.

Yet, if students with ADHD enroll in a traditional four-year college before their brains are mature enough, they are often unsuccessful and may be reluctant to ever return. Ultimately, many *young people with ADHD have the ability to earn a traditional degree* but are not ready to tackle higher education right after high school graduation.

The Myth of a Four-Year Degree

Fewer than half of all college students (44.1 percent) graduate within four years from the first semester. Another 20 percent graduate within five years, while an additional 29.9 percent graduate within six years (National Center for Education Statistics, 2022). And these statistics focus only on at students who reach graduation, not the 40 percent who drop out and never return to college (Hanson, 2022). Students with ADHD will find college more challenging and are at a much higher risk of taking longer to get to that degree. So, plan realistically.

Another important consideration is that for some students, a traditional college education simply *is not the best choic*e. The selection of advanced education after graduation should be based on the teenager's interests, talents and career aspirations, not on societal expectations.

So, we encourage you to take a step back and reexamine your mindset about the next step after finishing high school. This is the time to explore all the options open to your teen without preconceived notions of what is acceptable. Perhaps, your teen would benefit from taking a break for a year or so before deciding if a traditional two- or four-year college or a technical college is the best choice for her. Or perhaps the military, an apprenticeship or another path might be a better option. In this chapter, we offer an overview of these and other options your son or daughter may want to consider pursuing after leaving high school. With support and time your student can graduate (Figure 10.1). In the chapters ahead, we'll look more closely at specific choices.

DOI: 10.4324/9781003364092-10

Figure 10.1 Kendrick with proud mom, Karran.

PC: *He could have used a fifth year of high school to mature more, both personally and academically; plus, he needed more skills than they taught.*

Community College and Traditional Four-Year Colleges

Many of us are guilty of thinking of "real college" primarily as a traditional four-year institution where students sit in class, listen to lectures, take notes and learn from their textbooks. However, community colleges are real colleges as well and may offer a wider range of traditional classes as well as specialized professional or technical programs of hands-on study lasting from two years to a few months. Community college students attend classes, take notes, learn from textbooks, and then apply their knowledge in a hands-on profession such as licensed practical nurse (LPN), electrician, mechanic or welder—or go on to a four-year college if their chosen career requires a bachelor's degree. College can also include an institution of higher learning specifically designed to serve students who have learning disabilities or ADHD.

In addition to the technical training offered at community colleges, private technical colleges also prepare students for specific vocations. Training programs at either of these institutions have options that require fewer academic courses. A more detailed discussion of college options is provided in upcoming chapters.

PC: Having life experience and allowing him time to grow up have been essential. In retrospect, we could have saved a lot of money by not insisting on college before he was ready.

Risks of a Premature College Launch

There are serious hazards for teens with ADHD who go directly to college after high school graduation. Since they may be unprepared for more demanding independent work, they may drop out after the first year. In the process, they may amass school loan debt they'll be saddled with for years to come. Of course, with proper treatment, including medication, and supports in college, some students will do well. However, they may have to start with a smaller course load and may well take longer to graduate.

Experts report that up to 70 to 80 percent of students with ADHD may not finish college (DuPaul et al., 2021). The good news is that this percentage is trending down. A decade ago, we were reporting that 90 percent of students with ADHD were dropping out of college. Our students may be more successful if they delay college entry and take a year or more to mature and master independent work skills. By then they may also have a better sense of the career they want to pursue. Most college students with ADHD also benefit from additional supports and accommodations.

PC: Our daughter wasn't ready to go away to college until age 22. She began working with a life coach at 20, and that was helpful.

Because a college degree or further education after high school is a prerequisite for so many careers, we devote several chapters to discussing the issues related to attending college with ADHD as well as to choosing an appropriate college or educational program and getting needed supports if you and your teen decide to go the college route. See Chapters 11, 13, 14, and 15.

Gap Year Programs

A *gap year program* can be a wonderful option for students with ADHD who are late bloomers. Participating in a gap year program allows students to mature for another year or two after high school rather than sending them off to college or to a full-time job. Two options are generally available: (1) a paid gap year program with professional staff, or (2) a more personalized program that you and your teen design and implement. Carly, for example, worked with her family and designed her own gap year plan (Figure 10.2). Or you might consider adding an extra year to your teen's high school program and homeschooling her, as one parent we know did.

There are several good reasons to consider a gap year. The obvious one is to address the up-to-three-year delay in brain maturation. A gap year gives a young person more time for her brain to mature and time to explore potential career paths and build skills required to succeed in college. Gap year programs can also help young adults discover their talents, increase knowledge, learn to make better decisions, develop leadership skills and become more independent and self-sufficient. One major drawback to paid gap year programs is the cost, which may range from $10,000 to $40,000 a year.

By the time high school rolls around, you know your son or daughter better than anyone else does. So if you don't think he or she will be mature enough to successfully transition to

Figure 10.2 Carly, a gap year participant.

college, start planting the seed for the possibility of taking a gap year. The earlier you have this discussion during the high school years, the better. Ideally you'll introduce this option before your teen begins making plans about a future career. To be better informed, talk with other parents (and teens) whose children took a gap year. Here are some examples of how you might broach the idea to your teen:

Did you know that Carly took a gap year? She taught dance to younger children and participated in a local theater program. After the first year, she took a couple of courses at the community college and continued her other gap year activities. In the process, she discovered her true passion and now she knows what career path she wants to pursue. She wants to be a psychologist so she can help other students with ADHD.

I heard that Daniel's planning to take a gap year before college. He wants to be a veterinarian, so he's going to apply for an internship or part-time job, or he'll just volunteer at a vet clinic. He has also written to the dean of the Vet School at Auburn University and asked if he can tour their program. He wants to shadow one of the students for a day to see what they actually do or maybe even volunteer a couple of days a week.

Personally Planned Gap Year Programs

These are best if jointly developed by parents and the student. The plan could incorporate current extracurricular activities, such as working as a camp counselor or coaching youth athletic, debate or robotics teams, and include exposure to potential future career interests. Volunteering to work with people in various careers gives the student an opportunity to get a taste of what it's like to be an attorney, veterinarian, car mechanic, house painter or electrician.

Work jointly with your teenager and develop a plan for her to work or volunteer in a local agency or business related to her interests, especially one that might eventually lead to a career. For example, if your teen is interested in children, she might consider part-time volunteering in a school or working as a teacher's aide. Some students may apply for a part-time job or take one course at a community college in addition to their volunteer work. Spend time discussing your teen's career interests and create a plan that allows her to get firsthand experience working in that field. Detailed information on developing a personalized gap year program that combines education, personal growth and fun is in Chapter 12.

Formal Gap Year Programs

Check out accredited gap year programs first. These programs come in a variety of formats, and costs vary significantly. Programs may last from three months to a year. Some programs focus on specific interests such as robotics or on outdoor experiences such as wilderness survival, scuba diving or horseback riding. Another program offers an internship in Washington, D.C., with periodic lectures while also allowing the student to earn college credit. Others offer a semester of experiential community living in a foreign country and an opportunity to master a foreign language.

We are most familiar with the SOAR program, which was founded by Jonathan Jones, an adult with a learning disability. SOAR is an accredited educational academy and gap year program specializing in working with students with ADHD and/or learning disabilities. The gap year program is located in Wyoming at Eagle View Ranch. Each participant travels in the western United States and internationally, volunteers at a community organization and takes college courses on subjects such as workforce readiness and personal finance. Participants also take on real-life responsibilities such as doing laundry, cooking meals and planning trips. In the process, young people work indirectly on strengthening executive skills such as organization and planning ahead (SOAR, 2022).

USA Gap Year Fairs showcasing gap year programs are held annually during January and February in 40 different locations across the country. Scheduled locations are posted on their website. The USA Gap Year group has a directory of programs. You'll be amazed at the number and variety of programs available.

Income-Linked Opportunities

A variety of special programs are available for young people who have left high school and meet the income eligibility criteria. Two programs that may be appropriate for young adults with ADHD and/or LD are described here.

Job Corps

Young people may apply for training and work experiences at an area Job Corps program. Job Corps, a service of the US Department of Labor, provides educational and technical training for students ages 16 to 24. Two hundred of these programs offer training and work in a variety of specialties throughout the United States. Non–high school graduates can be accepted into the program and can work toward earning a GED while also taking training courses. Training is offered in a variety of areas: information technology, healthcare, automotive repair, construction, homeland security, and more (Job Corps, 2022).

Job Corps students live on campus and receive a biweekly living allowance with a transition allowance as they search for a job. A few programs allow students to live at home during training. Job Corps training is free to those meeting income eligibility criteria. For locations of Job Corps programs, eligibility requirements, and answers to other frequently asked questions, visit www.jobcorps.gov/questions.

Year Up

Year Up, a nonprofit program that has been featured on *60 Minutes*, was established to provide talented young people in urban areas the opportunity to enhance their knowledge and increase their incomes. High school graduates or GED recipients ages 18 to 26 may apply to the program, provided they meet income eligibility requirements and are legally allowed to work in the United States. (Students with DACA status are welcome to apply.)

During the yearlong program, students first take six months of courses in general business and professional skills and in skills specific to one of these areas: (1) information technology, (2) financial operations, (3) sales and customer support, (4) business operations and (5) software development and support. Students are supported by advisors from the program as well as by mentors who work in a related profession. Classes may be taken at freestanding Year Up locations or through local community colleges. (Students enrolling in a college-based program must also apply for admission to the college.)

In the second half of the program, students participate in a six-month internship. Students receive stipends during both the training and internship portions of the program. After completion of the courses and internship, the program actively assists in placing graduates in jobs. Graduates of the program have earned salaries averaging $22 an hour.

At present, locations are limited to larger cities in states on the East and West Coasts, as well as in Arizona, Texas and Illinois (Year Up, n.d.). More information is available on the Year Up website, www.yearup.com.

The Military: Army, Navy, Air Force, Marines, Coast Guard

The military could be a good choice for some young people with ADHD but a disaster for others. Typically, teens with ADHD who are successful military recruits loved high school ROTC or embraced the rigor and discipline of participating in sports such as football, basketball, soccer or swimming. For some, military service is a good short-term option (e.g., for one four-year enlistment), akin to a somewhat lengthy "gap year." The young person can often save a great deal of money for further education while maturing and honing executive functions and other skills. Others may find a lifetime vocation in the military, with options to retrain for a different job specialty at each reenlistment.

Generally speaking, the military doesn't want to accept anyone who is dependent on daily medication (e.g., for diabetes, asthma or ADHD) to function successfully. Ironically, the rates of ADHD among US military personnel are quite high—two times greater than in the general population. Note, however, that the rules changed significantly in 2018 for all the military forces and have made it much more difficult to enter the military with ADHD. The following conditions make ADHD a disqualifying condition:

- An IEP, 504 Plan, or work accommodations after the 14th birthday.
- A history of co-occurring mental disorders.
- Prescribed ADHD medication in the previous 24 months.
- Documentation of adverse academic, occupational or work performance.

Other behavioral and mental disorders have additional exclusionary conditions. The standards change periodically, so it is always worth checking with a recruiter or online to find out the current criteria (Department of Defense, 2022).

Don't let a recruiter tell your son or daughter to lie or omit any information about ADHD. Recruiters have quotas to fill and won't be there to stand up for your teen if and when the military sorts it out. Your young person can be discharged for withholding this information.

Chris's Lessons Learned: I've known several teenagers who successfully entered the military—but they did so before the more restrictive entry criteria were adopted. Most of them had milder ADHD and had stopped medication for a year. For them, increased physical activity enhanced brain functioning. In addition, the drill sergeant became the teen's "executive function brain," thus minimizing decision-making.

I've only known one young man who was released from the military, but he received an honorable discharge. He successfully completed basic training and was serving honorably when authorities discovered his ADHD. Talk with parents whose children with ADHD have gone into the military to learn more.

Apprenticeships and Full- or Part-Time Jobs

Apprenticeships: As discussed in Chapter 8, there are some well-paid, highly skilled careers such as electrician, plumber, solar panel installer, and heating and air-conditioning experts that don't require a college degree. Instead, workers are usually trained via apprenticeships and are typically paid a salary while they are apprenticing. If your son or daughter has an interest in one of these career fields, apprenticing may be a better option for him or her—at least right after high school. You can find out more about apprenticeships and search for opportunities in your area at www.apprenticeship.gov.

Full- or Part-Time Jobs: Earlier we discussed some of the benefits of working during the high school years. If your teen isn't ready for college or another postsecondary education program after high school graduation, she may want to get a job instead. This may be worthwhile, especially if she can find a job in a career field of interest or perhaps if she needs to earn money to go to college. For teens lacking career focus, it might be a good idea to work for a temp agency and sample different work settings and types of jobs.

What If Your Teenager Didn't Finish High School?

All hope is not lost. Encourage your teen to earn a GED: certification granted to those who pass a series of tests proving that they have the same academic knowledge as a high school graduate in the areas of language arts, math, science, and social studies. Several famous people have advanced their careers with a GED, including Dave Thomas, the founder of Wendy's; actor Michael J. Fox; and Bryan Jennings, a US congressman.

As mentioned earlier, students enrolled in a Job Corps program can earn a GED general education diploma that will give them access to more vocational options. Students can also study independently for the GED, enroll in in-person GED classes or elect to take online prep courses for the GED; however, the test must be taken in person at a designated facility. For the location of the GED program nearest you, visit the GED website: https://ged.com/

study/ged_classes/. After earning a GED, students can apply to a specialized professional and technical college or a community or four-year college. They will also have more success looking for a job, since employers generally look more favorably on hiring workers who have completed high school.

   The important lesson we have learned is that no path needs to be preordained. The needs of your young adult should be the driving force in the decision-making process. Start this discussion early in the high school years and let your teen know there are many acceptable choices. Many young people with ADHD will pursue several of these paths before finalizing a career direction. And these experiences will help them mature and do well.

References

Department of Defense. (2022, June 6). *DOD Directives Division.* Medical standards for military service: Retention. Retrieved January 18, 2023, from https://www.esd.whs.mil/dd/

DuPaul, G.J., Gormley, M.J., Anastopoulos, A.D., Weyandt, L.L., Labban, J., Sass, A.J., Busch, C.Z., Franklin, M.K., & Postler, K.B. (2021). Academic trajectories of college students with and without ADHD: Predictors of four-year outcomes. *Journal of Clinical Child & Adolescent Psychology,* 50(6): 828–843. https://doi.org/10.1080/15374416.2020.1867990

Hanson, M. (2022, July 21). *College dropout rates.* Education Data Initiative. Retrieved January 23, 2023, from https://educationdata.org/college-dropout-rates

Job Corps. (2022). *Careers begin here.* Retrieved January 23, 2023, from https://www.jobcorps.gov/

National Center for Education Statistics. (2022). *Fast facts: Undergraduate graduation rates.* Retrieved January 23, 2023, from https://nces.ed.gov/fastfacts/display.asp?id=40

SOAR, Inc. (2022, November 2). *SOAR: The world's premier ADHD and LD adventure program.* Retrieved January 23, 2023, from https://soarnc.org/

Year Up. (n.d.). *Job training to close the opportunity divide.* Retrieved January 21, 2023 from https://www.yearup.org/

11 Is College the Right Option for Your Teen (Now)?

Jennifer had been diagnosed in elementary school with ADHD and a reading learning disability, both well managed with support and treatment. She graduated from high school at 18 with a B average and was accepted at a college two hours from home.

The following September, her parents dropped her off at school with lots of encouragement and great expectations for her success. However, the lack of structure in her life on campus was very challenging for her. She stayed up late with her roommates, slept late and regularly missed her morning classes. She had difficulty staying on top of her assignments, particularly the long-term planning needed to complete two papers.

At midterms she was way behind and did poorly on her exams. She became stressed and depressed and fell further behind. She felt she could not tell her parents because they had such high hopes for her college experience. And her dad regularly reminded her how much money they were investing in her college years.

Jennifer's anxiety increased so dramatically that she was unable to take some of her final exams. She called her parents and asked them to come get her. To their shock, she had decided to drop out of college. Her dad was furious that $20,000 for tuition and room and board was wasted. She came home feeling like a total failure, depressed and reluctant to move forward.

Some version of this tale happens to thousands of students both with and without ADHD and/or learning disabilities. We can help our teens do better. The guidance in this book can help you avoid the disappointments that Jennifer and her family experienced. This chapter provides guidance to help teens and parents make a wise decision about when—and whether—to attend college. We cover some of the reasons that students with ADHD or learning disabilities may struggle and discuss several ways to assess your teen's readiness for college. Further help with decision-making is provided in Chapter 15, which describes specific college options in more detail. Also, don't overlook the potential value of giving your son or daughter more time to mature and clarify career goals by opting for a *gap year program*, as discussed in the next chapter.

Determining If College Is the Right Path Now

Keep in mind that going to college is not just about moving out on your own and pursuing a four-year degree. Some young adults may be better off living at home, pursuing a two-year degree, or enrolling in a shorter-term certification program with targeted instruction in specific job skills. And some may be better off putting further education on hold for a year or two.

The first thing to understand is that young adults with ADHD and/or LD absolutely can get through college and forge a satisfying career. The second fact is that completing college is hard, and there will be challenges. And third, it may take more time than you have

DOI: 10.4324/9781003364092-11

Figure 11.1 Alek, IT associate, California Department of Energy.

anticipated. By being focused as a family on the goal (a career) and continuing to provide a safety net for your son or daughter when he or she eventually goes to college, you are increasing the likelihood of success.

Keep sight of ultimate career goals. Be sure that college is really the right path and not just what everyone thinks your son or daughter should be doing after high school. College is a path, not a destination. Many of us have forgotten the true purpose of college: to prepare for a satisfying career in a field where you can earn a decent living. Alek found his ultimate job and is working in IT for the California Department of Energy (Figure 11.1). Far too many college students graduate with a major that doesn't lead to a career and still have no idea what they want to do. Remember, too, that there are plenty of satisfying careers that don't require four-year or even two-year college degrees.

Yet we persist in sending our young people off to a four-year college without any idea about career aspirations and paying huge amounts of tuition at great cost to the family or, worse, borrowing large amounts of money through student loans. A more thoughtful approach to the timing and choosing of a college can make a huge difference in both the student's life and the family's pocketbook. In other words, if your teen has absolutely no idea what sort of career he would like to have, or has only unrealistic ideas, that may be one very good reason to hold off on starting college right after high school.

PC: My daughter tried the first semester of college away from home and stopped attending classes and failed the first semester. She came home and was diagnosed with anxiety, depression and ADHD. She was completely unprepared for college work and study.

Why Is College Challenging for Teens with ADHD?

Every year, thousands of young adults go on to college immediately after graduation and then hit a brick wall. All young people find this a time of high anxiety. This is not just about our teens with learning challenges. Thirty percent of all first-year students don't return to college after their freshman year because they were not prepared to manage the freedom without the structure of home (College ExpressAtlas, 2017). When a student has a learning challenge such as ADHD, the likelihood of crashing is increased.

Keep in mind the everyday skills that make life challenging for teens with ADHD: organization, planning and problem-solving. Difficulties with these skills do not go away after high school graduation, and unless your teen has learned really good coping skills to compensate, he is probably not ready to set his own schedule, manage his finances, do his work independently and manage his own disability.

Remember how difficult transitions are for many young people with ADHD and executive function deficits? If your teen leaves home for college, it will likely be the largest and most disruptive transition he has faced. On top of that, he will be losing many of the supports he has had while living at home and attending school. This double whammy—severely decreased supports and significantly increased expectations—can be deadly for our young people who are not yet ready. With the proper academic supports and greater maturity, however, students with ADHD can successfully complete college.

Common challenges for students with ADHD and LD include the following:

- Difficulty handling social distractions and lack of structure.
- Procrastination.
- Executive functioning challenges.
- Disrupted sleep schedules.
- Poor study routines.
- Difficulty accessing treatment and/or medication.
- Lack of adequate supports and accommodations.
- Poor planning and follow-through on long-term projects.
- Little helpful feedback on performance from teachers.
- Social conflicts (roommate mismatch, relationship problems).
- Others asking to share stimulant medication.
- Financial hardships.

These challenges can make college tough, but anticipating and planning for these obstacles can make all the difference. On the other hand, forgetting about these challenges and automatically assuming the teen is ready to take that next really big step may be setting him up for failure.

PC: *When my son made the decision to attend a large state university, I was proud and scared all at the same time. He was awarded several scholarships and an athletic manager position with the football team. To be honest, it was the future he had heard us talk about his whole life. I tried to change his mind and tell him it would be fine to go to a community college closer to home, but he was firm in his decision. Looking back now, I believe he went to the large state university because he thought that was what was expected of him.*

The year and a half spent there was not at all what he expected. He was unprepared, even though he had been in the top seven of his class and had already taken several college classes before he graduated from high school. We felt like failures as parents. Why had we not prepared him better or forced him to make another decision?

Truthfully, we'd wanted him to attend that school since he was a baby. Again, our hopes and dreams became his because he heard them so much.

Assessing Your Teen's Readiness for College

So how do you know if your son or daughter is ready to enroll in college-level classes, leave home and tackle the world?

Key Indicators of Readiness for College: Students with ADHD who take medication, have had psychosocial treatments and have a higher GPA in high school are better prepared for college. Examples of psychosocial interventions include counseling, parent training, after-school programs, tutoring, accommodations at school, practicing self-advocacy, and daily structure provided at home. Teens may also be better prepared for college if they have learned and practiced good study skills, test-taking strategies and executive function skills.

When compared with students without ADHD, our children generally aren't as prepared. For example, they are often delayed in these areas:

- *Daily living skills.* Students with ADHD often are unprepared to manage daily living tasks such as organization (managing possessions and academic work, keeping an orderly living space, doing laundry, eating nutritious meals) and time management (balancing their schedule of socializing, getting adequate sleep, completing academic work and study).
- *Academic readiness skills.* The stronger the student's study skills—managing assignments, taking notes, preparing for tests and writing papers—the better prepared he will be for college. The ability to independently complete homework and organize and complete long-term projects is also a factor determining college success.
- *Self-awareness and self-advocacy.* Students who are self-aware and know their strengths and challenges are better prepared to advocate for themselves and seek accommodations or extra help. As a result, they are better prepared to succeed in college.
- *Vocational awareness/readiness.* Students who have explored possible career choices and have actually had work experience that they enjoyed are more likely to have direction and focus.

All transitions create periods of greater risk. Even well-functioning students may find the lack of structure and immediate feedback in college (and in adult life) to be highly challenging. The last year or two of high school is a good time to take stock with your teen and do a realistic assessment of his readiness to move on to postsecondary education (or a job).

Assess Daily Living Skills

Losing the support and structure provided by parents and in high school or college may set our teens adrift. The invaluable support and structure parents have been providing disappears when they leave home. No one will be sure they are getting up on time, getting to work or classes, finishing projects, getting the laundry done, getting enough sleep and completing the many other tasks that are part of everyday living. Don't assume that because your teen knows how to do things (skills and knowledge), he will actually use those skills (action). For example, your son knows how to set an alarm to wake up in the morning, but will he get up, get dressed and make it to class on time?

Focus on what your teen is doing now on his own. *It's also time to encourage your son or daughter to start taking more responsibility for everyday living tasks without your prompting!*

Chris's granddaughter, a college graduate, shares her insights regarding this challenging transition period:

PC: I have always been motivated to follow rules and adhere to guidelines or regulations so that I wouldn't "get in trouble." When no one is requiring me to be anywhere at any certain time and I have the financial support of my parents to fall back on, motivating and managing my self-appointed goals and tasks has proven to be nearly impossible for me. I have never ever, ever been accountable to just myself. This is very difficult for me.

You can prompt a conversation about needed skills by saying something like this: "I'd like to plan some time with you to think about next year and what we both need to do to get ready. How about the two of us sitting down tomorrow evening after dinner?"

You may want to do this in stages rather than all at once. You are likely to find that you and your teen have different perceptions of his abilities. Don't assume you're right. You'll probably underestimate your teen's abilities, while he is likely to overestimate. But do remind him (and yourself) that the answers should be based on what he *does* rather than what he *knows*.

Ruth's Lessons Learned: When my son graduated from high school, I told him we were now going to have "college rules" at home, which meant I was no longer going to nag him to clean his room or wash his clothes. Once he was away from home, he would have to do these things on his own.

Christopher had been doing his own laundry once a week since middle school, with a fair amount of reminding and structure from me. He absolutely had the knowledge. But once the structure was gone, the actions disappeared. That summer Chris discovered Febreze. There was a lot of grabbing clothes from the pile on the floor, shaking them out, and spraying them with Febreze before putting them on.

When my mother came to visit for Thanksgiving, she was appalled at the pile of clothes in the basement and in Chris's room, and upset with me for allowing this to happen. She promptly washed, folded and put away all his clothes. Once she went home, the piles began to grow again. But by January Chris began to do his laundry regularly and has been doing it ever since.

Basic Life Skills

When young adults leave home, they need to take care of the demands of daily life without much parental assistance. The more responsibilities your teenager can take in these areas while still at home, the better. Remember that you want to consider what skills he is actually using, not what he knows how to do. See the College Readiness Survey in the Appendix for examples of these basic life skills.

"Get Real" Tip: We need to give our teens opportunities to do things on their own as they will need to do as adults. But don't expect it will happen overnight or consistently. It takes time for them to mature, learn new skills and develop their own compensatory

strategies. And then there are always real-world consequences to prime the pump. As a parent, you can provide the structure and ask the questions to increase your teen's awareness of tasks he will need to do independently once he leaves home.

Financial Management

Managing money without parental supervision (and pocketbooks) is a challenge for most young adults. Obviously, you'll need to monitor your college student's finances. Here are some questions to ask to determine whether he has the most basic financial management know-how needed for college:

- Does he manage his allowance so he has sufficient funds to make it until the next allowance?
- Does he have a checking account? Is he careful not to overdraw the account?
- Has he managed a credit card without accruing lots of debt?
- Has he used an online payment app such as PayPal, Venmo or Google Pay?
- If he has bills, does he pay them on time?

Social Skills

The social life of a young adult is an important part of maturation. This is also a time of experimentation, of forging important long-term relationships and of developing the interpersonal skills needed in the workplace and in life. Helpful social skills such as being a good listener, cooperative, honest and unselfish are identified in Chapter 5, along with tips for enhancing those skills. To assess your teen's social skills for college, refer back to the section on "ADHD Challenges That Can Interfere with Likability" in Chapter 5. Has your son or daughter successfully overcome or made good progress toward managing all or most of these challenges? He should also be making strides toward controlling the emotional reactivity discussed at the end of Chapter 5.

Managing ADHD and Other Health Issues

If your teen is still living at home, it's likely that you are managing the ADHD treatment process. But once he reaches the age of majority (generally age 18 in the United States), you cannot legally participate in his health care without his permission. There are other changes as well. The pediatrician who has treated your child may now be ready to transfer him to an adult or family physician, and your teen will have to get to know and trust this new person over time.

If your teen goes away to college, be aware that some university health centers won't treat ADHD because of liability issues. That may mean finding a new doctor in a new location who is comfortable prescribing stimulant medication for young adults. This can be challenging because some family physicians fear drug abuse. It is possible your teen's current physician will agree to continue to treat him while he is away at college. Of course, if your teen lives at home while attending college or comes home often, he can continue to see his local health care provider.

Then there is the challenge of ensuring prescriptions are filled and purchased before medication runs out. And it is guaranteed that some college friends and acquaintances will ask your teen to share his medications. So, good health care management is a crucial skill for college-bound young people with ADHD.

In addition to questions on the College Readiness Survey, consider the following issues specific to teens with ADHD:

- Will your teen keep his medication safe and out of the hands of other people?
- Is he able to comfortably say no to those who want to buy or use his medication?
- Has he used self-help strategies to manage the symptoms of ADHD?
- Does he regularly get enough sleep?
- Will he be able to wake up and get to morning classes on time?

Assess Academic Readiness Skills

College and other postsecondary settings are a lot different from high school. The teachers don't usually insist that students attend class, give regular feedback about homework assignments or ask students who are struggling to see them after class. There are usually several big assignments and exams during the semester, and students are expected to work independently. High school students are in the classroom 30 to 35 hours a week, with 6 to 8 hours of homework. In college, a full-time student is in class only 12 to 15 hours a week, but has 24 to 30 hours of independent reading, assignments and studying every week. This switch is challenging for all students, but for particularly students with poor time management. Julien was able to master these challenges and received his degree in media studies (Figure 11.2).

Figure 11.2 Julian, media studies (film) degree.

However, extra supports and accommodations are available at colleges and at many specialized professional training programs. These supports are provided under the Americans with Disabilities Act (ADA) and Section 504 of the same antidiscrimination law that applies in high school. The difference is that students, not their parents, must ask for these supports and inform individual professors of needed accommodations. Guidance for applying for supports in college and specific accommodations to consider is provided in later chapters. Many colleges also offer tutoring to all students who request it. For example, Gadsden State Community College in Chris's community offers math tutoring for first-year students because failing math was historically the primary reason many students dropped out of school. At Howard Community College where Ruth works, a weekly hour of tutoring for each class is free.

Common academic challenges (e.g., writing essays and completing assignments and long-term projects promptly) and intervention strategies are discussed in Chapter 3 and in greater detail in Chris's book *Teaching Teens with ADD, ADHD and Executive Function Deficits* (see the Resources section).

Consider your teen's specific academic skills:

- Can he write an essay independently without any outside help?
- Does he initiate and complete class assignments in a timely manner without prompting?
- Can he successfully plan, organize and complete long-term projects without extra supports?

Also consider the following information to assess academic readiness:

- Do results of academic achievement tests indicate that your teen has mastered skills on grade level?
- What skill deficits and effective accommodations have been identified in any evaluations conducted for eligibility for services pursuant to IDEA or Section 504?

Assess Self-Awareness and Self-Advocacy Skills

A variety of self-awareness and self-advocacy skills are essential in college and in adult life. The lack of these skills often leads to problems in the young adult years.

Consider whether your son or daughter has these important skills:

- Is your young adult able to advocate for himself?
- Does he "own" his disability, and is he able to articulate how it affects him and what accommodations are helpful in managing his challenges?
- Does he have good problem-solving skills, and can he actively solve problems on his own?
- Does he ask for help when he needs it, without worrying about what other people might think?
- Does he decide on goals, make a plan to get there and then implement the plan?

Reviewing the ADHD Iceberg in Chapter 2 with your teen is one way to increase self-awareness of challenges. You can take this one step further by discussing and identifying challenges in the ADHD Iceberg chart and then listing your teen's challenges in the blank iceberg in the Appendix. Understanding and accepting these issues will be helpful for your son or daughter when it is time to discuss needed accommodations at college.

Assess Vocational Readiness Skills

Whatever path your teenager takes after high school, the most important developmental task for him is to prepare for a job or career. In addition to acquiring the knowledge and skills needed for a specific career, young adults need to learn "soft" skills such as regular attendance and punctuality to be successful in the workplace. The importance of "soft skills" is discussed in later chapters regarding challenges at work.

For young people who are considering going on to college, a crucial step in vocational readiness is to identify jobs that might be good fits for their interests and talents. Here are some questions you might ask when assessing your teen's vocational readiness for college:

- Does he have at least a general idea of a career field or two he might want to work in?
- Does he have a realistic understanding of the education and training needed to work in those fields of interest?
- Does he understand the long-term outlook for employment in his chosen career? In other words, will it be easy for him to find a job in that field?

See Chapters 8 and 9 for more information.

A Tool to Help Assess College Readiness

Ready for Take-Off: Preparing Your Teen with ADHD or LD for College, includes a tool to assess readiness: the College Readiness Survey (CRS; Maitland & Quinn, 2011). See the Appendix for the parent version of the survey. (Maitland and Quinn also include a student version in their book.) Completing the survey has several advantages:

1. The survey lists the essential skills necessary for college success.
2. The completed surveys create a helpful springboard for discussion between you and your child.
3. It identifies critical skills necessary to be successful in college and brings them to the forefront of your teen's awareness.
4. It increases your teen's awareness of skills he is lacking without your having to list his deficiencies.
5. For teenagers who have slow recall, it's easier for them to react to a statement than to an open-ended question.

Completing the College Readiness Survey will help decide the next best steps for your teen: heading off to college or taking a bit more time to figure out next steps. The survey results and your discussions with your son or daughter will be the foundation for developing a plan.

Still Not Sure About the Right Decision?

Think about what your teen is actually doing today. Also consider how well he has handled past transitions such as the one from middle to high school.

- Is he talking about what he would like to do after graduation from high school?
- Does your teen have some idea of possible careers?

- Has he shown interest in applying to college or for a job?
- Is he sharing information with you about his friends who are making college visits?
- Does your teen have answers when you ask about next steps?

If none of these things are happening, your teen may be telling you that he's not feeling ready for greater independence. So you may have to take a different approach in providing career guidance from that of other parents.

Consider all the options. If you insist that there is only one path immediately after high school graduation, such as college, you are unnecessarily limiting other potentially worthwhile career opportunities and creating undue stress for your teen. If you're open to helping your son or daughter explore multiple paths to a successful adulthood, the stress is decreased and the opportunities to build on strengths and successes are increased. Your teenager desperately wants to succeed, and you're the best person to provide the needed guidance for him to reach those goals.

If you find there is real reluctance to leave home and real confusion about what should happen next, let your teen know that getting a full-time job or seeking further education are not the only options. Maybe he needs a gap year to figure out what comes next. It's okay to not be sure what the next steps are, and he can have the time to figure it out. If that's the case, you can work together to plan a year that will help him decide. It can be a year of exploration and finding answers.

What if your teen is eager to leave home but has few of the skills necessary for living independently? Reviewing the key skills listed in the College Readiness Survey will help your son or daughter understand that he or she needs additional tools to cope with independence. Then the two of you can identify areas that need work in order to move forward.

"Get Real" Tip: So your teenager has his heart set on going away to college, but you have reservations about his maturity level and ability to juggle college life. What in the world are you going to do? Guidance on helping your teen succeed in college is discussed in Chapter 16. In addition, Chris's book Teenagers with ADD, ADHD, and Executive Function Deficits *includes helpful tips for setting up "safety net reminder systems" for a variety of potential academic challenges while your child is living away from home (Dendy, 2017).*

References

College Express. (2017). *College Atlas and Planner*. College Express.

Dendy, C.A.Z. (2017). *Teenagers with ADD, ADHD and executive function deficits: A guide for parents and professionals*. (3rd ed.). Bethesda, MD: Woodbine House.

Maitland, T.L., & Quinn, P.O. (2011). *Ready for take-off: Preparing your teen with ADHD or LD for college*. Magination Press.

12 Creating Your Own Personalized Gap Year Plan

So, you have worked with your child and done an assessment of the skills discussed in the previous chapter. Together, you've decided that it's not yet time for college or technical training. A gap year may sound like the right idea, but many gap year programs are very expensive, and your teenager isn't yet interested in leaving home or isn't ready to do so. So, what is the next step?

Creating a Positive Gap Year Program

First, it helps to keep in mind the purpose of a gap year and to be clear about what it is not. Consider the following as you and your son or daughter are developing and implementing a plan.

A gap year should accomplish the following:

- Help your teen choose some vocational options to explore. Remember, the clearer she is about a potential career, the better the next steps will be.
- Strengthen important life skills identified in your joint assessment. You and your teen should focus on just a few areas at a time (definitely not more than two or three). Think about skills such as managing money, handling medication and health care, dealing with social challenges or improving organization or time management.
- Gradually move the responsibility for life tasks and decision-making to your young adult.
- Give your teen more real-world, adult experiences. Activities should push her outside her comfort zone. That means doing things that are new and with less (or no) parental management, such as taking a trip without you or starting a part-time job.
- Allow more time for maturation in every aspect of life.
- Include fun and exciting activities as well.

A productive gap year *does not* include the following:

- Hiding in the basement (or bedroom) playing video games. This should be a year of activity and exploration, not avoidance.
- Traveling the world, experimenting with sex and drugs. Without a doubt, travel can give your teen a much broader worldview and can be exhilarating. But for some teenagers who struggle with making independent decisions, are impulsive or are easily influenced by others, there is some danger in sending them off to explore the world with little structure or accountability. So, if the gap year includes travel, be sure there is some structure and accountability built in.

DOI: 10.4324/9781003364092-12

- Time for parents to protect their son or daughter from the world. This is a time to help your teen expand her comfort zone and become more comfortable standing on her own. So be sure to include activities that move your teenager toward adult responsibilities.

The Parents' Role

As experienced parents, we encourage you to think carefully about your role in planning and implementing a gap year plan before you begin. Your job is to provide the structure, external support, and cheerleading, while your teenager's job is to provide the ideas and the decisions. You can suggest, but your emerging young adult needs to begin to take more responsibility for deciding what to do with her life. She will not always make decisions you would agree with or even make good decisions, but sometimes the best teacher is the real world. Remember, the plan is flexible and can be changed whenever it makes sense.

Developing a plan may not be your strength or your teen's strength, even working with the examples and template provided in the Appendix. If this is also a challenge for you, recruit a partner to work with you and your teen. The plan is a road map for the gap year. With no plan, or one with few details, the gap year can quickly become just a year off. Don't let that happen.

Division of Planning Tasks: The division of responsibility will depend a lot on your teenager. There is a dance all parents do when their child has ADHD or a learning disability. You need to be there to advocate and provide support. But you also need to let your son or daughter grow into an independent adult. This balance is by necessity not the same as it may be with children who don't have the challenges our kids do. And it's a constantly changing balance as our kids grow into young adults.

Be mindful of where you are in this dance and that now is the time for your young adult to lead as much as possible. Provide only as much support as needed, and allow room for exploration and mistakes. The message to your teen must be loud and clear: this is your life, and you must make the decisions. If the decisions end up being wrong, then you support your teen and begin to develop the next plan based upon what she has learned.

We also encourage you to provide a budget for gap year activities. As you will see in the examples later in the chapter, a number of useful activities may cost money. This can be a wise investment and provide a richer experience.

"Get Real" Tip: The bottom line reality is that you must start working with your son or daughter at his or her present level of functioning. If your teenager can't seem to come up with ideas, then ask questions and draw out her thoughts. Try something like this: "You've always enjoyed working on cars. Is that something you'd like to learn more about?" Or this: "You've always been so helpful taking care of people who are elderly and sick. I wonder if you'd like to learn more about nursing or other careers in the medical field?"

Developing the Plan

Here are the steps to developing a gap year plan with your teenager.

Step 1: *Review the discussions you have had with your teen about careers.* What passions did she identify? What personal strengths can an adult career and life be built on, and what challenging areas need improvement? If your teen has taken a vocational test, be sure to review the results together to spark ideas.

Step 2: *Develop three types of goals—vocational, life skills, and fun.*

- *Vocational goals* are intended to help your teen explore the career options that she thinks might be right for her. The possibilities for exploration are endless—for example, conducting interviews with people working in the career of choice, volunteering in the industry, taking a class or certification program, looking into apprenticeships, or getting a part-time, entry-level job. But plan something that will expose your young adult to the work she thinks she'll love.
- *Life skill goals* ought to be designed to help your son or daughter strengthen skills that are weak and can be practiced with a safety net still in place. Think about money management, getting up and out the door on time, managing health care and prescriptions, driving and all those other life skills discussed in earlier chapters that are often challenging.
- *Fun goals* should be a significant part of a year to grow on. Exploration should be exciting, challenging and stimulating. These are the things that our kids dreamed about doing when they grew up. Things like getting a car, taking a trip or having an experience that is special to them. And these fun items or activities can be rewards for making progress toward accomplishing life skills or vocational goals during the gap year. Kendall chose a trip out west camping and hiking as one of her goals (Figure 12.1).

Step 3: *Make a list of the goals and begin to add specific action steps.* Each action step should include information on the person responsible for implementing it, supports needed, initiation dates, and target completion date. Examples are given later in the section "Examples of Personalized Gap Year Programs." You can use the detailed examples and the form in the Appendix as a template, or create your own chart.

Figure 12.1 Kendall, camping and hiking during her gap year.

- Sometimes parents may be the ones who have responsibilities. Don't put everything on your teen.
- Remember to focus on only two or three areas at a time. A year provides time to address a number of goals as long as they are spread out over the year.
- The more specific the action steps and due dates, the better, because that provides a detailed road map for your teen.
- Explain in advance that if your son or daughter has difficulty working toward his or her goals, then certain privileges (internet, cell phone or allowance) must be earned and will be contingent on making progress toward goals.
- If a lengthy plan is overwhelming to your teenager, separate the goals so that it is easier to focus.
- You want some action to happen every workday, to keep up momentum.

Step 4: *Get to work and implement the plan.* Expect that there will be reluctance, bumps and things that don't work out. There is likely to be a fair amount of anxiety at times, as your son or daughter forges into new territory. Ask your teenager to describe any roadblock and try to figure out together what is needed to get past it. And be willing to step in and provide more structure.

If this leads to conflict, consider finding an ADHD coach or therapist to work with your teen and help her move ahead, removing the family conflict. Another trusted adult may also serve this purpose. As *a last resort*, if your teen is not actively working on her goals, then begin making some privileges contingent on making progress toward her goals. But above all, provide lots of recognition for progress and celebrate every step.

Step 5: *Change as needed.* Once a plan is developed and set in motion, be sure your teen knows that it's all right if things don't go as planned, or if she changes her mind about goals and/or priorities. Remember that this is about exploration. As your teen learns more about what her interests are, she will also learn what they are not. The path to a career is often meandering and changes over time. This is the norm. So be ready to go back to the drawing board as often as necessary and congratulate your teenager for her growing understanding of what her goals are and are not.

Ruth's Lessons Learned: When my son narrowed his career goal to working with young people, he did an internship in a public middle school, thinking teaching might be the answer. After several months he told me he hated school, no matter which side of the desk he was on. This was not a failure, but rather a really important insight. He still wanted to work with young people, but definitely not in a school setting. A year later he was majoring in parks and recreation, which led to his current job as a park ranger. Today he tells me he has the best job in the world. This is the ending we want for all our young adults.

Examples of Personalized Gap Year Plans

A sample detailed plan is available in the Appendix to help you and your teen think through what works for your family. You may want to share some of these examples with your teenager to give her an idea of what kinds of things to put in a plan. The following is an overview of the goals for these plans and a description of the outcomes.

Bryan's Plan

Bryan likes to work with his hands and be outside. He has combined type ADHD and has frequent bouts of anxiety. He graduated from high school but really did not like school, so currently he has no interest in attending college. He has no idea about what should come next in his life. Bryan has great social skills and makes friends everywhere he goes. In high school his grades were average. Bryan had several part-time retail jobs in high school. He has a checking account that is frequently overdrawn and wants to get a credit card "like everyone else." He has recently gotten his driver's license but has already had one fender bender. During high school he was easily influenced by his peers, and sometimes this led to problems—underage drinking, speeding, smoking, etc. But none of these problems continued after his parents intervened.

A recent vocational test suggested he might like being a carpenter, an electrician, a salesman or an installer of solar panels. Bryan did some investigation of these possible careers online and decided he was interested in finding out more about being an electrician or a salesman. Asked which he would like to start with, he decided an electrician was the way to go.

In helping Bryan plan his gap year, his parents discussed the following issues with him:

What are my strengths and challenges and what do I LOVE TO DO?

I love being outdoors and making things that are useful for people. I love having friends and people around.

Strengths	Challenges
Love hanging out with friends	Money management
Learn best by doing	Impulsiveness at times
Like working with my hands	Any desk work is tough
Love the outdoors	Reducing anxiety when stressed
	Getting speeding tickets

Vocational Goals

I will ...
1. Explore work as an electrician by "job shadowing" an electrician for a month. (Job shadowing is a volunteer, unpaid learning opportunity.)
2. Investigate apprenticeships for electricians.
3. Explore work as a salesman by "job shadowing" a salesman for a month.
4. Seek a part-time job as an electrician helper or as a sales assistant in the electrical equipment field.
5. Make a plan for next steps.

Life Goals

I will ...
1. Learn to budget money with no overdrawn charges for six months.
2. Open a savings account once I have started working and deposit 10% of my paycheck into savings.

3. Save for a 20% deposit on a used car. Mom and Dad will pay the remaining 80% if I have no traffic tickets or accidents.
4. Do my own taxes with assistance.

Fun Goals

I will …
1. Go backpacking on the Appalachian Trail with Kyle for 2 weeks.
2. Buy a used car.
3. Volunteer with the local Sierra Club, where I can meet other people who love the outdoors.

Notice that this is just an overview of the plan and not all the details. Some young people with executive function challenges may be overwhelmed by a detailed plan with lots of action steps. You still need a detailed plan, but we suggest making the action steps for each goal separately, so it is not an overwhelming document.

Bryan's Gap Year and Five Years Later

Vocational Goals: Bryan's dad was able to help him find an electrician willing to have him follow along and learn what he did each day. Bryan needed some assistance in getting to work on time each day, but the electrician left without him if he was late. After this happened twice, Bryan made sure he got to work on time.

While Bryan liked the work, he wanted to check out sales as well. The electrician introduced him to several equipment salespeople, and he was able to follow along with a salesman as well. Bryan liked the sales work better but learned that the best salesmen were also electricians. He got a part-time job as a sales assistant six months into the year and kept this job for the next six months.

Bryan then applied for and was accepted into a two-year electrician apprenticeship training program. After completing his training, he worked as an electrician assistant for another two years before he was eligible to take the journeyman licensing exam. He didn't pass the first time but retook the exam after more study and passed. There were times when he made mistakes on the job because of his drifting attention. Bryan talked with his supervisor about his ADHD, and now his boss checks his work regularly and gives him feedback. As a result, his mistakes have decreased significantly. His plan is to work as a journeyman electrician for at least a year and then decide if he wants to move into the sales area.

Life Skills Goals: Bryan struggled with the life skills goals during his gap year. He set up a budget but quickly abandoned it and overdrew his account several times. His father insisted he work it out with the bank, and his parents did not rescue him. Only when Bryan began to work and receive a paycheck did he start to take managing his money more seriously. He set up a savings account but often did not contribute to the account for his car purchase goal, despite reminders from his parents. At the end of the year, he had only $600 in the account. He also received two speeding tickets in the first six months. His parents helped him to revisit his goals and decide how to proceed.

Jointly they decided to use an app that would track his speed and emit a reminder tone if he was going too fast, silence his phone for texts or calls and notify his parents if he turned the app off. (You can google "apps for teen drivers" and find a variety of apps that may work for your family.) With this immediate feedback loop to his cell phone, Bryan became more aware of his unsafe habits and got no more speeding tickets.

The goal to purchase a car was modified to an exact dollar amount of $2,000, which was a much more concrete goal for Bryan. Eighteen months after the initial plan was developed, Bryan had saved enough and had been ticket-free for 12 months. His parents then helped him purchase a car. He has maintained the car well and took over the insurance payments after he went to work full-time.

When Bryan finished his two-year electrician's training class, he moved into an apartment with a friend. He has not always paid his bills on time, but he has gotten much better at it after paying a number of late-payment penalties.

Fun Goals: Bryan had a great time backpacking with his friend Kyle. He became an avid backpacker, and his love of nature deepened. Bryan was always popular with girls, and he developed a long-term relationship with his current girlfriend of two years. They are now talking about moving in together. She provides the external structure he needs away from work and helps him when he gets anxious. Bryan is now a successful, independent adult who is managing all his life tasks.

Amanda's Plan

Amanda has inattentive ADHD and a reading disability. She struggled through school and was somewhat of a loner. During high school, she was more comfortable staying at home rather than joining with other students in social and extracurricular activities. While she had made some friends, most were moving on to college or a job after graduation, leaving her feeling lonely. Amanda loves to bake at home and thinks she might like a career in the food industry. But she is not sure about next steps and is anxious about leaving home. In working with her mom to identify her strengths and challenges, she came up with the following:

What are my strengths and challenges and what do I LOVE TO DO?

I love to bake and make food for people. I am creative and a loyal friend.

Strengths	Challenges
Great baker, love to cook	Shy and make friends slowly
Loyal and supportive friend	Slow reader, difficulty retaining information
Creative	Can't drive yet
Good daily living skills	Have never managed my own money
Enjoy spending time with family and watching old movies with Mom	Never had a job

After reviewing this list, Amanda and her parents came up with the following plan:

Vocational Goals:

I will …
1. Work part-time in a restaurant.
2. Take a baking class at the community college.
3. Visit the nearby Culinary Arts Institute.

Life Skills Goals:

I will ...
1. Learn to drive.
2. Open a checking account and begin to pay my own bills.
3. Make a few new friends.

Fun Goals:

I will ...
1. Go on a baking tour in France.
2. Buy a used car after getting a license and three months with no accidents or tickets.
3. Visit my friend Judy at college.

Amanda's Gap Year and Five Years Later

Vocational Goals: The job search process was stressful, and Amanda needed lots of encouragement and some limit setting to get her résumé done and actually apply for jobs. Because the process was so stressful, with her parents' support, she went to the local American Job Center for assistance from a counselor in the job search process. She eventually got a job in an Italian restaurant near her home working as a prep cook. She found it difficult to handle the pressure, and the chef periodically yelling at her. After six weeks, she quit. Her mother and father refused to let her see this as a failure but helped her to view this as important information about her potential career.

Amanda really liked baking, so her plan was changed to looking for a part-time job in a bakery. She went back to the American Job Center, and one month later she found a job making pies three mornings a week, through a classmate in her baking class at the community college. Her hours were in the very early morning, and the work was much less stressful for her than the restaurant job. She loved it.

Amanda also signed up for a baking class at the local community college. She visited the college office of disability support services, though she did so with some reluctance. The staff determined she didn't need any accommodations for her current class but talked with her about the assistance and services she could use if she decided to take on more classes and work toward a culinary degree.

Amanda also visited the nearby Culinary Arts Institute with her parents in January. While it was very exciting, she was more comfortable at the community college, which also had a major in culinary arts. She decided to attend the community college the following year part-time as she continued her part-time job at the bakery.

Life Skills Goals: Amanda took driving lessons from a driving school and then practiced with her mom and dad. She logged twice as many driving hours as required in her state before taking the final exam. She flunked the first time but was encouraged to go back. The second time she passed with flying colors. She waited almost a year before getting her own car but was then able to cover the cost of her car insurance with earnings from her part-time job.

Once Amanda started working, her dad took her to the bank to open a checking account. Amanda didn't always keep track of how much money she had in the account, but a friend helped her to download the banking app so she could check her account whenever she needed. Six months later, she applied for and was approved for her first credit card.

Fun Goals: Amanda joined an ADHD support group for young adults and made several new friends there. She also made several friends at the community college and found a new social circle with other bakers. And her baking tour of France with her mom was the highlight of the year and really strengthened her goal of becoming a baker. She enjoyed the independence that having a car gave her. Her visit to Judy's college campus was fun but convinced her she didn't want to live that far from her parents' home.

A Happy Ending: Five years after beginning her gap year, Amanda has graduated from the community college with a major in culinary arts and works full-time at the bakery. She is the specialist for all custom-decorated cakes and has developed a real flair for this work. As a result, she is often requested to make special cakes. She has developed a website for orders outside of work and is making a decent living with her cakes, as well as a growing reputation for creativity and quality. She moved out of her parents' house after graduation from community college and is now sharing a house with two friends. She is dating but hasn't yet had a serious relationship.

But What If Your Teen Hasn't a Clue About Next Steps?

It is not unusual for a recent high school graduate to be living in the moment and not giving a lot of thought to plans for adult life. If your teen is in this category and is unable to come up with any useful ideas about a gap year or vocational interests, then you may need to do some preliminary work before developing a gap year plan. Vocational testing can be very helpful in identifying areas to explore. If you find it difficult to engage your teen in the process of exploring next steps, consider the services of a career counselor, a therapist or an ADHD coach to help your son or daughter think through options and develop a plan.

Your young adult may also have ideas about careers that are not a good match for her skills and aptitude. For instance, she may think she wants to be a forensic scientist because she loves watching crime shows, but she has never done well in any science classes. Some exploration of what a degree or training would involve will help clarify whether her career ideas are realistic. This is exactly what the exploration process is about. Encourage your teen to find out exactly what the educational and job requirements are and then think about whether she really is willing to tackle what is involved.

You may discover that your teen has a bunch of unrelated ideas that are all over the map. Ruth's son, Christopher, at various times thought he wanted to be a teacher, a police officer, a fireman and a park ranger. He did an internship in a middle school, volunteered for both the police department and the fire department at different times, and had a summer job in recreation and parks. He also worked as a plumber's assistant part-time for a year. By exploring all these options, he was able to zero in on the area that brought him the most joy and the best fit.

13 What's the Best College Option for Your Teen?

College can be challenging for students with ADHD, particularly right after high school graduation. That was the bad news. The good news is that young adults with ADHD and/or LD absolutely can get through college—whether it's a four-year college, a community college or a specialized professional or technical college—and forge a satisfying career. It's true there will be challenges, and it may take more time than you have anticipated. But by being focused as a family on the goal (a career) and continuing to provide a safety net for your son or daughter when the going gets tough, you'll increase the likelihood of success.

"Going to college" can mean different things to different students. In the United States today, "colleges" come in many flavors. Types of colleges include universities, four-year colleges, community colleges, independent private technical and career colleges and online-only colleges or universities. Depending on the type of college and course of study chosen, graduates of these colleges can end up with a certificate of competence in a particular field, a two- or four-year undergraduate degree, or a master's or doctoral degree.

Here are more details about these options that may help you and your teen select an appropriate type of college program.

Universities and Four-Year Colleges

Both colleges and universities grant bachelor's degrees, which are typically considered to be four-year degrees, even though many students take longer than four years to complete them. To receive a bachelor's degree, a student generally has to pass required core classes in a broad range of subjects (e.g., English, math, science, history, arts and perhaps a foreign language), plus classes specific to his major or specialty area. These core requirements can be a problem for students with specific learning disabilities in math, reading or writing.

Four-Year Colleges: Most four-year colleges only offer bachelor's degrees, although some may offer a few associate's (two-year) degrees. Classes are usually smaller than at universities and are taught by professors rather than by graduate students. In addition, the faculty's main responsibility is generally teaching rather than research.

Universities: Universities are made up of several colleges (e.g., college of liberal arts, college of public policy, business school). Each of these colleges generally offers both undergraduate programs leading to a bachelor's degree and graduate programs leading to a master's or doctoral degree. Programs leading to law and medical degrees are also considered graduate programs. Universities are usually larger than four-year colleges and offer many more degree programs than colleges do. They often have a major investment in faculty focusing on research rather than teaching. Graduate students may teach a number of

DOI: 10.4324/9781003364092-13

undergraduate courses (particularly lower-level classes for freshmen), and some classes may be quite large with hundreds of students.

Acceptance into colleges and universities is based upon students' grades, scores on tests such as the ACT and SAT, extracurricular activities, class rank and other factors. Admission to community colleges is often much easier, and in some systems, all applicants are accepted.

Colleges and universities offer students a chance to live away from home and fully immerse themselves in the college experience. If your young adult intends to get a bachelor's degree, attending a college or university from the start saves him from the disruption of beginning at a community college and transferring to another school. And your student can begin to take classes in his major earlier. For those students who have a good idea of the career they would like and are ready for more independence, this may be the right choice. Also take into consideration that students with ADHD may be more successful in a smaller four-year college than in a large university, because of the small classes and more personalized attention. The decision is all about what your young adult needs and how independent he is ready to be.

Is Your Teen Ready to Live Independently? Perhaps the biggest issue to consider in deciding between a four-year college or university and the other types of colleges described in this chapter is whether your son or daughter is ready to live away from home. If not, a better choice may be a nearby community college or technical college where he or she can live at home and benefit from continued support from parents.

Living at home may be a good choice for students who (1) need and are willing to accept additional academic supports from their family; (2) have limited financial resources; or (3) have family who are reluctant to pay tuition and related expenses when they aren't certain that their teenager can cope successfully with the demands of college.

PC: From 18 on has been a very challenging time. My daughter seemed poised to do well upon completion of high school and then got lost in college. It lacked the structure she seems to require; she didn't take medication as needed. Plus, she had a boyfriend who thought it was more important that my daughter spend time with him. It led to a downward spiral. However, at age 20, she is beginning to show some signs of independence and making better decisions than a few years ago. We feel like it is three steps forward, one step back.

Specialized Colleges for Students with ADHD or Learning Disabilities

A small number of colleges exclusively serve students with ADHD and learning disabilities. These colleges have designed their curricula to include smaller classes, and highly trained teachers provide support services specifically for students with learning challenges. Because of these specialized services, tuition tends to be high. These colleges include the following:

- *Landmark College* in Putney, Vermont, has a two-year program for students with ADHD, learning disabilities or autism spectrum disorders. Faculty members are experts in teaching students with learning differences. In the first year, students meet with an advisor weekly to ensure they are succeeding. In addition to the regular disability support services, coaching for executive function deficits is available (Landmark College, n.d.).
- *Beacon College* in Leesburg, Florida, provides a four-year college experience for students with learning disabilities or ADHD. The classes are small, and every student has access to personalized attention. Academic mentoring with learning specialists is available to all students. Life coaching and occupational therapy are included in the cost of tuition.

Developmental courses are offered for those who need to prepare for learning college-level material (Beacon College, 2022).

There are also a number of schools that have special programs for those with learning differences within a larger college/university context. Here are a few examples:

- *Lynn University* in Boca Raton, Florida, offers a program specifically for students with learning challenges. The Institute for Achievement and Learning provides coaching in time management, prioritization and goal setting to help students start on the right path, as well as academic tutoring as needed. The core curriculum is made up of small, seminar-type classes that engage students in developing critical thinking and problem-solving skills. Faculty are trained in learning style differences as well as their field of expertise. One in four students at the university has a learning challenge (Lynn University, n.d.).
- *Mount St. Joseph University* in Cincinnati, Ohio, has a special fee-based program to help students with ADHD and learning disabilities—Project Excel. It offers intensive supports including tutoring, executive function coaching, regular consultations to help with organization and time management, mentoring and more. This proven program is geared toward the student with learning differences and can make a considerable difference (Mount St. Joseph University, n.d.)
- *University of the Ozarks* in Clarksville, Arkansas, is the home of the nationally known Jones Learning Center. It was one of the first programs in the country specifically designed to help students with learning differences and has an extensive system of supports. Academic support specialists meet with students one-on-one as needed to help guide them. Tutoring, note-taking, training in academic and management skills, and assistive technology are offered to students as needed. It claims to offer more services to students with learning disabilities than any other college or university in the nation (University of the Ozarks, 2022).

In addition to visiting the websites of colleges that interest your son or daughter, you can find helpful information in the following resources, which identify colleges and universities that specialize in providing support for students with learning challenges:

- *K and W Guide to Colleges for Students with Learning Differences* (Kravets & Wax, 2021).
- Best Value Ratings for Colleges for Students with ADHD (Best Value Schools, 2022).

The cost and locations of these colleges and special programs are important factors for families who are deciding whether one of these schools or programs is the right choice. The resources listed in this section include both private and public schools, and tuitions that run the gamut.

Community Colleges

There are three broad reasons that a young adult might attend a community college:

1. As a stepping stone to a bachelor's degree from a four-year college or university.
2. To complete a two-year degree necessary to work in certain professions.
3. To complete a shorter-term certification program needed to acquire the job skills for a particular profession.

Stepping Stone to a Bachelor's Degree: Community college can be a great first step for students who know or think they might want to pursue a bachelor's degree. A student planning to get a four-year degree can take two years (or a bit longer) of general education requirements at a community college before transferring to a college or university to finish a bachelor's degree. Attending community college is often much less expensive than attending an in-state college or university (let alone a private college). This means that starting out at a community college can be an affordable way for a student to explore his readiness for college-level work and sample classes in a variety of subjects.

Two-Year Associate's Degree: Most community colleges offer programs leading to two-year degrees needed to obtain entry-level positions in careers such as licensed practical nurse, sign language interpreter, physical therapy assistant, electrician, dental hygienist or air traffic controller. Degrees available might include associate of arts (AA), associate of science (AS) or associate of applied science (AAS).

Certificate Programs: Community colleges also offer yearlong or shorter programs leading to certification in technical professions such as auto body repair, heating and air conditioning repair, and child care. Generally, salaries will not be as high as for those with a two-year degree. Certification programs focus on acquiring job skills and may not require academic courses such as English and algebra, plus they allow entry into a young person's career of choice more quickly.

Community and technical colleges can provide extraordinary career opportunities for our teens and young adults. Unfortunately, their true value often is not fully appreciated. Sadly, according to manufacturing researchers, *only 3 in 10 parents* would consider guiding their teen toward careers in auto body repair, heating and air conditioning, electrical work or plumbing.

Benefits of Community Colleges

Here are some facts to bear in mind as you help your young adult decide what sort of college (if any) to attend:

1. *Costs are cheaper* at community colleges than at four-year colleges and universities. Not only are tuition and fees lower, but students generally live at home and therefore don't need to pay for room and board. For students who are not yet sure about college or a career, this can be the right choice.
2. Students at four-year colleges or universities are often smothered with *heavy debt* after graduation, thus delaying their ability to buy a car or home or afford to have children.
3. Young adults can earn an excellent living working in many of the specialized professions discussed in the next chapter.
4. Students can live at home and still experience college life. They may be able to take classes part-time and work part-time.

Help Available at All College Levels: The good news is that federal law requires that all colleges and universities in the United States provide supportive services to students with qualifying disabilities. Each of these institutions must have an office that addresses these needs. While this office has different names depending on the school, look for Disability Student Support Services or staff who address the needs of disabled students. The counselors can help you identify needed supports and accommodations. Examples of beneficial supports and accommodations and information on requesting them is discussed in Chapter 16.

References

Beacon College. (2022, February 22). *For students with learning disabilities, ADHD, and other learning differences*. Retrieved January 23, 2023, from https://www.beaconcollege.edu/

Best Value Schools. (2022, November 14). *Best value colleges for students with ADHD 2021: Best value schools*. Retrieved January 23, 2023, from https://www.bestvalueschools.com/rankings/colleges-students-adhd/

Kravets, M., & Wax, I.F. (2021). *The K & W Guide to colleges for students with learning differences*. New York: Princeton Review, a Penguin Random House Company.

Landmark College. (n.d.). *The college for students who learn differently*. Landmark College for Students with Learning Disabilities, ADHD & ASD. Retrieved January 23, 2023, from https://www.landmark.edu/

Lynn University. (n.d.). *Institute for Learning and Achievement*. Retrieved January 23, 2023, from https://www.lynn.edu/academics/individualized-learning/institute-for-achievement-and-learning

Mount St. Joseph University. (n.d.). *Project Excel*. Retrieved January 23, 2023, from https://www.msj.edu/academics/disability-services/project-excel/

University of the Ozarks. (2022, February 21). *Jones learning center*. University of the Ozarks. Retrieved January 23, 2023, from https://ozarks.edu/academics/jones-learning-center/

14 Community College

Two-Year Professional and Technical Programs

Community colleges (CC) offer an often-unrecognized "gold mine" of opportunities and career options at a reasonable price for teenagers who just aren't quite ready to take on college full time. Attending a local college after high school graduation offers several advantages, especially for teens with ADHD. For example, taking courses locally gives students a couple more years to mature, learn to work more independently and master academic deficits. Plus, having family support and structure while still living at home increases the likelihood the teenager ultimately will be successful in college. The good news is that community colleges often serve as a bridge to help students transition, when they're ready, to a traditional four-year college.

These local colleges offer advanced educational training that will teach new skills and enhance the teen's ability to find a good-paying job. Some students will pursue a two-year degree with the ultimate plan to obtain a four-year bachelor's degree. However, others may enroll in a specialized professional field such as a licensed practical nurse (LPN) or computer technician. Students may pursue a third option to enroll in a shorter certificate program that *doesn't require English or math*, for example, to become certified as an auto collision repairman.

College Is Not the Best Choice for Everyone

For many years, obtaining a college degree has been touted as the ultimate goal for all students. Parents often embrace this same expectation; assuming that a college degree is the key to career success. Quite often, their children also subconsciously internalize this belief from an early age. So teens may head off to college, even though they aren't prepared for the rigorous demands of college work. Sadly, many students with ADHD will drop out, return home depressed and feel like a failure. Plus, the family may be burdened with significant college debt.

As you may have guessed, traditional four-year college may not be the best option for many teenagers with ADHD, at least not immediately after high school graduation. For those students with ADHD who lack the necessary academic skills and self-discipline to complete their work without supervision, community colleges offer an excellent alternative.

The lesson we've learned is that college is not for everyone and doesn't provide the only path to career success. Keep in mind, some students with ADHD have no interest in attending college and may prefer to take classes toward certification in a specialized professional or technical program, such as licensed practical nursing (LPN), cosmetology, culinary arts, massage, radiologic technology, computer science, auto collision repair, A/C and refrigeration, or

DOI: 10.4324/9781003364092-14

firefighting. Certification in one of these programs will enhance their job skills, making it easier to get a job and earn a good living. A list of these programs plus potential earnings is shown later in this chapter.

Pair Community College Classes with a "Gap Year" Program

One option for successfully bridging the transition from high school to a traditional college is to create a personalized "gap year plan." For example, take one or two courses at a local college while volunteering or working part time in a career area of interest. Students are more likely to identify a satisfying career path if they have some real-world work experience such as an internship, an apprenticeship, volunteer work or a job in a field of interest. Otherwise, students who enter college with no career path in mind may flounder. Consequently, they may graduate without a plan, won't be able to find a good job and ultimately must accept a lower-paying job.

PC: *My daughter graduated from college without really thinking much about a career path or what kind of job she wanted in the future. Sorority activities consumed her life. When signing up for an internship, she took the least demanding placement, not realizing she was missing out on building a potential stepping-stone to a future job. After graduation, she floundered and couldn't find a job that interested her. Ultimately, she accepted a low-paying job as a receptionist for a lawn maintenance service.*

One young adult who implemented a gap year plan described the experience as follows:

My gap year plan included taking one or two classes each semester at my community college. In addition, I'm teaching dance fundamentals to three- and four-year-olds, creating their dance routines plus organizing their annual dance recital. I've learned to develop lesson plans, plus hold the attention and interest of these wiggling young children. Also, by volunteering with a school-based program known as Extended Family for Kids (Extended Family for Kids, n.d.), I'm gaining experience in facilitating group discussions. Ultimately, I plan to earn a degree in psychology. My gap year has given me a year or two for my brain to mature and has made a huge difference in my schoolwork. Now, I understand concepts better and the classes seem easier.

What Programs Do Community Colleges Offer?

Parents may familiarize themselves with the full range of classes and programs offered by community colleges in subsequent paragraphs. Program availability and graduation requirements at community colleges vary across the United States. Generally, however, community colleges offer both degree and certificate programs. The next two sections offer an overview of the requirements and costs for these two types of programs in Chris's home state of Alabama.

Public Career College Programs Are Highly Ranked: In 2018, Forbes ranked the nation's Top 25 two-year technical and career trade schools. The good news is that 21 of the 25 technical and career colleges are public, offering training at a more affordable rate. One example of a private trade school is the number one–ranked Pittsburgh Institute of

Aeronautics. (PIA), a private aircraft maintenance school. In-state tuition for PIA is roughly $25,500 (Coudriet, 2018).

Two-Year Degrees

To earn a two-year degree in Alabama, 60 to 76 credit hours of coursework (about 20 to 26 classes) must be completed satisfactorily, including one course each in composition, humanities or fine arts, science and math, and one class in history, sociology, etc. Next, 7 technical courses are required, plus 13 work-specific classes (e.g., fundamentals of gas and electric heating, commercial systems, etc.).

Costs: Average costs of associate degrees and certifications as of 2020 are shown in the next section. A student from out of state must pay extra tuition unless there is a reciprocal agreement with neighboring states. For example, any student who lives within 50 miles of the Gadsden State Cherokee campus pays regular tuition. So, a student living just across the state line in Rome, Georgia, could attend this Alabama community college without paying out-of-state tuition. Other states may use different criteria for determining costs. For example, in Maryland, each county has its own community college. County residents pay the lowest rates; Maryland state residents from other counties pay the second-lowest rate; and out-of-state students pay the highest rate.

Degrees: The following degrees can be earned in Alabama (depending on the concentration chosen). Some two-year degrees prepare the student to transfer to a four-year college, or the degree may be what is known as a "terminal degree," allowing the student to immediately begin looking for a job. Examples of these "terminal degrees" include computer science technology (AAS) or registered nursing (AAS). Typically, one semester-long class earns a student three credits, four credits if it includes a lab.

- Associate of Arts (AA) (60–64 credit hours; cost $8,704).
- Associate of Science (AS) (60–64 credit hours; cost $8,704).
- Associate of Applied Science (AAS) (60–76 credit hours: cost up to $10,366).

Certificates

Shorter programs award *certificates*, rather than degrees, to students who fulfill the requirements. Hours in class are shown, and that equals a certain number of courses plus one for college orientation.

Certificates (average of 46 hours; 15 courses, *including written composition and math*); cost $6,256.
Short-term certificates (average of 28 hours; 9 courses, *no math or written composition*); cost $3,808.

Depending on the specialty, students may be able to choose whether to work toward a two-year degree or a short- or long-term certificate. Here's one example: In Alabama, a student in air conditioning and refrigeration may earn one of three levels of training: (1) an AAS degree, (2) a certificate or (3) a short-term certificate. Higher-level certification requires completion of more classes but will result in higher pay.

Specialized Professional and Technical Programs Available

Here are examples of programs that may be offered at your local community college:

- Air conditioning and refrigeration.
- Auto collision repair.
- Automotive manufacturing.
- Certified nursing assistant (Figure 14.1).
- Computer science.
- Commercial truck driver.
- Cosmetology.
- Court reporting.
- Culinary arts.
- Electrical technology.
- Emergency medical technician.
- Engineering technologies.
- Firefighter.
- Graphic design.
- Industrial maintenance.
- Legal transcription.
- Machinist: mill and lathe.
- Massage therapy.
- Medical lab technology.
- Paramedic.
- Paralegal.
- Radiologic technology.
- Salon and spa management.
- Surgical and operation room technician.
- Teen development.
- Welding technology.

Figure 14.1 Tatum (with proud parents Sandra and Steven), cosmetologist and certified nursing assistant (CNA).

Visit your community college's website to see what programs are offered in your area.

Advantages for Students with Learning Challenges: Most community colleges offer non-credit *developmental classes* for those who are not ready for academic content at the college level. Students who struggled in high school can get a college experience while shoring up their skills in English (reading and writing) and math. If students decide to transfer to a four-year school, they have mastered the skills necessary to succeed—both the academic content and the study skills.

Community colleges often have smaller classes and a strong commitment to help students succeed. The extra supports offered may include tutoring programs, classes in study skills, classes in executive functioning skills, counseling, career planning, internships and even alert systems to identify struggling students. Programs that support first-generation college students, students from minority groups, low-income students and single parents may be available. Check out your local community college to find out what types of support are offered and encourage your young adult to take advantage of these programs if appropriate.

One final advantage of community colleges for those with learning challenges: in several states, students who complete an associate degree with a certain grade point average are guaranteed acceptance in at least one of the four-year colleges within the state university system. For example, in Maryland, community college students who complete an associate degree with at least a 2.0 grade point average will be accepted into the public four-year university system, although they will not necessarily get into their first-choice major. For students who have difficulties with tests such as the ACT or SAT, this can be another path to a four-year college or university. Check to see whether your local community college has agreements with four-year schools within the state system.

Supports at Howard Community College in Maryland

Ruth is a Disability Support Services Counselor at Howard Community College in Maryland. Her summary of the supports available at HCC should give you an idea of the supports available to students at many community colleges in the United States:

We have programs to identify and reach out to any student who is struggling, including a course for new students on how to study and cope with college life and an early alert system for faculty to identify students who are struggling. The college has staff designated as completion specialists, whose mission is to help students in peril to complete their degrees. And we have programs to support high-risk groups: single parents and first-generation students, for example. We have mentoring and support programs for African American and Latino students. Our disability services, tutoring, and counseling services, which are available at most colleges and universities, are both effective and proactive. Look for these types of supports at any college your teen is considering.

(Howard Community College, 2020)

The Need for Graduates of Specialized Professional or Technical Programs

It's worth giving serious consideration to attending a community college offering specialized professional and technical training programs, or a private specialized technical school. This is true especially if your teen is ambivalent about whether or not a four-year college is the right choice for her.

A major complaint of business industries today is that they can't find enough *highly qualified employees*. So if your teen is interested in working in the business or manufacturing industry, it's important to know more about employer expectations and prepare accordingly.

With increased automation, highly skilled employees are in short supply. That means good-paying positions are sitting empty. For example, over 500,000 jobs are available in the manufacturing field. And significant shortages are facing the country in construction, nursing, plumbing, heating and air conditioning, auto mechanics and auto body repair. So consider the incredible value to your teenager if she earns a specialized professional or technical certificate or degree in one of these fields.

Our Parent Survey Results: *Only 10 percent of our teens with ADHD sought vocational training.*

The Shortage of Highly Skilled Workers: Thousands of manufacturing, construction, nursing and other jobs requiring highly skilled staff are available right now. Most people don't really "see" the shortage of professionals in specialized fields and trades until they need to hire a plumber and then must write a substantial check for payment, or they go to the hospital and recognize the shortage in the nursing staff.

In short, there is a shortage of skilled employees in many fields. In the nursing field, the US Department of Health and Human Services (Haines, 2022) projected a shortage of nurses even before the pandemic hit. HHS has projected that 3.6 million registered nurses will be needed by 2030 to avoid a further shortage. Obviously, the demand for additional qualified medical personnel, including travel nurses, LPNs and CNAs (certified nursing assistants), will also increase. Similarly, 81 percent of construction companies have trouble finding qualified workers (Association of General Contractors of America, 2020). Since record numbers of baby boomers are retiring, the need for skilled employees in the home health industry is also growing exponentially.

Mike Rowe, host of the TV programs *Dirty Jobs* and *Somebody's Gotta Do It*, pushes a strong message reminding us that manufacturing industries always need "skilled somebodies to do the dirty jobs." Of course, most of these jobs aren't really dirty and are a perfect match for some young adults with ADHD. Through his foundation, mikeroweWORKS (www.mikeroweworks.org), Rowe, a Baltimore native, has amassed millions to award scholarships to deserving students (mikeroweWORKS, 2021).

The lessons learned from the COVID pandemic in 2020 have made all of us more aware that job markets can change rapidly. Perhaps it would be wise for your teen or young adult to consider professions that can't be outsourced or eliminated and will have plentiful job openings in the coming years. The US Bureau of Labor Statistics projects current job growth (and salaries) in every industry. For more information, check out employment projections on www.onetonline.org (O*NET online, n.d.).

Manufacturing Misperceptions: Many young people and their parents are under the misguided perception that manufacturing is dull, dirty, tedious work. In a Deloitte report, fewer than half of those surveyed realized that jobs in manufacturing are often interesting, rewarding, clean, safe, stable and secure (Giffi et al., 2017). These highly skilled jobs are not your grandparents' boring, repetitive activities of old.

With increased automation in industry, highly skilled employees who know how to use a computer to set up machines to operate properly are in high demand. For example,

Chris's son Steven, who is in manufacturing management, hires highly skilled staff to design the product, die-cut a template and then print, fold and glue the final product. All these complex steps are required to produce paper products for restaurants and other stores—for example, Chinet plates and Popeye's and Church's chicken boxes. Like most manufacturing companies today, Steven's company hires unskilled employees, too, then "trains them up" to be highly skilled staff.

Examples of Jobs and Average Salaries: Spend some time reading about technical training programs offered in your community and check out some of the annual salaries these professionals earn. Examples of skilled job salaries were obtained from two sources: (1) average national salaries in 2019 (US Bureau of Labor Statistics, 2022), which will vary depending upon where you live; (2) an interview with Steven Dendy, Director of Operations of Huhtamaki in Kansas City).

Profession	Typical Annual Salary
Industrial electrician	$80,000
Dental hygienist	$73,000
Welder, offshore	$67,000
Respiratory therapist	$65,000
Offset printing press operator	$62,000
Folding carton gluing operator	$60,000
Surveyor	$60,000
Electrician	$58,000
State highway patrol officer	$51,000
HVAC technician	$47,000
Web developer	$47,000
Plumber	$46,000
Industrial maintenance	$45,000
Printing operator	$45,000
Licensed practical nurse (LPN)	$42,000
Welder, regular	$36,816
Phlebotomist	$32,000
Certified nursing assistant (CNA)	$26,000

Many students think in terms of hourly salaries rather than annual income. So let's give some perspective on annual salaries as compared with the current federal hourly minimum wage of $7.25. For example, an electrician making $58,000 a year is paid $27.77 an hour. Or an LPN making $42,000 earns $20.11 an hour. Please note that workers in jobs that are paid hourly may also earn significant overtime pay. Some industries also certify their own employees and pay them more as their skills become more advanced (e.g., from Class C up to Class A, the highest-paid level).

Skills and Professions in High Demand

Since so many industries have adopted some level of automation, the need for technology-savvy employees has increased significantly. So, if your teen is interested, encourage her to take classes that emphasize these skills. The skills will be invaluable regardless of the career path chosen:

1. *Technology computer skills*: for example, training on cloud computing, information security or CAD (computer aided design), and AutoCAD used by many engineers.
2. *Digital skills*: skills collecting and analyzing data and working with AI (artificial intelligence).
3. *Programming skills for robots/automation*: monitoring robot performance and giving feedback to programmers or working as robot team coordinators (RTD).
4. *Working with tools and technology*: interacting with technical equipment and digital tools to support productivity and decision-making.
5. *Analytical problem-solving skills*: being able to troubleshoot issues as they arise and correct them.
6. *Ability to adapt to new technology*: being aware of new technology on the horizon and knowing how to adapt it to use in the industry.

No matter the ultimate goal of your young adult, community college can be a stepping stone. And for many students with ADHD, it may be the best step after high school. Community colleges prepare students to transfer and succeed at a four-year school, or prepare for a career after getting an associate's degree or a certificate. The student supports in most community colleges are often greater than in colleges and universities offering bachelor and graduate degrees. And the faculty focus is on teaching and helping students, rather than on research and publications. Your student can continue to live at home, receiving the critical support of family. In short, community college can be a win-win scenario for students with ADHD.

References

Association of General Contractors of America. (2020). *2020 construction outlook survey results national results – AGC*. Retrieved January 28, 2023, from https://www.agc.org/sites/default/files/Files/Communications/2020_Outlook_Survey_National.pdf

Coudriet, C. (2018, August 16). The top 25 two-year trade schools: Colleges that can solve the skills gap. *Forbes*.

Extended Family for Kids. (n.d.). *Support system for families of prisoners*. Support System For Families of Prisoners. Retrieved January 28, 2023, from https://www.extendedfamilyhelp.org/

Giffi, C., Rodriguez, M.D., & Mondal, S. (2017). *A look ahead: How modern manufacturers can create positive perceptions with the US public*. The Manufacturing Institute. Retrieved January 28, 2023, from https://www.themanufacturinginstitute.org/research/a-look-ahead-how-modern-manufacturers-can-create-positive-perceptions-with-the-us-public/

Haines, J. (2022, November 1). The state of the nation's nursing shortage. *US News & World Report*.

Howard Community College. (2020, June 2). *Howard Community College*. Home. Retrieved January 28, 2023, from http://www.howardcc.edu/

mikeroweWORKS Foundation. (2021, May 26). Retrieved January 28, 2023, from https://www.mikeroweworks.org/

O*NET online. (n.d.). O*NET OnLine. Retrieved January 28, 2023, from https://www.onetonline.org/

US Bureau of Labor Statistics. (2022, September 8). *Fastest growing occupations: Occupational outlook handbook*. Retrieved January 28, 2023, from https://www.bls.gov/ooh/fastest-growing.htm

15 Selecting and Applying to a College

If your son or daughter has a decent idea of what career would be satisfying and you have mutually decided that it's the right choice and the right time for college, deciding where to go is the next step. For students with ADHD and/or a learning disability, the goal is to find a school that will (1) give them the very best chance of a successful college experience and (2) lead to a career that is fulfilling and pays a living wage.

PC: I regret her high school and college choices, which were too academically pressured.

Selecting a College

Forget how prestigious a college is, how beautiful the campus is, or who in the family is an alumnus. The best criteria for choosing a college are the factors that will enhance the likelihood of success for your son or daughter, given his or her personal strengths, challenges, career aspirations and potential obstacles. For example, Sophie found a school where she could succeed and also play lacrosse (Figure 15.1).

Factors to Consider When Selecting a College

Ultimately, *your student's priorities* are the most important consideration. You can help your son or daughter crystallize priorities by talking about what he or she wants to get out of college. Do lots of listening. And you can prompt your student's thinking by discussing the following issues:

- *Size of the college or university.* Some students with ADHD or LD do better on small campuses where they can get individualized attention and smaller classes. Others need the stimulation and variety of a big campus. Think of the pros and cons of each. For Ruth's son, a smaller university was a perfect fit. It gave him lots of contact with his instructors and more of a hands-on learning experience than a larger school could have provided.
- *Major.* Does the institution offer a major in the area your teen is most interested in pursuing? Are there opportunities to actually work in this field while at school, through internships and work experiences?
- *Office of Student Services (Disability Services).* In the United States, any postsecondary institution that receives federal funding—including two- and four-year colleges and professional and technical colleges—must provide accommodations for qualifying students with disabilities. At most colleges, accommodations are authorized by an office

DOI: 10.4324/9781003364092-15

Figure 15.1 Sophie, lacrosse scholarship.

of disability or student services. (See "Applying for Accommodations and Supports at College" later in this chapter.) Some schools have wonderful disability support services, while others offer more limited services. You, of course, want a school that will really help your student. Visit college websites to determine what services they provide for students with ADHD or learning disabilities. Be sure to visit whatever office provides disability services when you make a campus visit, and ask what they do in addition to approving accommodations.

• *College career services*. Career services can often help a student sort out the best major and a future career. And as your son or daughter nears graduation, this resource will be invaluable in helping him or her create a résumé, learn interview skills, apply for jobs, etc. Make sure the colleges your teen applies to offer a full range of career services and encourage your student to use them.

• *Unique career opportunities*. Check into unique courses of study that may be attractive to your son or daughter. For example, in Alabama, 65 percent of farm revenue is from the poultry business. Gadsden State Cherokee College offers a poultry science degree in partnership with Auburn University. Students take two years of basic core courses at Gadsden State Cherokee and then transfer for the last two years to Auburn University (Gadsden State Community College, 2019). The starting salary for someone with this degree is around $47,000.

• *Counseling services*. Anxiety and depression are huge problems on most college campuses and often present significant challenges for young people with ADHD and LD. What counseling services are offered, and how easy is it to obtain them? Usually these services are free, but costs and availability may vary from school to school.

• *Academic difficulty*. Too often, students choose the most academically rigorous school that accepts them. But for students with learning challenges, it may be better to choose a school with good support services and less rigorous academic standards. After graduation from college, few employers are concerned about which college job applicants attended.

- *Size and instructional approach of classes.* If your student will be in classes of 200–300 students, you can anticipate that there will be very little individual attention. Size matters. And online classes can be extremely challenging for students who are not self-starters, which includes many students with ADHD.
- *Research versus instruction.* Do the faculty put more emphasis on research and publishing, or instruction of students? What is the reputation of faculty in assisting students with disabilities? During a campus visit, ask students about the willingness of instructors to give extra help to students. You can also check out instructors' reputations on www. ratemyprofessors.com.
- *Student health center.* Most student health centers don't treat ADHD. Where can your student receive medical services for ADHD? Where can prescriptions for medication be filled? If off campus, how easy is it to get there?
- *Living arrangements.* Does your student need a room by himself? If so, are single rooms available for freshmen, and are they affordable? Are there potential social difficulties with roommates? If the roommate situation isn't a good one, what alternatives are there?
- *Social culture.* Does the college have a reputation as a party school? Do fraternities and sororities dominate social life? How much drinking is on campus? What about drugs?
- *Nearness to home.* The ability to go home when times get tough can be helpful for some students. Others are ready to be truly independent and want to be farther away.

Applying to College

Ideally, during the junior year of high school, you and your teen will identify a few schools or colleges, visit their campuses, and talk with student services staff. Granted, it is sometimes difficult to do things in an ideal sequence with our children. So, if you start the planning process later, during the senior year or even years after high school graduation, don't panic. It's never too late. Bear in mind, however, that most four-year colleges and universities have strict deadlines for applying for admittance for the fall or spring, and applications and test scores must be submitted months in advance. Many community colleges and professional and technical colleges will admit students weeks or days before classes start, however, as long as there are openings.

Check important application deadlines for each of these steps. You can't afford to miss critical deadlines.

College Aptitude Testing

The two tests most often required for admission to a four-year college are the SAT (College Board, n.d.) and the ACT (ACT, n.d.). If your teen is seeking accommodations such as extended time for taking either of these tests, be sure to investigate the current rules for qualifying for accommodations. Visit the SAT and ACT websites and talk with a counselor at school. Both the documentation required to prove the need for accommodations and the process change over time. Here are some tips that will help you be successful:

- Start early. It can take several months to receive approval for accommodations.
- Consult with the person at your high school (often a guidance counselor) who is an expert on the ACT and SAT. Most schools have staff members who work with these testing companies and are up to date on the rules and processes.

- Be prepared to describe what accommodations your teen needs during the test and why. Common accommodations are increased time, breaks, large-type text, or braille.
- Your school can work with your student and actually submit the documentation for him. Both testing firms recommend this.
- If your student doesn't have a current IEP or 504 plan, he may need an external psychological evaluation to qualify for accommodations. Find out early what documentation will be required. This takes time.
- Encourage your student to take online practice tests so he will be familiar with the format and type of content.

Placement Testing

Many community and technical colleges don't require SAT or ACT tests. But they are likely to require placement testing in English and math after a student has been accepted. These tests are typically given on campus. The placement tests are to ensure that students are enrolled in the right classes, given their current level of knowledge. Many students aren't ready for college-level English or math and are usually offered developmental classes to prepare them for college-level work.

Completing the College Admission Application

Filling out college applications is almost a rite of passage for juniors and seniors in high school. Some applications are short and easy to complete. Others are more complicated and will require the student to write one or more essays. Most can be done online. Here are some suggestions for getting through the process successfully:

- *Deadlines.* Know the deadlines and start early. Don't wait until the last minute, or the quality of your student's application will suffer.
- *Admission instructions.* Follow the instructions carefully and be sure your teen provides all the information requested.
- *Required essay.* Struggling with the essay? A parent can be a good sounding board for your teen's ideas, but the essay needs to come from him.
- *Proofreading.* Encourage your student to proofread the application several times and then ask someone else to look at it as well.
- *Recommendations.* Help your son or daughter decide who to ask for a recommendation letter and practice how to ask. Then encourage your teen to check back to be sure her references have sent the recommendation in.
- *Keep copies.* For online applications, make a copy of everything before hitting the submit button.
- *Transcripts.* Help your teen find out the process for requesting transcripts from his high school and ensure that he has them sent to the colleges he has applied to.

Reminders Must Be Given for All Deadlines: Most parents must help their son or daughter compensate for executive planning deficits during the college application process. For example, you may need to remind him or her of key deadlines. Keep in mind that teens with ADHD tend to have working memory problems and an impaired sense of time, so most likely will not remember the deadlines. If needed, sit with your teenager and complete the application together.

Chris's Lessons Learned: I realized my son couldn't gather and organize all the documentation the college required, so I collected all the materials, he filled out the application, and I mailed it for him—to ensure that he met the submission deadline.

Financial Aid

Most families will need some financial assistance to help pay for college. Start by going to www.studentaid.gov (Federal Student Aid, n.d.). This is the site for the Free Application for Federal Student Aid (FAFSA). Before students can receive any financial aid, most institutions require them to submit a FAFSA application online. This is your teen's gateway to low-interest government loans and grants as well as to need-based scholarships offered by the specific school(s) he is applying to. This is also a great site for learning all about the various kinds of financial aid and how to apply.

The FAFSA application must be completed online well before the fall semester and requires that you provide detailed information about your household income, your child's income, most recent tax filing, family size, other kids in college, etc. Unless your son or daughter is self-supporting, this is information that *you* must provide. Be sure to check deadlines—there are federal and state deadlines, but the most important one for your teen is the college deadline. Awards are for the academic year starting in September, and the deadlines usually range from early February to June.

Always start by looking for grants and scholarships, which provide financial aid that does not need to be paid back, as long as it is used as intended (e.g., for tuition, fees or other specific college costs). It is often much easier for students to get loans, but few college students understand the impact of a student loan on their future lives. And if a student drops out of school, the student loans still need to be repaid. But do fill out the FAFSA. And be careful about cosigning a loan unless you are truly able to repay the loan in full. Tim earned a soccer scholarship which helped to defray the cost of college (Figure 15.2).

The FAFSA needs to be completed each year, not just before the first year of college. So, pay attention to deadlines and be sure the FAFSA is submitted every year until your student leaves school. Students who receive financial aid also need to be aware that dropping classes, withdrawals and poor grades often affect financial aid for the next semester. Students need to show sufficient progress toward graduating in order to keep financial aid.

Applying for Accommodations and Supports at College

Section 504 of the Rehabilitation Act (a civil rights law) ensures that Americans with disabilities have the same access as everyone else to opportunities and activities that receive any federal funding (Office of Civil Rights, 2020). And the Americans with Disabilities Act (ADA) requires that both public and private postsecondary institutions provide students with disabilities with equal access to their buildings, programs and activities (ADA National Network, 2023). Thanks to these laws, colleges and other postsecondary programs must provide needed accommodations for students with a disability. But you need to demonstrate that a disability exists. In case you're wondering, after high school graduation, IDEA (the special education law) no longer applies.

Most colleges and universities in the United States have an office that serves students with disabilities. The eligibility process and accommodations offered are different from those in

Figure 15.2 Tim, soccer scholarship.

high school. The most important change is that the student is now in the driver's seat. While you might accompany your son or daughter to the first appointment, the disability counselor will be directing questions to the student, and final decisions will be made by the two of them. Most disability services staff will not talk with the parent without the student, unless special permission is given by the student. Another important difference is that now the student is responsible for asking for assistance and for making sure the notice of accommodations is up to date and given to the student's instructors each semester. And the third change is that the types of accommodations allowed may differ to fit into the college curriculum and place greater responsibility on the student.

Well before your student arrives on campus, you should check the college website and contact the Student Disability Service Office and find out what documentation your son or daughter needs to submit to be eligible for accommodations. Then encourage him or her to schedule an appointment with someone in the disability support office.

Typically, documentation consists of a form filled out by a medical professional, an evaluation by a medical professional or psychologist that has been completed within the last three years, and/or an IEP or Section 504 plan showing accommodations the student had in high school. Depending on the disability, the school may require that the documentation come from a professional in a particular medical specialty; for instance, a disability such as ADHD, anxiety or depression may require a mental health professional to provide the documentation. But the requirements vary dramatically from school to school. So before investing in an expensive evaluation for this purpose, find out exactly what your teen's school requires.

Chris's Lessons Learned: During a campus visit to the college, my son and I went by and met the director of student services. Visiting her office and meeting her personally made it easier for my son to go meet with her after he started college. Otherwise, he would have been intimidated by initiating a meeting and finding the office and never would have sought supports or accommodations.

To determine what accommodations the college will provide, the disability staff person will look at the documentation and talk with the student about his challenges in school. The accommodations will reflect what a student needs based upon the disability. However, just because something was offered in high school does not mean it will be provided in college. For example, it's less likely that a college will permit flexibility for deadlines as an accommodation. It will be really helpful if your son or daughter thinks about what accommodations are needed before this meeting. Typical accommodations for students with ADHD are listed in the next section to help you and your student think about what would be most useful.

Once the counselor and student have agreed upon the accommodations, an accommodations memo or statement is developed and given to the student to share with instructors. These accommodations are not retroactive, and the memo must be given to the instructor before the accommodations take effect. Some schools now send the accommodation memos directly to the faculty. But many do not, and expect the student to share this information with the instructor. By having the student make the decision, he is able to decide who he wants to share this information with. If your student is embarrassed and uncomfortable with giving the accommodation memo to an instructor, suggest that he email it. That works as well as delivering the memo in person and actually provides evidence that it has been shared with the teacher.

Remember, an accommodations memo is useless to the student if it does not get to the instructor. For example, even though a student might be approved for extended time for tests, if he does not give the accommodations memo to her English professor at the start of the semester and then fails the midterm because he didn't have enough time to complete it, he can't belatedly produce the memo and get additional time.

A student can go back to the disability services office at any time and request changes to the accommodation memo. Often college freshmen underestimate how challenging classes will be and realize that they need additional supports after school has begun.

Common Accommodations

Here are several accommodations recommended in Chris's book *Teenagers with ADD, ADHD, and Executive Deficits* (Dendy, 2017):

- *Extended time on tests and assignments.* Most universities allow qualified students extra time to complete tests and can usually offer these tests in a quiet place, such as a test center. If needed, tests can be read to a student, or a scribe can record the answers.
- *A laptop in class for notes or compositions.* Students who have ADHD and slow processing speed can have a hard time finishing a composition in a one-hour class period. Your teen may want to consider requesting allowance to write essays in a separate room and use a computer.

- *Technology.* When used wisely, technology can be the saving grace for students with ADHD. Computers, smartphones, smart pens and apps can help them be better organized, remember key events, edit or spell-check written work and manage time more wisely. There are programs that will translate text (reading assignments) to voice so a student can hear and see reading assignments at the same time. And there are programs that do the opposite—take a recording and turn it into text—to help students who are poor notetakers.
- A *notetaker or note taking app.* Colleges may make arrangements for a notetaker for a student or allow the student to record the class. In addition, some professors may be willing to give the student a copy of their class notes or PowerPoint slides. Many colleges now give students text-to-speech apps to assist with note taking.
- *Early registration and selection of classes and instructors.* Students who qualify for Section 504 supports may be eligible for early registration, which gives them first choice of class times and professors. If your teen has a sleep disturbance or trouble getting organized in the morning, being able to choose classes with a later starting time can be a real boon. He can also ask his advisor or disability support coordinator for help selecting professors who work well with and are supportive of students with learning challenges. And any student can check out ratemyprofessor.com to see what other students think of the instructors teaching the courses he needs. Look for ratings that are high (positive) and comments that indicate flexibility and concern for students.
- *Tutoring.* Most colleges and universities offer free tutoring to all students who feel they need it in at least a few core classes (e.g., freshman English or algebra). There are often special programs that offer tutoring as well. Not only does tutoring help a student learn the content for the class, but it also provides one more bit of structure for the student— dedicated time each week for focusing on the class. Sometimes teens with ADHD have trouble getting started on new initiatives without an external reminder. You may need to make the initial call to find out details about tutoring and then give your teen the phone number to schedule an appointment.
- *Waivers.* Some colleges allow students with serious learning problems to apply for a waiver and exempt a subject related to their learning deficit. But students can't usually get a waiver for a class that is required for their major. However, if a student struggles with a subject outside her major that is required for graduation, the college may allow her to make a course substitution, such as Spanish art appreciation for a foreign language. Or a computer programming language or sign language course could count as a foreign language. The willingness of schools to provide waivers is highly variable. So, your teen should not count on a waiver unless he has actually talked to advisors at the school.

Chris's Lessons Learned: My son attended two smaller colleges that both provided wonderful supports: West Georgia College and Jacksonville State University (Alabama). We both met with the director of student services at each college, and they were incredibly positive and helpful. His most helpful accommodations were early registration, guidance on selecting teachers who understood ADHD and learning challenges, and extended time on assignments and tests. Some instructors also gave him copies of their notes and PowerPoint presentations.

References

ACT. (n.d.). *Requesting accommodations: The ACT test.* Retrieved January 29, 2023, from https://www.act.org/content/act/en/products-and-services/the-act/registration/accommodations.html

ADA National Network. (2023, January 31). *What are a public or private college-university's responsibilities to.* Retrieved January 29, 2023, from https://adata.org/faq/what-are-public-or-private-college-universitys-responsibilities-students-disabilities

College Board. (n.d.). *Accommodations on College Board exams.* Retrieved January 29, 2023, from https://accommodations.collegeboard.org/

Dendy, C.A.Z. (2017). *Teenagers with ADD, ADHD and executive function deficits: A guide for parents and professionals.* (3rd ed.). Bethesda, MD: Woodbine House.

Federal Student Aid. (n.d.). *Federal student aid.* Retrieved January 29, 2023, from http://www.studentaid.gov/

Gadsden State Community College. (2019). 2+2 *poultry science program.* Retrieved January 29, 2023, from https://www.gadsdenstate.edu/programs-of-study/poultry-science.cms

Office of Civil Rights. (2020, January 10). *Students with disabilities preparing for postsecondary education.* Retrieved January 29, 2023, from https://www2.ed.gov/about/offices/list/ocr/transition.html

16 Helping Your Teen Succeed in College

The college is chosen, and the first semester is approaching. What steps can you and your teen take to ensure success? Too often we send our sons and daughters away to school, hoping for the best, and then react only when they hit the wall and are experiencing major difficulties at school. By anticipating possible problems up front, you can often forestall disasters later.

Remember that there is no longer a feedback loop to you as a parent. No one will call you when your son doesn't show up for class or your daughter doesn't get her term paper in on time. You will not even be sent a report card at the end of the semester. Only your student will be able to give you any information about problems. And she won't do so if she feels that she'll disappoint you or create a conflict. A positive relationship between you and your student can make a world of difference (Figure 16.1).

The message needs to be clear: "Life is full of problems, and you'll have your fair share, as everyone does. I want you to know that we are always here for you. So please let us know if you experience some difficulties. We are here to help and always will be."

Chris's Lessons Learned: My son struggled in high school, and I knew he'd need more guidance and support in college. So when he went away to college his freshman year, I told him I'd help him as much or as little as he liked. Then later I said, "I'd like to learn more about the courses you're taking, so if you don't mind, please send me a copy of your class syllabus." The day before a big test, I'd call and say, "Good luck on your test tomorrow"—in fact, reminding him that he even had a test.

Accommodations and Other Supports

Yes, we discussed accommodations in the previous chapter. That's because we want to emphasize how critical accommodations are to the success of college students with ADHD and/or a learning disability. Also, it's one thing to check out the disability services office when your student applies to college. But you need to ensure that she is actually able to receive needed services and accommodations once she is enrolled. Each semester your student must request her accommodations be sent to her instructors. This does not happen automatically. Ruth's experience is that many students forget this step despite many email reminders from the disability office. The result is they aren't receiving the accommodations they are entitled to and they think they have. Asking if this request has been made can be an important reminder.

DOI: 10.4324/9781003364092-16

Figure 16.1 Andrew with proud parents, Tina and Keith, manufacturing and engineering degree.

It's always wise to apply for accommodations well before your student leaves for college, even if she may choose not to use them. Otherwise, she may be in crisis during the first semester, and it will take time to qualify for needed extra supports. You can phrase it like this: "Let's submit the application just in case. You don't have to use any accommodations, but if needed, you'll have them."

Think back to the process you went through with your teenager when selecting a college. What are the potential pitfalls and areas where support needs to be available? Begin the first semester with as many supports in place as your student will agree to, and then she can drop them when she feels they are no longer needed.

Review the list of accommodations at the end of the last chapter. You may want to consider the following supports in particular:

- *Reduced course load.* Fewer classes in the beginning can help a student adjust to the academic expectations of college. Your student is more likely to adjust to college well and finish sooner than if there are failed courses that need to be retaken.
- *Tutoring.* Those challenging classes in high school will become more challenging at the college level. And tutoring is available to everyone, not just students with disabilities.
- *Counseling.* Does your son or daughter have difficulty managing emotions? Problems with anger, depression or anxiety? The school probably has a counseling service, and there is frequently no charge.
- *Courses on how to study.* Many schools offer a special freshmen class on how to study. Encourage your student to take it even if he feels it is unnecessary. If so, it will be an easy class.
- *Single room.* It is unlikely the college will agree to a single room as an accommodation, but you may want to look into the cost and availability of single rooms if sharing with another student seems problematic. This may be the case if your son or daughter has social problems, difficulty with emotions, a sleep disorder or a variety of other issues.
- *An academic or educational coach.* You might want to look into hiring an ADHD coach or a professional who specializes in ADHD for your son or daughter. A coach can be

especially helpful if disorganization and time management are problems or if your teen has difficulty adjusting to new situations. Coaches or professionals who specialize in ADHD help their clients learn strategies and techniques to deal effectively with the symptoms of ADHD. Some coaches specialize in working with students who have executive function deficits. They help with problems with time management, organization, scheduling of study time and any other academic impediment due to ADHD. Coaches can meet with their clients in person or online, so you don't need to limit your search to the vicinity of the college.

These organizations may help you find a coach:

- The ADHD Coaches Organization (adhdcoaches.org) represents coaches who specialize in ADHD. They have a directory of coaches that you can search online.
- The Edge Foundation (edgefoundation.org) specializes in training and providing ADHD coaches specifically for college students.

Look for a coach who is certified and has been through special training for ADHD. Also look for one who specializes in serving college students.

Ruth's Lessons Learned: Be a supportive partner for your college student, but the student needs to take the lead and be invested in any accommodation plan for it to work. When my son was a freshman at the community college, I made the appointment with disability services and literally dragged him to the meeting kicking and screaming. (This should have been a clue that he was not ready to attend college, but I didn't get it.) It was not a pretty sight, and the disability counselor wisely separated us after about 15 minutes. Christopher was given accommodation memos to give to his professors, but he never presented them to all his teachers.

At that point he didn't want everyone to know about his ADHD. Several weeks later, a professor asked him if he would be willing to share his notes with a student who was deaf. The professor had noticed that Christopher brought a laptop to school each class. Christopher was delighted to agree to be the helper rather than the recipient of help. And despite my concerns, both Christopher and the student he shared his notes with did well in the class. Christopher then began to use his accommodations (test in a quiet environment, extended time on tests, teacher notes) when he felt it was needed, and I learned to take a step back.

Remembering to Notify Instructors of Accommodations
As explained in the previous chapter, after being approved for accommodations, your teen must share information on the need for accommodations with each professor, usually in a memo created by the disability services office. This memo doesn't include any mention of your student's disability. It's doubly hard for our students to follow through with asking for these supports; sometimes they're embarrassed to ask, or they simply forget. So be sure your son or daughter understands the need to share the memo with instructors as needed.

Auburn University's campus in Montgomery, Alabama (AUM), is one of many universities that now send emails notifying instructors that a student is eligible for accommodations.

The list of accommodations is stored online and is accessible to both the student and faculty members. Of course, the student with ADHD and/or LD still must meet and discuss the accommodations with each instructor. Tamara Massey, director of the AUM program, explains that "this generation was raised on technology and has been more accepting" of discussing accommodations their instructors have already seen online rather than having to hand-carry a memo listing needed accommodations. Massey also notes that faculty are reviewing accommodations memos more frequently during evenings and weekends since they have 24/7 access. Considering our teens' difficulties in remembering to hand-deliver accommodation letters to their instructors, this simple action is a godsend.

"Get Real" Tip: *If your teen is likely to forget, give a tactful prompt. "Did you decide to ask for extra time in your algebra class? Great! Do you have to give your instructor a letter from Student Services, or do they notify him?" Obviously, it may take more than one prompt. Nagging her about this is unlikely to work. If she begins to struggle to pass a class, however, be sure to raise the issue of taking or emailing the letter to his instructor.*

ADHD Medication Management at College

This is a time when many young people with ADHD want to stop taking medication. Negotiate with your son or daughter to continue for at least the first semester until it is clear how challenging classes and life will be. If your student does well the first semester and feels medication is no longer necessary, going medication-free the next semester may be worth a try. But talk about possible outcomes first. What is the agreement if her grades slip or she stops going to classes? Having this discussion will give you the opportunity to discuss possible problems and give your student the incentive to make sure problems don't happen.

Finding a Physician and Pharmacy: If your teen is going away to college, jointly develop a plan for ensuring that he gets his medication regularly while away from home. Simplifying this process is critical to ensure that she takes her medication when needed. Hopefully, his local doctor or pediatrician will continue to treat her until she graduates from college. If not, help her find a doctor near the college who is willing to treat her ADHD. For students who attend a college within easy driving distance of home, making a trip home every month to pick up medication and check in with their doctor may be a good option.

- Check to see if the *college health center* can provide treatment for ADHD. Unfortunately, most college health centers do not.
- If your teen needs a *new doctor*, help expedite the search. Perhaps the student health center can suggest a physician who specializes in treating ADHD. Or perhaps your pediatrician can recommend a doctor in that community. As you might guess, some physicians are reluctant to treat a young person with ADHD at all, because of concerns about stimulant abuse.
- Help your teen select an *easily accessible pharmacy*. If she doesn't have a car, perhaps a friend will drive her or she can call an Uber or Lyft. Don't be surprised if the local pharmacy staff treat your young adult with suspicion until they get to know her better.
- Once your teenager finds a new doctor, your local physician can *transfer relevant medical records* to that office. Or you could send a complete copy of her treatment record with her to college so she can take it with her on her first visit.

Remembering to Refill and Take Medications: Any barriers to getting prescriptions filled will likely result in your teen running out of medication and then spiral into further problems related to the untreated ADHD. You won't be there to offer daily reminders once your teen leaves home. Talk with her about a reminder system and figure out what works best for her. She might want to set up reminders on her cell phone. Or she could put her weekly pill container in a place that is out of sight but that she will still see each morning—for example, in a dresser drawer if possible inside a lockbox. Suggest that she plan to refill the prescription several days before she runs out of medication so there is no lapse. If her reminder system isn't working, a simple reminder text from you might be helpful until she can establish a regular routine for getting prescriptions filled.

Potential Medication Abuse: If your student is currently taking stimulant medications, she needs to be prepared for the challenges of using prescription drugs on campus. Hopefully she won't advertise the fact that she's taking medication for ADHD. If others know about her ADHD and medication, other students will ask her to share or sell her pills. If caught unaware, many students agree to share, either because they want to be helpful or are embarrassed to say no.

Potentially, this is a felony (dealing drugs). Help your teen understand the possible ramifications. If caught sharing her meds, she can be expelled from school and even face criminal charges.

Your son or daughter needs to be prepared to say no to other students with a clear, rehearsed response: "Sorry, but I need all my medication for my ADHD or I'll run out by the end of the month. So I don't have any medication to share." The medication should be kept in a lockbox, and your teen should always keep the key with him or her. This will also discourage stealing. If your student has supportive roommates, she can ask them to help her discourage others from asking for her meds. Most college students don't think that it's right for fellow students to take stimulants without a prescription but are reluctant to speak up. If your teen asks friends or roommates to help her say no, most students will be there for her.

Remember: This Is About the Path to a Career

The ultimate goal of college is to enable students to find a job in a career that will provide adequate financial support. The path there may meander a bit, but a career or job should always be the goal, not just going to college because that's what everybody is supposed to do. Don't get distracted by what other families are doing. If you jointly make decisions based on this aim, your student's path will be easier and more focused.

Ruth's Lessons Learned: I didn't understand these lessons when my son went to college. He did indeed go because I insisted and other choices were not clear. But he still found his way to success almost in spite of my pushing.

The first meandering step was community college and part-time work (for five years), then a gap year where he began to get clear about career goals. With more clarity, he then transferred to a small state university in western Maryland with a faculty emphasis on teaching rather than independent research. Both schools were his choice, and he had a good sense of what he needed, better than I did. After transferring, he lived in an on-campus apartment with three others but had his own bedroom. And his major department (Parks and Recreation) was very hands-on and experiential in its teaching approach. Within the first month my son was engaged in planning a citywide Halloween party. He made use of the college support services when needed.

The faculty assisted the students in finding summer jobs in parks and recreation. His summer job was at a camp that eventually hired him full-time as assistant director after he graduated. And the department required a five-month full-time internship and helped place students all over the world. My guy spent his internship working in a camp on the North Shore in Oahu, Hawaii.

To this day Christopher still communicates with the faculty members who are mentors for him. It was the perfect setting for him to learn the skills of his career choice. With these supports, he graduated magna cum laude. Today he is a park ranger, a highly competitive field, and loves his work. My late bloomer is blooming beautifully.

An Underutilized Treasure Trove: Career Guidance

College career service centers offer invaluable guidance for students who are uncertain about a major or are approaching graduation. Unfortunately, fewer than 20 percent of students take full advantage of the services. And yet many young people who graduate from college with no clear career path in mind end up underemployed at low-paying jobs with few advancement opportunities.

The services provided by the Career Center at Georgia State University are representative of what your student may find at her college career center (Georgia State University, n.d.):

- *An interactive online career assessment* that includes tests to identify potential job paths, integration of test results, a rating of entrepreneurial attributes and an overview of 27 business career paths.
- A section on the website called *"What you can do with a major in ..."* that offers information on nine different areas (computer science, information, finance, hospitality, managerial science, marketing and real estate) including a career description of each, possible job titles and possible employers.
- Information on *conducting informational interviews* with people who are already working in the field, including guidance on how to prepare and interact during and after the interview.
- *Job search strategies*, including guidance on identifying the ideal industry, ideal employers, geographic areas of interest and ideal job roles.
- *Conducting employer research*: how to prepare by reading about the potential employer, including key personnel, mission statements, products and services, key clients, and trends in the industry.
- *Targeting your résumé*, including essential elements of a good résumé and additional qualities to highlight, plus sample résumés for various major fields of study.
- *Selecting references* to support your job application.
- *Preparing for a career fair*, including suggested dress, tips on behavior, strategies for speaking with as many representatives as possible, following up with a thank-you letter or email.
- *Suggested business attire for interviews*, including proper dress and personal grooming tips for both formal business interviews and interviews where business casual dress is the norm.
- *Sample questions that might be asked in an interview.*

Ashley, a young adult college graduate with ADHD who is searching for a career path, gives this advice (Figure 16.2):

Figure 16.2 Ashley, college graduate.

I think the most important thing to figure out when you choose a college major and even once you're in your program is not what you *can* do with your major but what you *want* to do with your major. That's where I messed up. My double degree gives me endless opportunities, but I never explored one avenue over another when it came to choosing a career.

Create a Safety Net

To the extent possible, try to create a safety net for your college student. Monitor his progress in these areas and text reminders if necessary:

- Working with the Student Disability Services Office.
- Selecting the best accommodations, scheduling classes, and finding tutors.
- Applying for student housing.
- Remembering test dates or dates big projects are due.
- Remembering the last day to drop or add a course and not get a failing grade.
- Taking medication and getting prescriptions filled.
- Dealing with an emotional crisis (create a plan beforehand for helping long distance).
- Paying fees (including tuition!), bills and parking tickets on time.
- Applying for graduation before the deadline date.

Remember: when teens and young adults are forgetful or disorganized, it's not simply laziness; it's a brain chemistry issue, so don't feel guilty about helping out with reminders.

PC: I wish I had checked in more thoroughly with her and let her know it is okay to let us know if anything is really troublesome to her.

Of course, you can monitor and remind your son or daughter only if he or she is receptive to hearing this information from you. One strategy is to talk to your teen as a partner, giving her choices about your level of involvement. Another option is to make regular check-in phone calls or texts with a *camouflaged reminder question.* Examples include "Good luck on your test tomorrow," or "Did you have any trouble picking up your medicine from the pharmacy?"

Here's one of Chris's favorite "safety net" stories:

When Alex was in college, I talked to another mental health professional who also had a son in college. We were both struggling with similar feelings. *When do we let go of our children with ADHD?* She told me that her son had called from college, really upset about his first big test in history, a subject that was very difficult for him and required a lot of memorization. They agreed she would drive to the college and help him study. After they made the decision, they both cried. She decided then that *you stop helping your child when they no longer need help.* He was making every effort to make it academically on his own. There was no reason to feel guilty for helping him.

Chris's Lessons Learned: I put several safety features in place for my son. He and I visited the college he would attend and met with the director of student support services. He was eligible for several accommodations, including early registration, pick of the teachers, and consultation with staff in student services regarding which teachers worked best with students with learning challenges. He came home every weekend, so we filled up his medicine case at that time. He had a system where he put the medicine container by his bed so he would see it first thing in the morning.

When Problems Occur

And they will, so don't be surprised. Many parents are totally unaware of the problems until their son or daughter is on the brink of a disaster. Regardless of when problems occur, don't overreact. Listen closely and help your child consider her options for next steps. Let her know that you are there for her. Help her manage her pain, embarrassment and feelings of failure. And then guide her through developing a plan. Continue to work with her as she implements the plan.

PC: It's hard being an adult anyway. Our kids will get there; it just takes more time, so let them go slow. We have a fifth-year senior in college, but we have a fifth-year senior! He's so close ...

A fair number of students drop out of college at some point. This isn't necessarily the end of a college career, but rather a point in time when your son or daughter is telling you, "This is not the right place, time, or goal for me now." Your young adult has developed a better picture of what works for her and what does not. You can use that information to move onto a new path. Chapter 19, "Hitting the Speed Bumps of Life," provides helpful guidance. Returning to college at another time or location, or with a different major, or switching to a different sort of college, is always an option. Better to sort out what is the best path while not paying tuition. Coming home is not a failure!

Often parents are unaware of academic difficulties until a student is on the brink of a disaster. You can help avoid last-minute surprises by making sure your son or daughter is comfortable coming to you with problems, even though it may be upsetting. The message you want to give frequently is "We are always here for you, in good times and bad."

Ruth's Lessons Learned: Think carefully before making any decisions on behalf of your son or daughter. Your job is to guide, not decide. This is the time that a teen or young adult will make his own decisions. I can clearly remember times I was certain that my son was making a bad decision, and I was wrong. He usually made the right choice. Give your college-aged child the opportunity to learn from his own decisions (and mistakes) and to mature. My rule of thumb for intervening was "Are there safety issues or potentially devastating consequences?" I absolutely intervened if my son was doing anything I thought might be dangerous or have serious consequences. I would offer support for the other stuff but let it be if my son went in a different direction. More often than not, he was fine and pursued a different path from what I would have recommended.

PC: *After three semesters at a large university, our son came home, still unsure about what he wanted to do. As a family, we spent time talking, regrouped, and developed a new plan. He began classes at a community college while living at home. He was happy again and began to experience success. During this time, he worked on his coping skills and study strategies.*

When he finished his basic classes at the community college and he was ready to transfer to a smaller four-year university to finish a degree, we used several resources to help him develop ideas about career choices. During this time, he met with the head of the engineering department to discuss their programs and his options. When he sat down and talked with the department head, it was like a light clicked on and he knew what direction he wanted to go.

Some young people are ready to make a decision about their future when they graduate from high school, but my son with ADHD didn't make that decision until two and half years later. This decision was not on our time schedule, but his. Remember, our children may be two to three years behind their peers. This is OK.

As in this example, returning to college at a different location and with a clear idea of a major field of study can be the best option. To repeat: Better to sort out what is the best career path while not paying tuition. Coming home is not a failure!

You can find more detailed guidance on common challenges at college in Chris's books, *Teenagers with ADD, ADHD, and Executive Function Deficits* (Dendy, 2017) and *Teaching Teens with ADD, ADHD, and Executive Function Deficits* (Dendy, 2011). This includes tips on the following:

- Helping students address their disorganization and forgetfulness and get started on assignments.

- Setting up a reminder system to take medication or pay bills.
- Helping your son or daughter cope with an emotional crisis while living away from home.
- Deciding how much you should be involved.

Here's an example of the guidance you'll find in the book:

> **Dropping and Adding Courses:** Most colleges have a cutoff date after which a student may no longer "drop" a class without receiving an F. It is important for parents to be aware of this date, especially if your child is forgetful and has enrolled in a difficult class. Give your teenager permission to drop a course she is failing. Receiving an F significantly lowers a student's grade point average, which could impact their ability to earn a degree in their major.
>
> **One Caution:** If the student has grants, double-check to determine if dropping a class will endanger their grant funds.

This chapter has only touched on some of the ways you can help your son or daughter succeed in college. There are many publications, videos, and organizations that can help you learn additional strategies, and some of the best are listed in the Resources section at the back of the book.

Many young adults with ADHD do graduate from college and move on to successful careers, although the path is often meandering. With your guidance, understanding, collaboration and love, your son or daughter can also complete the journey through postsecondary education to a satisfying and fulfilling job.

References

Dendy, C.A.Z. (2011). *Teaching Teens with ADD, ADHD and Executive Function Deficits*. Bethesda, MD: Woodbine House.

Dendy, C.A.Z. (2017). *Teenagers with ADD, ADHD and executive function deficits: A guide for parents and professionals* (3rd ed.). Bethesda, MD: Woodbine House.

Georgia State University. (n.d.). *University career services*. Retrieved January 24, 2023, from https://career.gsu.edu/

17 Helping Your Son or Daughter Launch a Career

Just because your son or daughter has graduated from high school or even college doesn't mean your job is finished. When your young adult seeks her first "real" job (not a summer job or casual part-time job), don't be seduced into thinking that because he's an adult, he no longer needs the support and/or treatment he had in the past. In truth, young adults with ADHD need help and support more than ever as they face this huge transition filled with stress and challenges.

Not only have job search strategies changed dramatically in recent years, but the process is much more complex. The sheer volume of information about jobs posted online is overwhelming to all young adults, not just those with ADHD. If it has been years since you last applied for a job, be prepared to take a quick crash course to learn the best job search strategies for today's world. Since sifting through all the information is such a daunting task, this chapter provides a summary of online job sites and resources. This information will be helpful to both of you as your son or daughter plans his or her next steps.

We recommend following the wise lead of veteran career counselors: meet regularly with your son or daughter and give needed information in smaller chunks when he or she is ready to move forward. Hopefully, you'll have casual discussions around progress updates so you may anticipate what resource is needed next. For example, you might say something like this: "I saw a good format for developing a résumé in some of the material we gathered. I'll email it to you." Then later, you could say, "If you like, I'll help you polish your résumé, or "Here's a summary of possible job board sites you may want to search." Sydney found a job that was a great fit for her as a bilingual human resources associate (Figure 17.1).

Chris's Lessons Learned: When my son was nearing graduation from high school, I laughed and told friends that "we" were graduating from high school. His high school years were incredibly challenging for a variety of reasons, and it took us working as a team to successfully reach graduation day. The same team approach and lots of patience were required to help him find his first job.

The Benefits of Professional Guidance

Career guidance is available from many sources, including high schools, colleges, state agencies, county or state unemployment agencies and private businesses. And many resources for career guidance are available online.

If your young adult has graduated from college or will graduate soon, hopefully he has worked closely with the career services center to prepare for his job hunt. If not, he may still

DOI: 10.4324/9781003364092-17

Figure 17.1 Sydney, Amazon Canada, bilingual HR associate.

be able to contact the center and use some of their online resources or schedule a consultation after college graduation. Many universities offer free consultation for one year after graduation and beyond. Typically, these centers offer guidance in résumé writing, information on job fairs, tips on job searching, and information on key employers by career field.

The Georgia State University (GSU) Career Advancement Center (Georgia State University, n.d.) is an example of a college career services center that offers an excellent multistep pathway to career planning and job searching. GSU has generously made this information available to the general public. You'll find step-by-step guidelines like those listed in this section for addressing key aspects of the job-hunting process in Georgia State's *Undergraduate Student Career Guide*.

Your local community college may also be a resource even if your young adult has not attended the school. Ruth's college offers free guidance to anyone in the community. And if your son or daughter has used the state rehabilitation services, they can also offer career guidance.

An Overview of the Job Search Process

In this chapter, we assume that your son or daughter has at least a general idea of jobs that would be a good fit for his or her skills, strengths, and interests. If not, please refer to Chapter 8 on career exploration and Chapter 9 on finding your passion. If your young adult hasn't already taken a vocational interest inventory such as the *Strong Inventory* or the *Focus 2*, as noted earlier, discuss the benefits to be gained from test result information and encourage him to complete one of these inventories. When you review the results, discuss the strengths identified and the importance of matching them to job descriptions.

The number one factor determining job success for our young adults, especially on a first job, is that their strengths must align with the job description, according to Dr. Jason F. Aldrich, assistant dean of strategic partnerships and career advancement at GSU's Robinson College of Business. Bearing that in mind, here are the general steps in conducting a job search:

1. *Identify job openings of interest.*

   - First, select three to four cities in which you'd like to work and live.
   - Identify the top ten employers in those cities within your field of interest.
   - Within these companies, what job requirements best match your skill set and strengths?
   - Begin a job search via the resources available on the internet: review job postings, post your résumé and use social networking sites such as LinkedIn to connect with people in the field. (See below for specific sites that may be helpful.)

2. *Make good use of job search time.* Rarely do we teach job hunting and job keeping skills to young people until they are faced with the need. But with some forethought and planning, your son or daughter can be better prepared for this stage of life. Experts suggest splitting job search time roughly into thirds between these three activities:

   - *Researching and strategizing* regarding a job to pursue, as described in "The Hardest Part" section later in this chapter.
   - *Networking in the community*, such as meeting people, attending events, joining clubs of interest and volunteering.
   - *Searching and applying for jobs* online (this should be limited to only 20%–30% of the total job search effort).

Online Resources

There are a variety of online resources that can help job seekers identify job openings and give them broader exposure.

Job Boards and Job Search Engines: Job seekers can search job boards or use job search engines to find job openings. Job boards post openings listed by employers, and job search engines consolidate listings from multiple job boards and company websites.

Job seekers can upload résumés to any of the sites, but first they should check submission requirements for each site. Several of these sites offer unique services such as research on salaries or job trends or comparison of your résumé with a job description to determine if it's a good match. For example, if there's only a 20% chance that your résumé will make the cut for an interview, the résumé must be tweaked to match the buzzwords in the job description.

- Traditional job boards like *Monster* (Monster World Wide, 2023) and *CareerBuilder* (Career Builder, 2023) post lists of available jobs from potential employers.
- *Indeed.com* (Indeed, 2023) (offers expanded access to multiple job boards for companies, career sites, associations and other job sources.

Industry-Specific Job Boards: Industry- or agency-specific websites will also post jobs. These include positions available at businesses; local, state, and federal agencies; and local school systems. Typically state agencies require submission of an application to determine if you are eligible to be placed on the state registry of qualified employees. Potential state employers then review this list and select job applicants to interview.

- *Dice* (Dice, 2023) posts openings for tech positions such as tech developers, engineers, programmers and tech writers.
- *CareerBank* (CareerBank, 2023) lists jobs in the financing and banking industry.

- *Adzuna.com* (Adzuna, 2023) specializes in marketing and advertising jobs, including their designing and creative aspects.
- *Health eCareers* (Everyday Health, 2022) features jobs in the medical field.
- *Lawjobs.com* (law.com, 2023) posts attorney, paralegal, and other legal jobs.
- *Creativehotlists.com* (Coyne and Blanchard, Inc., 2023) and *Craigslist.org* (Craigslist, 2023) are good places to find job postings in creative fields such as graphic design and writing.

Professional Social Networking Sites: In contrast to job boards, where job hunters go to look for employers, social networking sites may be visited by employers looking for employees. LinkedIn (LinkedIn, n.d.) is by far the most popular networking site. Work with your son or daughter to create and polish a LinkedIn page. Employers and recruiters frequently review this popular social media site looking for prospective job candidates.

LinkedIn is like Facebook for professionals. Members add "connections" by asking people who are working in their career field to "connect" with them. You can also contact other professionals to ask for job tips or possibly to arrange an online "meet and greet." Members may create the equivalent of an online resume (CV) that lays out their education, training and previous work experience. The site recommends specific job openings that match your education and work experience.

If writing is your teen's strength, you might suggest he showcase his skills by blogging on key issues related to his field.

Social Media Sites: Remind your son or daughter that job applicants have been rejected because of compromising posts on sites such as Facebook and Instagram. Suggest that he review his sites to make certain there are no unflattering posts, pictures, profanity or politically inappropriate messages. Perhaps he'll even welcome your quick review of his page to confirm it's in good shape.

The Hardest Part: Actually Hunting for a Job

Once your young adult has decided on a career path and received the necessary training at college, a local employment agency, a training program or an apprenticeship, it's time to find a job. For most young people, job hunting is quite stressful, resulting in high levels of anxiety regarding their ability to not only get but select the "right" job. Parents should anticipate that some key job search tasks may be particularly difficult for a young person with ADHD. Let's look at the potential challenges so you can plan how to navigate through them.

Job Hunting

The biggest challenge of job hunting is doing it. No one enjoys this activity, and the process is full of rejection. It's hard for anyone to be persistent, but it's especially difficult for people who need immediate feedback, clear expectations and positive support. It's also terribly isolating. Here are some suggestions to make the process easier.

Set Up Daily Goals and a Reward System: Suggest that your son or daughter create his or her own reward system. Make it simple initially, then add additional rewards if needed. Your young adult can set goals like those listed here, then reward himself with an activity he enjoys. If helpful, work with him to create a chart, so he can check off each step.

Or suggest using a goal-setting app such as Coach.me or Habitica that can make the process easier. Start with achievable daily goals such as these:

- Identify three interesting job leads.
- Complete two online job applications.
- Contact two people in the field and ask for an interview to learn more about the field (networking).

Network: Remind him to keep a balance between applying for jobs and networking with people in his community. Grabbing a cup of coffee and asking for advice from someone in the field can offer an opportunity for your young adult to get his foot in the door. Networking is often the most productive way to find a job and is a break from the isolation of job hunting.

Attend a Job Fair: Search for nearby job fairs. Job fairs may be sponsored by local high schools, colleges, businesses, counties, employment agencies or chambers of commerce.

Join a Job Club or Job Support Group: Look up *Career One Stop* (Career One Stop, n.d.) and *American Job Centers* (American Job Centers, n.d.) both programs of the US Department of Labor, on the internet and search for job clubs. These centers provide a full range of job search services free of charge, including helping young adults find a job. Ruth found 11 job clubs near her midsize city. In Chris's small town, the closest job club is an hour away. If there is nothing near you, check for groups online on sites such as Meetup and LinkedIn. Sharing experiences with other people going through the same thing can give the job seeker the support and structure lacking in the typical job search.

Hire a Job Search Coach or a Career Counselor: This may help your son or daughter structure the process and stay on task. It will be money well spent and removes potential conflict within the family if parents are feeling they need to nag about job search activities. You can search online for one near you, but most coaches offer virtual services. To locate a job search coach, check out the professional associations for Career Coaches. Try Certified Professional Career Coach (2022) or the International Association of Career Coaches (n.d.).

Check Out Your State's Department of Vocational Rehabilitation: Young people who have a disability that makes it difficult to find a job can contact the state office for vocational rehabilitation to see if they qualify for services, which generally include help creating a résumé, practice with interviews, and job search assistance. A young adult with ADHD or LD may be eligible for services if he had an IEP or Section 504 plan in high school, but there may be a long wait for services (even years) unless his disability affects his abilities in many areas (e.g., communicating, walking, taking care of daily needs), not just job hunting. There may not be a waiting list in your locale, so it's worth investigating the availability of services.

The Interview

After a successful application process, the next step, a job interview, is a huge one. Understandably, your son or daughter will probably experience high levels of anxiety and a fair amount of panic before the first couple of interviews.

Practice: Encourage practicing for an interview with a nonjudgmental and neutral person. If there is someone in your family's circle of friends who has experience interviewing job applicants, don't hesitate to ask that person for help. Preparation is key, and there are some wonderful resources to help your job seekers prepare for the typical questions. The Muse, a job search and career counseling website, has a wonderful list of typical interview questions and suggestions on how to best answer them (The Muse Editors, 2023).

Work with your young adult to prepare some questions to ask the interviewer about the job or company. This lets the interviewer know that he has given serious thought about this job and has a real interest.

Many interviews are moving online, and initial interviews may be done by phone or a video chat app. Getting comfortable with online programs like Zoom is important. In addition to preparing for the interview itself, video interviews involve paying attention to lighting, the backdrop (not your young adult's bed, please!) and sound. And don't forget to dress professionally! (Figure 17.2). Practice will help your job seeker feel much more comfortable.

Approach Each Interview as Practice for the Next One: Seldom is a job applicant hired by the first person who interviews him. That means your young adult is facing several interviews, with several discouraging rejections. He will really need your support and encouragement during this job interview phase.

There are no failed interviews, but rather learning experiences. Your son or daughter will learn from each experience and be better prepared for the next interview. Help him or her understand that this is a marathon, not a sprint, and to anticipate having multiple interviews

Figure 17.2 Nathan, preparing for a virtual interview.

before finding a job. Be a sounding board afterward as your young adult thinks through which questions were hard for him or what caught him by surprise. And be sure to ask about the questions he answered well. It's so easy to concentrate on the negative and lose sight of her growing interview skills.

Look for a Good Work Environment: Although difficult to assess in an interview and office visit, these are characteristics to look for in potential work environments:

- Is the work atmosphere pleasant? Do workers seem happy?
- Is the work culture receptive to differences and diversity? Do employees seem supportive of one another? Is there a willingness to help one another? Is there diversity in the workforce? Once your young adult has been on the job for a while, she will have a much better sense of the informal culture and whether her colleagues will be receptive and accepting if she needs extra help.
- Is the job supervisor supportive and flexible? The supervisor is the key person who makes work life tolerable. If the supervisor has rigid expectations and is not tolerant of individual differences, it will be harder to develop a positive working relationship if your son or daughter needs to ask for accommodations. On the other hand, a supervisor who works with each staff member individually and supports growth on the job will be a godsend.

Do Not Disclose ADHD or Other Disabilities in the Interview: It's generally not recommended to disclose potential job challenges in an interview unless a job applicant has an obvious disability or needs immediate accommodations. This is a very different environment from public school or college. Although employers may not discriminate by law, subtle attitude changes can adversely affect the chances of getting a job. Problem-free employees are the Holy Grail for bosses, though very rare. After your young adult is hired, there'll be time to consider sharing information about ADHD or a learning disability.

Once your son or daughter has been on the job for a while, he or she will have a much better understanding of the challenges. If a work obstacle significantly affects her work but could be addressed with some extra supports, then it may well be worth the risk of sharing information about ADHD and/or LD. However, if the work environment is likely to be unsupportive or the obstacles are minor, it may be better not to disclose the disability. Only the employee himself can make this decision, so offer support and help him weigh his options carefully. He should give himself time to decide what's best for him.

Accepting a Job

It's very tempting to accept the first job offered. And perhaps your son or daughter needs to begin work immediately for financial reasons. But encourage him or her to revisit some of the questions she considered when doing her career exploration:

1. Is this something I can do successfully?
2. Does it capitalize on my strengths?
3. Can I make a decent living with this job?
4. Do I love this work?

If the answers to these questions are yes, then the job is probably a good fit. If the answers are no, then your young adult should seriously consider the pros and cons of the position. Keep in mind that this job may be a stepping-stone to a better position or provide needed income while he looks for something better. Whether he takes the job or not, he should consider continuing her job search for something that will be a better match for his talents.

Starting a New Job

Yeah! Your son or daughter has a job. At this point, everyone celebrates and often assumes all will be well. Not so fast. Every job has its challenges, and having ADHD and/or a learning disability can magnify those challenges. Remember that our young people have difficulty with transitions, and starting a job is a huge one.

Getting Off on the Right Foot with the Boss: Encourage your young adult to try to make the boss look good by learning what the boss needs from him. Employees who learn to do this are highly valued. That means anticipating what the boss will need and how others perceive them. New employees shouldn't assume that the boss knows everything about their job responsibilities. So your son or daughter should be prepared to keep the boss informed about the latest reports and critical aspects of his or her work.

In school, students are often more concerned about peer perception than about what the teacher thinks. It is important that your young adult understands that on the job, it is all about the supervisor's opinion, so he should not get caught up in the gossip mill at work. His coworkers can't help if her boss is unhappy with his work or on-the-job behavior.

Ruth's Lessons Learned: I will always remember the day my son came home from a new job and said, "I hate my boss. He's even worse than you." (Secretly, I was overjoyed it was someone other than me.) For him, it was the beginning of learning how the real world works.

Last but Not Least: Keeping the Job

The Georgia Department of Labor surveyed over 770 employers regarding reasons for employee turnover. According to the survey, the primary reason an employee was let go was *a lack of work ethic* and so-called *soft skills* (rather than technical skills). These critical soft skills include attendance, punctuality, attitude, respect, discipline, character and appropriate mobile phone usage. Eighty-seven percent of employers indicated that they also highly valued two additional skills: *critical thinking* and *problem-solving skills*.

Unfortunately, most of our teenagers receive little or no instruction regarding the importance of soft skills such as the ability to think critically and problem solve. So the job may fall to you as a parent or another trusted adult to make your teen aware of the critical importance of practicing these skills. You could make a list of soft skills, hand it to your son or daughter, and then discuss it. Explain that surveys have found that failure to demonstrate these skills is a huge reason that employees are let go.

Of course, many of our young adults with ADHD still grapple with managing symptoms and executive function deficits that can present challenges on the job. Be sure to check out the next chapter, "Signs that Trouble May Be Brewing at Work," to see how you can help your son or daughter with challenges in the workplace.

Trying to Juggle It All

If your son or daughter is still living at home, you'll be available if he or she needs help managing classwork and/or a part-time job. However, young adults who relocate to attend college or accept a job face greater challenges.

Offer help with details. The whirlwind surrounding adjusting to a new college or job, finding an apartment, setting up utilities and internet service, paying bills, getting to class or work on time and staying on top of work may well be overwhelming. You might help your son or daughter set up autopay for bills so they will always be on time. Or you might offer to work together on getting utilities and internet/cable service set up. You could even volunteer to house sit when someone has to come to the house to install new services.

If your young adult has moved to another city, that means finding a new doctor and a new pharmacy and often dealing with a new health insurance plan. Help your son or daughter identify several doctors who are experienced ADHD treatment professionals and are taking new patients. If you have friends or relatives in the area, ask them for suggestions of a new physician or psychologist.

At some point, your son or daughter will probably need help managing the health insurance aspects of treatment. Insurance companies are not always consumer friendly, and you have far more experience dealing with them than your young adult does. Switching to a new insurance company, learning how insurance networks work, getting referrals when necessary, meeting deductibles and budgeting for copays and other medical expenses can disrupt ongoing treatment and a young person's ability to function well in a new and stressful environment.

Offer to work with your young adult to develop a plan to take care of all the details. If he accepts your offer, then ask him what he wants you to do. The "ADHD Medication Management at College" section in Chapter 16, "Helping Your Teen Succeed at College," may be helpful as you finalize medical treatment plans.

Your role as parent is to be the cheerleader, supporter and to offer guidance when your young adult needs and requests it. Rarely do young people get training in how to look for a job. So look for the resources and support that will make job hunting less mind-boggling and difficult.

References

Adzuna. (2023). *Job search—find every job, everywhere with adzuna.* Retrieved January 26, 2023, from https://www.adzuna.com/

American Job Centers. (n.d.). *American Job Centers.* United States Department of Labor. Retrieved January 26, 2023, from https://www.dol.gov/general/topic/training/onestop

CareerBuilder. (2023). *Find a job.* Retrieved January 26, 2023, from https://www.careerbuilder.com/

Career One Stop. (n.d.). *Career One Stop: Your Source for Career, Exploration, Training and Jobs.* Retrieved January 26, 2023, from https://www.careeronestop.org/

CareerBank. (2023). *CareerBank—find the best jobs in finance, banking and accounting.* Retrieved January 26, 2023, from https://www.careerbank.com/

Certified Professional Career Coach. (2022, December 1). *Certified career coach directory.* CPCC Career Coach Certification. Retrieved January 26, 2023, from https://cpcc-careercoach.com/need-coaching/

Coyne and Blanchard, Inc. (2023). *Job search: Creative talent: Creative hotlist.* Retrieved January 26, 2023, from https://www.creativehotlist.com/

Craigslist. (2023). *Craigslist.* Retrieved January 26, 2023, from https://www.craigslist.org/about/sites

Dice. (2023). *Find jobs in technology.* Retrieved January 26, 2023, from https://www.dice.com/

Everyday Health. (2022, June 16). *Healthcare eCareers.* healthecareers.com. Retrieved January 26, 2023, from https://www.healthecareers.com/

Georgia State University. (n.d.). University Career Services. Retrieved January 26, 2023, from https://career.gsu.edu/students/

Indeed. (2023). *Job search\indeed.* Retrieved January 26, 2023, from https://www.indeed.com/

International Association of Career Coaches. (n.d.). *International Association of Career Coaches.* Retrieved January 26, 2023, from https://www.iacareercoaches.org/

Law.com. (2023). *Start your job search here.* Home\Lawjobs.com. Retrieved January 26, 2023, from https://lawjobs.com/

LinkedIn. (n.d.). *Suggested job searches.* Retrieved January 26, 2023, from https://www.linkedin.com/jobs

Monster World Wide. (2023). *Monster jobs—job search, career advice & hiring resources.* Retrieved January 26, 2023, from https://www.monster.com/

The Muse Editors. (2023, January 4). *Your ultimate guide to answering the most common interview questions.* The Muse. Retrieved January 26, 2023, from https://www.themuse.com/advice/interview-questions-and-answers

18 Signs That Trouble May Be Brewing at Work

After high school graduation, John got a job with a real estate firm as an administrative assistant and hoped to someday get a real estate license. His duties included answering the phone, taking messages, filing, and making sure all the agents had the paperwork they needed. Since many of the agents were out of the office much of the day, his work was essential to the smooth functioning of the office.

John had been treated for ADHD since he was ten, with medication, a 504 plan for school support and periodic counseling when times were tough. After graduating and getting a job, he felt confident in his ability to manage his ADHD and stopped taking his medication. Soon afterward, John started having trouble keeping track of the phone messages and visitors. Then John misfiled and lost a contract that had been signed for a house sale. His boss was so upset that he fired John immediately. John not only lost his job, but he could no longer pay for his apartment and was forced to move back home with his parents.

Every job has its challenges. There are many poor supervisors and difficult coworkers, and work may be too challenging, too boring or just not right for a particular employee. Be aware that there are often some rough bumps in learning the job duties, the culture at work, the quirks of the supervisor and the behavior of coworkers.

After the initial excitement of a new job has worn off, you may see signs that your son or daughter is worried, stressed or unhappy. Although most employed adults have faced problems at work, that doesn't mean your young adult should feel stuck in a bad situation or that the situation can't improve. But what can you do to help besides letting him know you're concerned and offering encouragement? This chapter offers some real-life strategies that may work for you and your young adult.

When Problems Arise at Work

Your job as a parent is to support your young adult and encourage a problem-solving approach to her employment dilemmas. You are now the coach and cheerleader, not the doer. Sharing some stories of your own struggles on the job can help relieve some of the stress and is a great way to impart wisdom and potential solutions without taking over.

When problems occur, it may be for several different reasons, and it's helpful to sort out the source(s) of the problems. If your son or daughter is experiencing difficulties during the early months on the job, help identify what the major challenges are and then discuss steps he or she can take to correct the problem.

DOI: 10.4324/9781003364092-18

A Bad Job Fit: If the problem is that she doesn't like the work, it's definitely not what she expected, or it's consistently boring, then she should start looking for another job. Help her see that she doesn't need to stay in a position that is a bad fit and makes her feel terrible about herself every day. But remind her, *don't quit until you have another job lined up.* It's always easier to find a new job when you are working.

Encourage your young adult to soldier through the tough parts and put her energy into finding a new position. Help her learn from her experiences to be sure she finds a job she'll really like. This is not a failure, but rather another step in the job exploration process. She'll have learned things about herself and the employment world that will help down the road.

Conflict with Peers: Sometimes the work is great, but the people are not so much. The typical workplace has its share of gossip, bad attitudes, jealousy, competition and sometimes even backstabbing. Caution your son or daughter to avoid getting caught up in gossip about fellow employees. Seek out the veteran staff who seem more mature, have a positive attitude and are supportive, then follow their example.

Conflict with the Boss: When there are problems with the direct supervisor, it can make anyone's work life miserable. Before giving up entirely, here are a couple of suggestions for living with a difficult boss:

- *Try to see things from the boss's point of view.* Help your young adult understand that she'll probably have a steep learning curve before she masters the new job. If she is struggling to meet deadlines and goals, her bosses may be supportive and help set up a structure to be successful. However, the typical boss's criticism is often direct, embarrassing, anxiety-provoking and hurtful. It's always difficult not to take criticism personally. Offer encouragement, and after listening to your son's or daughter's concerns, discuss ways to improve his or her job performance. Often criticism is not personal, but rather about meeting the bottom line financially.
- *Seek help from a supportive fellow employee or mid-level manager.* Ask them for the best way to interact with the boss. For example, if the boss isn't pleased with your son's or daughter's reports, he or she could ask the manager to review and make suggestions for improvement.

Unethical or Inappropriate Behavior from Coworkers: Don't hesitate to draw on your own life experiences to help your young adult sort out these very difficult situations. If a boss or another coworker makes sexual advances, asks your son or daughter to do things that are unethical or illegal, or makes racist comments, then it's time to take action by scheduling an appointment with HR staff for guidance on handling the problem. This is a very difficult decision, and your support will be essential.

Problems Outside Your Control: A lot of stuff happens at work that has nothing to do with individual employees. For example, the boss may be under major pressure from corporate headquarters and get angry more easily or place unreasonable expectations on all staff. Help your son or daughter learn to step back and stay uninvolved. Learning to let go of what he or she can't control is one of life's great lessons.

When ADHD or LD Gets in the Way

If the work is too challenging, or your son or daughter is finding it difficult to meet work expectations, stop and consider whether ADHD or a learning disability is getting in the way. If your young adult is having problems focusing, meeting deadlines, getting along with coworkers, remembering instructions, getting to work on time or struggling with anything else related to his disability, he may need to ask for extra supports or supervision in order to work more effectively.

Help identify the major reason the boss is unhappy with your young adult's work and come up with suggestions (accommodations) for addressing the problem. For example, if meeting deadlines is the major difficulty, then identify two or three supports that are most likely to help (see the next section for suggestions).

Talk with the Supervisor: Your young adult should schedule time with her supervisor and identify the problems she is struggling with, then discuss her thoughts on possible solutions. *It's not necessary to disclose ADHD or a learning disability at this time.* Instead, she can try to impress her supervisor by being proactive in addressing the challenges at work and suggesting potential solutions. The informal solutions she suggests must be easy to do, inexpensive, and have little impact on coworkers.

Seek Help Early: Too often the employee with a major challenge at work waits until the job is in jeopardy before asking for assistance. Waiting to seek help is often counterproductive and often doesn't work. Suggest that your son or daughter take action as soon as he or she hits a barrier that interferes with success on the job. It's extremely unwise for an employee to wait until her performance has deteriorated to the extent that her job is in jeopardy. Remember—early intervention can make all the difference in her ability to do the job.

In addition, your son or daughter may need to see a physician for a medication adjustment. New challenges, increases in stress, and transitions can indicate that treatment and/or medication need reevaluation.

Consider Disclosing ADHD or LD Now: If your son or daughter may need multiple accommodations, it may be wise to disclose the existence of a disability sooner rather than later. See "Is It Time to Disclose ADHD?" at the end of the chapter.

Common Work Challenges and Strategies That May Help

Often the primary reason the boss is unhappy with an employee is that she's not meeting her job requirements. Frequently an employee with ADHD can do the work but lacks the focus, structure and persistence to finish a given task. The boss may be angry when:

1. An employee is consistently late to work and meetings.
2. Written reports are incomplete or late repeatedly.
3. Tasks are not finished in a timely manner.
4. Sales productivity goals are not met.
5. Work time is misspent on lower-priority, more enjoyable work.

Strategies for handling the difficulties that can contribute to these and other common problems are listed next.

1. Frequently being late:

   • Organize all materials needed for work the night before.
   • Put all work materials near the door to the garage or exit to the street.
   • Set a wake-up alarm 15 minutes earlier than usual.
   • Lay out work clothes the night before.

- Calculate commuting time to work during regular work hours and add 15–20 minutes' "oops time" to allow for traffic, stopping to get gas, a delayed bus or subway, etc.
- Set an alarm on a cell phone for 10 minutes before time to leave for work.
- Set a second alarm that signals that it's time to walk out the door.
- If these strategies don't work, talk with the doctor about taking a short-acting (immediate-release) ADHD medication early each morning. These ADHD meds will help the young adult get ready for work and out the door more quickly.
- Another possibility is to ask the boss for a change in arrival time (and a later time to leave work) to better accommodate the ADHD internal clock or to avoid heavy morning traffic. The important thing is to be there for all meetings and to get the work done.

2. Difficulty setting priorities:

- Make a checklist of all task assignments.
- Start on the tasks that are most important and most urgent.
- Mark which two or three tasks are most important.
- Identify which important task is the most urgent and make note of the due date.
- Identify which task is most important to your boss or supervisor.
- Post due dates on a calendar that is visible from your desk chair.
- Make a separate list of two or three important tasks that must be done today.
- Set aside uninterrupted time to work on the most important/urgent task.
- If there is an important task that requires minimal time and effort, complete this task first. Clearing this task will give you a sense of accomplishment and allow you to move on to a more time-consuming task.

3. Missing deadlines:

- Create a plan beginning with the project due date and planning backward. Note all dates on a frequently reviewed calendar.
- Consider using project management software for any long-term project. Designate deadlines for each step of the project.
- Use a planner (on a cell phone, computer, or paper) religiously and add warnings of all upcoming deadlines at least a couple days in advance.
- Set alarm reminders of each due date on the phone or computer.
- Break the task into chunks and schedule when each segment should be completed. For example, by the end of tomorrow, collect all data necessary to write the report.
- Find a sympathetic staff member who might be willing to be a mentor—someone to check in with periodically regarding progress and due dates.

4. Forgetting a job assignment or deadline:

- Try the free app Remember the Milk (Remember the Milk, n.d.). Enter each task and its due date and schedule a reminder email to be sent the day it's due.
- Add a reminder of all due dates to a project management program, phone, computer, or a month-at-a-glance calendar and review it first thing every morning.

5. Procrastinating:

- End each workday by making a list of the most important work priorities for the next day.

- Begin each day with work on the most important tasks.
- Resist the temptation to take care of less important items first.
- To get over the initial difficulty in starting a task, set a timer for a small amount of time (like 15 minutes) and do as much work as possible within that time frame. Most people with ADHD will continue working once they have gotten started. This will help your young adult work more efficiently and get her over the hump of beginning a project.

6. Trouble managing interruptions:

- Set aside a designated time slot to return phone calls and emails. Then mute the cell phone and don't check any emails or answer texts until all the tasks are completed. Email and text are huge time gobblers.
- Use a timer on the computer or phone as a reminder to avoid any interruptions during a certain block of time. "Time Timer," a time management app, makes the passage of time concrete and visual (Time Timer, n.d.) For example, set the timer for a 45-minute uninterrupted work session. In addition to the visual cue of time winding down, an alarm will sound when time elapses.
- Put a "Please do not disturb" sign on the door or outside the cubicle.

7. Difficulty following and remembering oral instructions:

- After each supervisory session or staff meeting, send a brief bulleted email to the boss outlining an understanding of the work assignments. This gives the boss an opportunity to correct any misunderstandings and also provides a written guideline for the task.
- Write a list of specific responsibilities for each project.
- Don't start a new task until a list of all the components of the assignment and due dates are entered on a calendar. In other words, focus on the overall project before jumping into a particular task.
- Record planning meetings (with permission) and use a speech-to-text app such as Otter to turn the recording into text. Review the text and highlight all the tasks you need to follow up on. Then add all the tasks to your planner or to your "to-do list."

8. Losing things frequently:

- Organize and declutter desk; designate places for key reports or other important documents, works in progress and completed work. If your son or daughter doesn't have a regular workplace but is mobile, consider using a crate with all the work materials in one place so they can be taken from desk to desk or from site to site. For employees who are working from home, it is important to set up a space that is exclusively for working, and definitely not the bed. Too many college students get used to doing everything from their bed, but that's not acceptable for a work environment.
- Place personal items in the same place each day: put car keys in the side pocket of a purse or in a designated bowl or box; hang keys for the work vehicle on the designated office hook.
- Consider using a tracking device for keys, wallet, purse, phone, laptop, and any other easily lost item. There are many available that will sync with a phone or computer and send an audible signal.

- Handle papers once, do what has to be done with them, and put them away in their designated spot.
- Color-code files—for example, use red to designate the most important ones.
- Use open shelves that can be "seen," thus giving a visual reminder of important assignments.
- Avoid storing important documents in drawers and closed cabinets; unfortunately "out of sight, out of mind."

9. Easily distracted:

- Ask to work in a quieter area with less traffic, even if it's a file or storage room.
- For special projects, work in an unused conference room temporarily.
- Use a white noise machine to cover up background noise.
- Occasionally ask to work at home to wrap up a major project.
- Use a noise-canceling headset.
- Do one task at a time before starting another.

10. Problems reading and understanding large amounts of material:

- Highlight key points in a written report.
- Discuss important points with a colleague (particularly useful for those who have problems absorbing verbal information).
- Review any diagrams or drawings in the material to clarify points.
- Use text-to-speech software (with headphones) to read and hear it at the same time.

11. Forgetting names and numbers:

- Before going to an important meeting, take a minute to review the names of key people who will be there.
- Practice using word associations linking the name to things that are known—e.g., Jeff is also the name of a favorite uncle.
- Keep a list of key phone numbers on a cell phone.
- Before attending important meetings, make notes of key points, including important data.

More Accommodation Ideas

A great resource for identifying what accommodations would be most useful at work is the Job Accommodation Network at www.askjan.org (Job Accommodation Network, n.d.). The site has lists of the types of accommodations that have been helpful to others who have specific disabilities. If you don't find what you are looking for, send JAN your questions and get some expert consultation for free.

New Habits Require Time and Practice

The hardest part of implementing any of these suggestions is making sure they stick. All of us have made a "to-do list," used it for a few days and then stopped. It's best to focus on one challenge at a time. So encourage your young adult to avoid overwhelming himself with too many ideas. A new habit requires practice for 30 to 60 days to really become a routine part of life. During that time, there will be lapses. The key is to recommit to the strategy as often as needed until it becomes a natural part of work life.

Develop a Plan for Success

If a young person with ADHD is really struggling to succeed on the job, it can help to take a step back and pinpoint all the difficulties that are contributing to problems at work. Then he can develop a plan to address each difficulty and monitor his progress toward resolving the problems. The following is one young man's plan for success.

> Aaron was on the verge of being fired ... because of most of the work challenges mentioned earlier. His boss gave him an ultimatum: "Get your last three months' expense reports submitted and meet your sales quotas, or you're fired."
>
> A recently diagnosed adult with ADHD, Aaron had not pursued treatment. Aaron finally told his boss that he had been diagnosed with ADHD, but it wasn't being treated. He didn't formally request accommodations but rather created his own intervention system with help from others. Aaron realized he needed to immediately schedule an appointment with a physician to discuss treatment options. In addition, a supportive supervisor recommended that he contact a treatment professional who could help him develop behavioral strategies to ensure he completed his monthly reports and hopefully enhance his sales numbers.

Aaron's Plan for Success

1. *Schedule an appointment with a physician.* After some discussion, Aaron decided to try medication to see if his work productivity improved.
2. *Develop a corrective action plan.* With the help of an ADHD job coach, Aaron developed a plan that included several action steps to ensure he completed his required reports.
3. *Manage time better.* Aaron realized he was spending more time on aspects of his job he liked (consulting with the superintendents at golf courses) and postponing the unpleasant task (writing expense and sales reports) until late in the day when he was too tired to focus. He decided to schedule report writing earlier in the day and then reward himself with a visit to a golf course later that afternoon or the next day.
4. *Minimize distractions.* Aaron selected an isolated workroom in the business warehouse to work on his expense reports.
5. *Improve focus at work.* He made his work environment more user-friendly by taking a "brain break" after completing a report (walking around, stepping outside for fresh air, drinking water). Sipping Gatorade also enhanced his attention (increased blood glucose sugar). He interspersed working on reports with absentmindedly petting his dog, Jack, who accompanied him to work. Petting his dog was the equivalent of using a "fidget toy."
6. *Create a chart to monitor progress.* Aaron created a list of reports that were due and checked each one off when it was completed. He wrote a weekly summary of his office product sales and submitted that to the boss.
7. *Report progress.* To reinforce his new work habits and make sure he was implementing his plan for success, the first few days Aaron texted his job coach with an update on each step he was taking. "I started." "Finished first report." "Taking a break." "Starting the second monthly report."

By following the steps in his plan, Aaron was able to complete all three months of his travel expenses and submit them to the boss. However, his customers hadn't placed many orders for the products he was selling, even though they loved the expert advice he offered. Aaron continued to visit the superintendents at several golf courses, walked the course with them, identified the disease culprits and suggested products that could help resolve their problem. As a result, his sales numbers steadily increased.

One of Aaron's greatest strengths was that he was a true expert on diseases on golf course greens and best treatments. Aaron was also a "people person." During his first six months on the job, he established his credentials and built strong relationships of mutual trust with the superintendents. He loved walking the course with them and actually seeing problems firsthand, then suggesting the best treatment strategy. Once Aaron got a handle on paperwork requirements and deadlines, he truly excelled at his job. Ultimately, due to constant pressure for sales performance, Aaron left the company and opened his own business that allowed him to do the things he loved while also making a decent living.

Is It Time to Disclose ADHD?

If informal intervention strategies and extra supports aren't adequate and your son or daughter needs more help, now is the time to consider the ramifications of disclosing ADHD or a learning disability at work. If your young adult believes the problem he is experiencing could eventually threaten his job, then suggest he act now.

First, schedule a meeting with someone in human resources (HR) and ask for advice about the best approach to use in asking for accommodations. HR staff should know whether the boss will be receptive to the request and, if so, the best way to phrase a request for extra help. If a supervisor has had a good experience working with another employee with ADHD or a learning disability, then he or she is far more likely to be receptive. A human resources department's job is to make sure the business abides by the law in all matters related to employees and that personnel practices are fair. HR staff will be knowledgeable about the Americans with Disabilities Act (Equal Employment and Opportunity Commission, n.d.) and can help guide your young adult and her supervisor. *Second*, ensure that your son or daughter knows his or her rights under the law, as explained in the next section.

What Rights Do Employees with Disabilities Have?

In the United States, employers with more than 15 full-time employees may not discriminate against people with disabilities in any employment practices. Employees have a right to be free from harassment because of a disability, and an employer may not fire or discipline an employee for asserting legal rights under the Americans with Disabilities Act (Equal Employment and Opportunity Commission, n.d.). Most importantly, an employee has a right to request reasonable accommodations in order to do the job, provided that he or she is able to perform all the *essential functions* of the job. A "reasonable accommodation" is an adjustment to the work environment or to the way the work is done that allows the employee to successfully perform the job duties. But it also must be "reasonable," which means that this is fairly easy for the employer to do and not unduly expensive.

Choosing Accommodations to Request: For employees with ADHD, reasonable accommodations might include written instructions to reinforce verbal directions, access to a quiet workspace with few distractions, using a checklist instead of writing reports, or more frequent reminders of deadlines. For employees with LD, reasonable accommodations might include text-to-speech software for reading problems, speech-to-text software for writing problems, or a specialized calculator for a math learning disability. These are just a few examples of the many accommodations that can be helpful.

The important thing is to ask for accommodations that will directly address and provide support for the job skills the employee with ADHD and/or LD is struggling with. The Job Accommodation Network at www.askjan.org (Job Accommodation Network, n.d.) has extensive lists of accommodations categorized by disability and is a great resource for sorting out what accommodations to consider.

Asking for Accommodations: After identifying a few accommodations to try, your son or daughter can schedule a meeting with the supervisor. At this meeting, he or she should disclose ADHD and/or a learning disability to the supervisor and ask for one or two key accommodations under the Americans with Disabilities Act. The ADA was created to prevent job discrimination on the basis of a disability.

Your son or daughter should follow up with a written memo or email stating his or her request so there is a written record. If all goes well, the supervisor will agree, and accommodations will be formally implemented.

When to Request Accommodations: *When* an employee asks for help, is as important as *if* he asks. Too often employees with disabilities wait until they are about to be fired before disclosing a disability and requesting accommodations. This is often too late in the process. If the informal requests for support and the strategies in the earlier sections of this chapter aren't working, problems are continuing and the supervisor is concerned, then it is time to consider disclosing a disability.

What If the Business Has Fewer than 15 Employees?

In a small business, the office culture and the attitudes of the boss make a huge difference. Businesses with fewer than 15 full-time employees are not required to give employees accommodations under the Americans with Disabilities Act. However, a small business can still be very accommodating to individual differences. But employees must pay attention to the office culture. If supervisors are not flexible and accommodating, it may be wise to avoid disclosing ADHD or a learning disability. Or if there is not much tolerance for diversity and difference among employees, it may be best not to share information about ADHD.

Potential Downsides to Disclosing ADHD or LD

There can be a downside to sharing, too. Some supervisors may change their expectations and assumptions about an employee's work ability once a disability has been disclosed. In the worst case, stigma about a disability may raise its ugly head. There is a lot to think about when considering the options. You might offer to discuss the pros and cons of asking for accommodations before your son or daughter makes a final decision. Or perhaps suggest that requesting a transfer within the company might be an option.

Coping with Stigma at Work: While the disclosure of ADHD or a learning disability should be confidential, it is best to assume coworkers will figure it out. Some coworkers may feel as if the employee with ADHD is getting special treatment.

The most effective way to deal with stigma or resentment at work is for the employee to demonstrate that he is a productive worker and a good team player. Suggest that your young adult identify coworkers who may be supportive and become potential allies. She can also make a special effort to develop friendships—for example, by inviting a coworker to go to lunch with her. She could then ask this person for tips about working at this firm.

If there are social conflicts, she can look for a friendly "caretaker" among fellow employees and ask this person to informally provide feedback and, if needed, be a mentor.

It's highly likely that some coworkers have no information or erroneous information about the challenges related to ADHD or learning disabilities. You might be able to give your son or daughter the words so that he or she can educate others in a gentle manner: "You know, Bob, I need a quiet space to work just like you need your glasses to read." It may help to explain that accommodations don't in any way exempt an employee from having to do the job to the supervisor's satisfaction. It simply gives the employee a workaround to be more successful.

Ruth's Lessons Learned: Ruth once worked with a very forgetful staff member. The secretary agreed to check him out each morning to be sure he had on matching socks, buttons were buttoned and he was appropriately attired for the activities of the day. This step took away any discomfort in letting him know if there was a problem and saved him from some embarrassment.

Our Final Reminders

Too often young people with ADHD never disclose, problems arise, and the employee makes no effort to find a better way to do the tasks. Remind your son or daughter: *DO NOT WAIT until your job is in jeopardy to ask for extra support.* Way too many times we've heard from people who were on the verge of being fired before asking for accommodations as a last-ditch effort to save a job. That approach is rarely productive in the long term. And by that time, work relationships are already damaged.

If your son or daughter can't decide whether to request accommodations or which accommodations to request, suggest talking with a healthcare provider, others who have ADHD or learning disabilities, an educational consultant, and groups like CHADD, the National Resource Center on ADHD, and ADDA. As mentioned previously, you can also send the Job Accommodation Network (www.askjan.com) your specific questions, and they will help. Also check out the listings in the Resources section.

When all else fails, start job-hunting again. Refer to the previous chapter regarding "launching a career" for tips on helping your son or daughter.

References

Equal Employment and Opportunity Commission (n.d.). *Your employment rights as an individual with a disability.* Retrieved January 29, 2023, from https://www.eeoc.gov/laws/guidance/your-employment-rights-individual-disability

Job Accommodation Network. (n.d.). Retrieved January 29, 2023, from https://askjan.org/

Remember the Milk: The smart to-do app for busy people. Remember the Milk: Online to-do list and task management. (n.d.). Retrieved January 29, 2023, from https://www.rememberthemilk.com/

Time Timer. *The original visual timer.* (n.d.). Retrieved January 29, 2023, from https://www.timetimer.com/

19 Hitting the Speed Bumps of Life

Life rarely goes as planned for any of us, but this is particularly true for our children with ADHD and executive functioning challenges. Both you and your son or daughter can anticipate that there will be challenges along the way, some of them big—but you'll be there for him or her when the problem occurs. This chapter will give you information on a number of typical challenges young people with ADHD may face. More serious problems such as anxiety and depression were discussed in Chapter 6.

Our suggestions in this chapter are for general guidance. Keep in mind that ultimately, you know your teen best. You are aware of his skills, challenges, and level of maturity. After reading our suggestions, you can decide which ones are most appropriate for your young adult. Most young people with ADHD haven't mastered all the skills discussed here but will master them over time or learn to compensate.

Do not feel that you're a failure as a parent or make your teen feel guilty because he hasn't mastered all these skills. Select key skills to work toward improving and be satisfied with taking small steps forward. You get to determine the pace at which you encourage practicing new skills. The bottom line is to treat your son or daughter as a partner, discuss issues, and make final decisions together.

Lifelong Support Strategies

There are a variety of ways you can help your son or daughter weather life's storms. One of the most effective ways is by being a good role model—modeling how to handle common challenges (Figure 19.1). Other all-purpose strategies to begin using as early as possible are described in this chapter.

Support Your Child in Good Times and Bad

First, when problems arise, as they do in everyone's lives, it's important that you support your son or daughter and keep your relationship strong. That means handling your anger, disappointment and irritation in ways that don't alienate him or her. Young people make impulsive decisions without regard for the potential ramifications. Our job is to help them manage the consequences and learn from the experience. *Maintaining a strong relationship beginning in childhood is the key!* Listen carefully to what your child is communicating (both with words and behaviors). This was the resounding message from our survey of parents who had already gone through the transition to adulthood with their sons or daughters with ADHD.

DOI: 10.4324/9781003364092-19

Figure 19.1 Sophie with Mom, Jeremy.

PC: *The relationship between you and your child is more important than grades or success in school or work. If the relationship isn't strong, where else will he or she go for help and support, especially when they most need it?*

PC: *I would advise parents to do whatever they can to make their home a sanctuary and a place of peace for their sons or daughters with ADHD. They have grief everywhere, so give them a place where they can come and rest, talk or sleep, because life is tough out there.*

PC: *[What helped most was] open dialogue about what was happening at school, bullying and isolationism.*

PC: *Talk, talk, talk to your child about how to help themselves as they get older. Keep communication going at school and at home. Always be the soft place for your child to land.*

PC: *She started to starve herself and get very depressed. I wish I had talked to her more in depth, somehow seen that this was coming on as well as helping her to identify what she was feeling and what we could do to help her before it got that bad.*

PC: *Just love them no matter what.*

PC: *Stop blaming them; listen carefully to what they say they can and can't do. There's a good life out there for each of us. They need to find theirs. No anger; it doesn't help at all.*

PC: *I would advise others to actively listen to their adult children. As they talk to us parents, they are figuring it all out in their minds, and communication helps them do that.*

Always do your best to be patient, and remember they are still learning (as we all are). Tell them you love them and that you are proud of them daily! Positivity helps in a world that often does not give of that freely. Be your child's biggest fan!"

Teens and young adults may avoid telling you disappointing news. Too often young people don't share their problems with their parents because they're worried about angering or disappointing Mom or Dad. Throughout this book there are suggestions to help strengthen communication between parent and child and handle conflict effectively. When problems can be discussed safely without anger, serious consequences can be prevented. So, find the ways you and your teenager can communicate frequently and safely about successes and challenges.

Ruth's Lessons Learned: Early on in Christopher's life we developed a special meaning for "time out" in our house. It meant that we were in a spiraling argument and needed to back off. Either one of us could declare a time out, and we would decide on a time to come back to discuss the problem. I called a time out more often than Christopher did. I needed to calm down, call my best friend to vent, and decide how to handle the situation. Christopher would often leave home to go to a neighbor's or just get out of the house until he felt calmer. He even learned early on to call me on the phone with bad news, so I had time to calm down before we talked face-to-face. When we came back together, we were both much calmer, able to listen to each other and eventually settle the issue.

Another way we coped as he got older was to have serious discussions at restaurants, where both of us were less likely to lose it and create a scene. When he was younger, I had the final word, but I listened and seriously considered his input. Now as an adult, he has the final word. Both of us recognize that we can come back and renegotiate if things change. Find what works for you and your son or daughter so the lines of communication are always open.

Model Asking for Help

An important behavior to model beginning when your child is young is requesting help when needed. We have a strong culture in the United States of each person handling problems without outside assistance. As a result, millions of people suffer in silence when help is often a phone call away. Too often we wait until things really get bad before considering outside assistance with rough spots and major challenges.

If you have a tendency to try to handle your own challenges, recognize it and push yourself hard to get help earlier. If your child learns to cover up problems because that's what you do, you can anticipate there will be a time when she keeps vital information hidden from you and other important people. This can sometimes lead to devastating consequences such as self-harm, school failure, job loss or even suicide. We know that the sooner extra support or treatment is provided, the more likely a major disaster will be averted. This message is crucial: *Ask for help when you need it!* A willingness to accept help from others is an amazing strength, not a weakness.

Many professionals can help you and your son or daughter deal more effectively with challenges: school counselors, therapists, ADHD coaches, advocates, religious leaders, doctors and others. Model seeking out assistance from a professional or even a trusted friend when you encounter a difficult personal problem. Often a neutral, trusted person can be far more effective with your teen or young adult than you can. If your son or daughter is younger and unwilling to accept help, then seek it for yourself so you'll have some expert guidance in dealing with what's going on in your child's life.

Avoid Making Ultimatums

Often when we feel desperate as parents, we are tempted to issue an ultimatum: "It's my way or the highway." These ultimatums are often unenforceable or do lasting harm to the parent-child relationship. But if you take the time to back off, calm down and reconsider, there are often intermediate steps that will be more effective. We highly recommend Ross Greene's collaborative problem-solving approach if you find your family up against a truly difficult situation. This works best if you have used this method as your son or daughter has been growing up, but it can be a game changer at any age (Greene, 2017; Lives in the Balance, n.d.).

Dr. Greene views the challenges our children and teens face as "lagging skills and unsolved problems." His most well-known quotation also expresses his philosophy: *"Children will do well if they can!"* Here are the three basic steps:

- *Empathize.* Take the time to listen and empathize with your teen's concerns, and understand what is happening from her point of view. Say, "We have a problem, and I really want to hear what you think about it."
- *State parental concerns.* Next, clearly define your concerns. Be specific: "The current situation is a problem. These are my concerns ..."
- *Suggest brainstorming a solution.* Finally, brainstorm a path forward together. "We have to come to an agreement on how to fix this problem. I want to hear your ideas on what we can do together to make it different."

Without a doubt, following these steps is not an easy task to do well. But it can be a way forward when you have reached an impasse with your teen. For more guidance on problem solving, visit Dr. Ross Greene's website: www.livesinthebalance.org. Here you will find tools for assessment of lagging skills and unsolved problems (ASLUP). This tool offers families guidance and a springboard for discussion of these types of issues. If your family is in a place where this discussion can't happen successfully, then consider finding a therapist or family counselor to help you sort it out.

Perils After High School Graduation

Teens and young adults with ADHD often can't accurately evaluate their abilities and challenges, according to Dr. Russell Barkley. So parents and teens may not see eye to eye about readiness for the next steps after high school graduation. Some of our young people are overconfident, while others are too anxious to try something new. That doesn't mean that the parents are always right, either, so be careful in assuming that you're right. We sometimes lag behind in seeing our children's growth. Let's look at some of the common problems faced by our young adults.

Differences of Opinion about Readiness for College

Sometimes parents have very different perceptions of college readiness from that of their teen. For example, they may disagree about the young person's ability to independently handle the increased workload and lack of instructor feedback, her willingness to request and use needed accommodations, or her ability to finish work on time in the face of many distractions.

If you and your son or daughter haven't already completed the College Readiness Survey (CRS) in the Appendix as suggested earlier, then do that now. Next, spend some time discussing the results. Results of the survey provide a neutral springboard for discussion that doesn't put you in the position of having to tell your teen her shortcomings with regard to college readiness. Rather, taking the survey gives her the opportunity to come to her own conclusions and increase her self-awareness.

- *Discuss whether she can handle academic responsibilities.* Attend class regularly and on time, keep up with assignments, complete homework/reports, do required lab work or long-term projects, study for tests, notify instructors of accommodations, register for classes by the due date, and seek tutoring or ask the instructor for help if struggling academically.
- *Plant a seed regarding different options.* Suggest that your son or daughter consider getting a part-time job and taking one course at the community college. Or the two of you could create a personalized gap year program. A gap year would give her more time to figure out exactly what she wants to do with her life.
- *Be careful of underestimating your young adult's skills.* Our children may overestimate their abilities, but parents often underestimate what they can accomplish. Over many years Ruth learned to trust her son's assessment because he was right more often than she was. As a parent, you are looking at the past, while your young adult is looking at the future. If there is significant disagreement, ask your son or daughter to demonstrate ability in a particular area before leaving home.
- *Ultimately, the decision may not be your teen's.* The decision may actually be determined for her. For example, if her grades and scores on entrance exams are low, she may not be accepted to the college of her choice. Or your family simply may not be able to afford all the expenses associated with attending college and perhaps living away from home.

Disagreements About Readiness to Live Away from Home

Perhaps you and your teen agree that the next step ought to be college but disagree about whether she should live at home and take classes at a local college or technical institute or go away to school. Hopefully the two of you can agree upon a solution.

Spread out discussions over time. Break up discussions about life skills into smaller chunks to avoid overwhelming your teen. As you talk about independent living skills, you may ask her if she thinks she's ready to take on all these responsibilities. Is she currently doing a good job of handling them? Is she willing to take on more of these tasks now? Discuss how she might handle specific tasks such as getting prescriptions filled when she is away at school or being on time to class every day.

- *Manage daily living.* Discuss her ability to independently ensure that she gets adequate sleep, gets up on time, keeps an orderly living space, does the laundry, eats healthy meals on a regular basis, manages her time wisely and balances time spent on academics and socializing.
- *Act responsibly.* Can she follow college rules, drive responsibly, avoid excessive partying and drinking and avoid drug use? If there is a possibility of a public health emergency, can she follow the guidelines for wearing a mask, social distancing or other precautions set by the college?

- *Manage medication.* Can she take medication daily, refill prescriptions in a timely manner, properly store medication, and not share meds with others?
- *Manage finances.* Can she live within a budget; avoid overdrafts; responsibly use a credit, debit or ATM card; pay required fees promptly; keep records of specific amounts paid for books, tuition, lab fees and other expenses that parents need to keep track of when using a 529 plan (a tax-advantaged college savings plan started years earlier); pay rent, utilities, internet and phone if living off campus?

Most likely, your son or daughter is not currently handling all these tasks. So have her take on some additional responsibilities like filling her own weekly medicine container, washing her clothes, or getting prescriptions filled. For other tasks, identify which supports she needs to successfully make the transition to handling them independently. For example, bills such as rent can be paid through the bank's automatic bill payment system.

- *Identify an area that needs improvement.* Ask her which daily living skills she'd like to practice first.
- *Start early and small.* Tackle one thing at a time. You are building success, not setting her up for failure.
- *Don't expect perfection*, but look for improvement. Being late to school one day a week is much better than being late three days a week.
- *Celebrate successes.*

"Get Real" Tip: If your teen has mastered many readiness skills and is adamant about living away from home, find ways to help her compensate so that she can be successful. For example, just managing academics was about all that Chris's son could manage his first year in college. So medication containers were filled, clothes were washed and prescriptions refilled when he came home on weekends. Most routine bills were automatically paid online.

Academic Failure

Many, many students with ADHD and learning challenges experience difficulty in college. Far too many drop out. Forty percent of all freshmen, not just those with ADHD, don't make it to graduation within six years. The best intervention is prevention, but if your son or daughter fails or drops out of school, he or she will be coming home with a huge sense of failure and embarrassment and will probably be depressed. This is a high-risk time for acting out impulsively and may result in complications such as an unwanted pregnancy or dangerous behavior such as drinking excessively or driving recklessly. Some young people may even consider suicide.

Home needs to be a safe harbor, a place to recover. Again, this doesn't mean hiding, but rather coming home to a place where your son or daughter feels valued and loved and is in a safe setting for planning next steps. As a parent you may feel disappointed and upset about all the money you spent on college costs. But no matter how bad you feel, your young adult feels many times worse. So put it in perspective and be there to help her.

Here are some steps to take now:

- *Monitor your young adult's mental health.* The period after dropping out can be a *high-risk time*, so be assertive in making sure your son or daughter gets whatever assistance is needed sooner rather than later. In addition to the academic ramifications, she's likely to be depressed and anxious and in need of professional help. Because of the depression, it will be harder for her to initiate the steps needed to ask for assistance. She may need your help to move forward.

- *Identify causes of bad grades.* Sort out what the problems were that led to failing grades. Was it lack of studying, too many social activities, the wrong school for your student's needs, lack of direction, a need for different accommodations, or a need for medication or counseling? Your student is telling you through her actions that attending college at this time did not work. Something needs to change. Figuring out what must change is essential.
- *Regroup and identify passions.* Help your young adult identify what she is passionate about so she can begin planning next steps as soon as possible. If there is a clear goal and a high level of interest, she is far more likely to be successful. Refer to an earlier chapter on helping teens find their passion.
- *Plan a gap year.* If she is not ready for total independence, start working on a gap year plan with activities to help her mature and identify career interests.
- *Explore pursuing a career without a degree.* If the career path she selects doesn't require a college degree, begin planning what the next steps are to pursue this career. Refer to guidance in Chapter 10 regarding options after high school.
- *Look for a college that is a better fit.* If her desired career does require a college degree, consider whether she should immediately get back into a college with the supports needed to be successful. This may mean finding a school that is a better fit. Your goal is to help her find a school where she will be successful.
- *Add supports upon returning to school.* If your son or daughter is returning to a college environment, then overload on supports in the beginning. Your student can back off from the supports when they are no longer needed. Helpful supports and accommodations are discussed in earlier chapters that focus on success in college.

Medication Mismanagement

Your teen or young adult will discover that stimulant medication has monetary value among her peers. Once your young adult leaves home, if not before, she will be asked by others to share or sell her stimulant medication. If she is not prepared for handling this, the easiest thing to do is to say yes. Young people want to be liked by their friends, and saying no is difficult. This is particularly common on college campuses. Discuss strategies for handling these situations.

- *Practice managing meds.* Have your teenager begin managing her medication while still at home. That means filling her weekly medication container, taking medication regularly, picking up new prescriptions and making doctor appointments. Start with one or two steps and then add others. The time to learn these routines is not *after* your son or daughter leaves home. Do it sooner.
- *Keep medication in a lockbox.* Discuss the best way to keep medications safe while away from home. The goal is to keep others from helping themselves to your student's medication. Many young people with ADHD have lost some or all their medication when it was stolen.
- *Keep meds in original prescription containers.* Some people think that keeping medication in an unlabeled bottle is a good way to discourage other people from taking it. But if your son or daughter is stopped by the police for any reason, having stimulants in an

unlabeled container could lead to legal problems such as questions regarding possession or selling of illegal drugs.

- *Don't ever share or sell medication.* Be sure your son or daughter understands that sharing or selling stimulant medication is a felony and can lead to school expulsion. Stimulants are a controlled substance, and sharing is a serious crime.
- *Give the words to say no.* Discuss possible answers to use when someone asks for medication: "I have exactly enough medication to cover me each day. If I give any away, I won't have enough medication for myself." The most common scenario is that a young person who takes stimulant medication is approached the night before an exam or on the weekend before a party and asked to share her stimulant medication. Figuring out how to say no and still be cool is a challenge.
- *Educate friends to say no.* Encourage your son or daughter to enlist the help of others in saying no to sharing meds. Most college students don't approve of sharing stimulant medication but stay silent when they see it happen. Roommates and friends can chime in and provide support to your teen if others ask her to share her meds.
- *Be aware of potential health risks.* Young people need to know that stimulants can have a serious effect on friends with some health conditions. If a student has an undiagnosed heart condition, for instance, stimulant medication can make it worse. That's why an individual should never take an ADHD medication unless a doctor has prescribed it for her.

Poor Financial Management

One of the challenges for many young people is managing money successfully. If a young adult is impulsive, it will be hard for her to budget and manage her finances so that all the bases are covered.

Ruth's Lessons Learned: When my son, Christopher, first started working, I helped him open a joint checking account for students. And of course, an ATM card came with the account. The ATM was this magic machine that supplied money whenever he needed, resulting in large fees for overdrawing from his account, often by small amounts.

At first, I covered the fees and talked with him about the importance of checking what was in his account. Not surprisingly, this was not an effective intervention. But the real world can be a wonderful teacher. I forewarned my son that he would need to cover future overdraft fees from his own funds. And my charismatic son talked the bank manager out of the fees the first couple of times. But after paying the fees multiple times, he began to modify his behavior. Today he is responsible with his funds. It is crucial our offspring learn to manage their money while they are still at home.

Here are some steps to follow to help your son or daughter master money management skills:

- *Educate about checking and savings accounts.* Help your son or daughter set up accounts with the bank. Explain how to use ATMs, deposit funds (with a cell phone or at an ATM or bank), and schedule automatic payment of bills as much as possible.
- *Proceed cautiously with credit cards.* Every young person wants a credit or debit card, and every credit card company wants her to have one, too. Consider a prepaid credit card as the first step to preventing runaway debt. Studies have shown that a person with a

credit card will spend, on average, 8 percent more than the same person using cash. If possible, go over bills with your son or daughter and point out how quickly interest accumulates.

- *Explore electronic payment options.* If you are not already experienced in using payment options like PayPal and Venmo, you may need to learn along with your young adult. Or this may be an opportunity for her to teach you. But using these systems is increasingly important in our changing world.
- *Work out a spending plan.* Help your young adult list all her expenses and sources of income and create a budget.
- *Expect difficulties living within a budget.* Work with her on money management skills including responsibly using credit cards and spending within her financial resources. If she overspends her budget while she's still financially dependent on you, find ways for her to earn money to repay you or encourage her to get a part-time job so she'll have more spending money.
- *Don't dictate how monetary gifts should be spent.* When your teen or young adult receives a gift of money, allow her to decide how to use these funds. While she may not use the funds the same way you would, she will learn from the experience.
- *Carefully consider taking on student loans.* Getting a student loan can be a wonderful idea if it's the only way a young person can go to college, but beware of higher interest rates that may saddle your son or daughter with a lifetime of debt. Find out what interest rates your bank offers and compare them with government student loans. Income-eligible students are eligible for subsidized and unsubsidized student loans with relatively low interest rates that can be paid back over many years, but debt can add up quickly. It's important for both you and your teen to understand the various kinds of loans and the implications of debt after college. If possible, pay upfront for as many expenses as possible and then borrow the remainder. A great resource from the federal government is "Federal Student Loans: Basics for Students," (Federal Student Aid, n.d.) The entire Student Aid site at https://studentaid.gov is full of good information on paying for college.
- *Avoid too much student debt.* Seventy percent of college graduates have student loans, and the average debt in 2017 was $37,172, although some graduates had debts closer to $100,000. Heavy debts can significantly delay other financial milestones—marriage, buying a home or having a baby. Milestones are often occurring at a much later age for today's millennials, largely because of the impact of student loans on their lives. The harm is greatest for those who don't graduate and have difficulty getting a good job but still have significant student loan debt.

Losing a Job

Despite our best preparations, sometimes a job is a bad fit or a young person is not ready to do the required work, and it all falls apart. So how can you help your son or daughter recover if he or she has lost a job?

- *Plan an exit strategy when possible.* If an employee anticipates being fired and plans to quit, it's crucial to give two weeks' notice. One of the most common mistakes made by inexperienced employees is walking off the job with no notice. This is almost always an emotional and impulsive decision. If you know your young person is struggling and anticipating leaving, be sure to work with her to plan a positive exit strategy.

- *Don't vent anger and frustration about the firing at work.* The person fired needs to leave in as professional a manner as possible. If your daughter calls from work to say she has been fired, your most important job is to help her get to a calm place where she can exit with as little drama as possible. For instance, you could coach her to say to the supervisor, "I'm really surprised and upset. Could I please come back tomorrow to finish this conversation when I can think more clearly?"
- *Help your young adult grieve the lost job.* But encourage her to express her anger and mourn the job loss at home and with friends not connected to the job. Then she can safely vent all she wants. It is likely to be a combination of anger, hurt, fear about what comes next, regret and frustration. Eventually it also means taking a step back and learning from what happened. It means taking ownership of the things that she had control of and letting go of those that she had no control over. Help her know it's safe to vent and mourn for a while, but then it's time to move on.
- *Apply for unemployment benefits.* Every state has different eligibility requirements, so be sure to check out what the rules are in your state. Just because a person has been fired doesn't mean she's ineligible. It may well depend on the circumstances. Not only does unemployment provide some financial relief, but the rules provide the structure and support for looking for a new job.
- *Figure out what happened.* When the anger and frustration have calmed down, talk about what happened. This is not about blame but about learning from the experience. Even if the supervisor was the problem, your son or daughter needs to learn how to manage problematic bosses. There will undoubtedly be other difficult bosses at some point. Explore if any accommodations would have helped your young adult do the job more effectively (ADA.gov, n.d.; Job Accommodations Network, n.d.).
- *Renew the search to find the passion.* Revisit the process of helping your young adult find her passion. If she loves the work, other job difficulties become more manageable. It will help to find a job in her area of interest, even if it's a part-time position.

If your son or daughter is having difficulty, go back and reread Chapter 17 on launching a career. It's important that he or she begins to apply for other jobs fairly soon after losing a job. The guidance provided for job searching, preparing for an interview and getting help with the job search will be helpful.

Ruth's Lessons Learned: I once had to fire a young man who was chronically late for work and didn't get his work done. When leaving, he took ownership of his work problems and thanked me for the experience of working for our company. He thanked his coworkers and wished them well. I know he was able to get references from some of our staff, including me, and it was due to his professional demeanor when he left. The message to your young adult: *don't burn your bridges*.

Reluctance to Accept or Ask for Needed Help

Just when our young adults are experimenting with independence and are most likely to deny they need help from a parent or a professional, the rules change and the responsibility to ask for accommodations, medication and counseling now belongs to them. Paralyzing anxiety and depression may well play a role in reluctance to ask for help. Parents will need lots of patience to help their son or daughter get through these difficult times.

What do you do when your adult child won't talk with you about next steps? Hopefully, her reluctance to accept your help will not spiral downward into a destructive power struggle. If you have to resort to imposing consequences for inaction, life will become unpleasant for you both. If she is living at home (or financially dependent on you), you still control many aspects of her life: cell phones, internet access, rent, allowance, etc. If you suspect a power struggle may erupt, encourage her to seek outside help from an ADHD coach or treatment professional.

Remember that you actually have more influence than you think. Try not to descend into shouting matches. Stay calm but insist that she work with you to plan the next steps.

- *Discuss plans for the future.* Talk about your son's or daughter's plans for the next year. Listen carefully to his or her thoughts and concerns about the next steps. If she is reluctant to discuss her plans, ask why: "Help me understand why you don't want to talk about your future plans." She may be confused and overwhelmed. Plus, it may be a combination of embarrassment, fear of failure, anxiety, a push for independence or a plea to "accept me as the person I am."
- *Acknowledge concerns.* Acknowledge her concerns and feelings once you understand them. Figure out how you can work together to allay concerns.
- *Suggest options.* Always suggest two or three solutions or possible actions. Make it clear that inaction is not a choice. Hiding in the basement playing video games all day is not an option.
- *Develop a plan.* Work with her to develop an action plan of small steps that will create some positive momentum.
- *Get help.* An ADHD coach or therapist can work with her (or you) to make progress.
- *Take advantage of real-world consequences.* When real-world consequences underscore problems, that gives you an opening. Don't place blame, but use this as an opportunity to suggest a different path.

Getting Help. If you are unable to help your young adult resolve her problem or she would prefer to get assistance from someone else, help her figure out where to get help:

- Identify the problem and what kind of help is needed.
- Talk to other parents who have children, teens and young adults with ADHD and find out what local resources are available.
- Check with ADHD advocacy groups for suggestions of local resources.
- Call a couple of professionals, do a quick phone interview, and look for folks who specialize in serving people with ADHD. Ask them:
  - Do you have a waiting list?
  - What services do you provide?
  - Have you received specific training in ADHD?
  - What percentage of the people you serve have ADHD?
- Suggest that your young adult choose from a couple of professionals, if possible. Ideally, it would be great for you to meet and interview the professionals. However, limited time and money and privacy laws may not allow this as an option. Giving your son or daughter a choice of professionals can be a good way to overcome resistance.
- If your son or daughter is not making any progress in resolving the problem, suggest finding someone else to assist him or her.

Refusing Medication or Treatment

Once teens are legally considered adults (age 18 in most states), they become responsible for consenting to medical treatment without a parent's involvement. And not surprisingly, some young people decide they no longer need treatment for ADHD or for other conditions like anxiety or bipolar disorder. It's a period in their lives when they desperately want to be like their peers and are rebelling against the things their parents insisted upon. Ruth's son Christopher would mimic Popeye, saying, "I am what I am," when she discussed his desire to stop medication at 18.

As parents, we need to remember the ultimate goal is to have our young people manage their own lives. Their bodies change as they mature, and a few may be able to function well without medication. If they have learned good coping skills and have the ongoing support of a doctor, counselor or coach, they may be successful without medication. Ultimately our teens need to figure out the role of medication and treatment in their lives as adults.

Here are some suggestions for navigating this time:

- *Suggest a trial without medication.* If your son or daughter wants to stop taking medication, try proposing a time-limited trial without medication or treatment. In other words, honor her concerns, but also try to reduce the chances of potential negative outcomes. Make a very short list of major problems that might develop, and see if she will agree to go back to treatment if they occur. Examples of major problems might include grades dropping significantly, speeding tickets or a car accident, or angry outbursts that are consistently out of bounds.
- *Negotiate a medication plan.* Often the emotional baggage between the parent and young person makes this a difficult process. A treatment professional can provide information about the possible outcomes in a much more neutral manner. Suggest that your teen or young adult ask the doctor or counselor to work with her to develop a plan for a medication-free trial. A doctor will also help her understand that some medications (some antidepressants) need to be tapered off instead of stopping cold turkey. Hopefully this discussion will include reasons why your son or daughter should consider using medication or seek counseling again.
- *Clarify expectations.* Develop reasonable expectations for academic success, safe driving and other behaviors. Parents need to be clear about baseline expectations of behavior and under what circumstances they will continue paying for tuition, car insurance, etc. Young people with ADHD have to work harder to limit impulsiveness, focus on studying, and keep on task. They need to understand that these expectations will not change if they're no longer taking medication.
- *Don't expect your son or daughter to be perfect.* Stuff happens. Be careful not to attribute any changes in behavior to stopping medication. But do respond to any behavior that is extreme or can cause serious consequences.
- *Assess progress.* Agree ahead of time to a date to jointly evaluate how the medication-free trial has gone. Try to do this in as objective a manner as possible. Hopefully your young adult will be able to see the benefits of medication or counseling and evaluate what she needs in the short term. And it's possible that she'll have developed the skills to cope successfully without medication most of the time. Counseling or coaching is not intended to be a lifelong process. Young people may need some time to test out what they have learned on their own. If counseling ends well, they will be open to returning when needed.

- *Ask for permission to speak with her therapist.* You might consider asking your young adult if she is willing to sign a HIPAA privacy release. This would allow the treating professional to share information with you, particularly if she's struggling to manage her own health care needs. Check out this link for more information and a release form you can use: www.simplemost.com/parents-rights-under-hipaa-when-kids-arent-minors.
- *Watch out for crises.* Because life is challenging, there will be times when the symptoms of ADHD become problematic and affect functioning. Major life transitions, like leaving home to go to college, starting a new job, breaking up with a significant other or getting married, for example, may be times that medication and or counseling will be helpful.

And When All Else Fails

If your son or daughter is in trouble and isn't willing to accept help or hear your concerns, then consider seeking therapy or counseling for yourself as a parent. This support can help you think through any actions you are considering taking and the possible consequences more carefully. Therapy can also help you to grieve the (hopefully temporary) loss of your relationship with your young adult.

Our Most Important Role

The list of possible problems in this chapter is not comprehensive and doesn't address some of the more serious problems that young adults with ADHD may face, but the same concepts apply in helping your young person survive most bumps along the road and begin to thrive again. Remember, our most important role is to help our children heal and learn from the crisis they are experiencing. You'll have to process your own feelings of disappointment, anger and frustration. But remember that your son's or daughter's experience is much more intense than yours. If counseling or a medication adjustment is needed, be sure to take action and help make it happen.

There Is Light at the End of the Tunnel

When our sons were struggling through their teen and young adult years, we felt incredible fear and anxiety. We worried about how they could possibly cope in the future. At times the journey was made even more difficult because family and friends thought our parenting strategies were all wrong. Sadly, you've probably experienced these same ambivalent emotions.

But there is good news: our sons have not only survived but are happy and thriving as adults. We as their parents feel such incredible joy seeing their achievements and knowing in our hearts that all the hard work and loving support to see them succeed was well worth the long wait. In addition, parents of now-grown children with ADHD who completed our survey have mirrored our experience. Over and over again, we heard stories of their grown sons and daughters who have been quite successful.

Here are a few final words of advice:

- Don't ever stop believing in your child, in yourself and in your ability to cope with whatever challenges arise.
- Do whatever it takes to help your child succeed in school and life.
- Be patient; give your son or daughter the gift of enough time to mature.

- Remember that the immature child or teen of today will be a more mature young person in five years—and even more mature in another five to ten years.
- Make your home a safe haven.

While the transition to adulthood can be more than a bit tumultuous for our young people, they will find their way. Our late bloomers *can* thrive and usually do.

Our next chapter is a celebration of hope and highlights the achievements of many young people with ADHD who have made successful transitions to their adult lives. This can be the outcome for your son or daughter, too. Hopefully we have helped you with information, strategies and insights that we both wish we had had years ago when our young men were transitioning to adulthood. It's our greatest hope that our learning experience may make your son's or daughter's transition to young adulthood a bit easier, not only for him or her, but for the whole family.

PC: When trying to help your teenager with ADHD prepare for life after high school, please remember this is their future and it may look different from the one you have planned for them. This is OK. Teenagers with ADHD may not be ready to make those life decisions when their peers are. This is OK. Remember, you want your child to find the best educational or career fit for them so they will be successful in their own time. Always remember, it is not their job to make us happy. It is our job to accept our child as they really are, love them for who they are and see the potential for who they can become. They can't do it alone. They need our unconditional love, support, guidance and acceptance.

References

ADA.gov. (n.d.). *The Americans with disabilities act protects people from discrimination.* Retrieved January 27, 2023, from https://www.ada.gov/

Federal Student Aid. (n.d.). *Federal student aid basics for students.* Studentaid.gov. Retrieved January 27, 2023, from https://studentaid.gov/sites/default/files/direct-loan-basics-students.pdf

Greene, R.W. (2017). *Raising human beings: Creating a collaborative partnership with your child.* Scribner.

Job Accommodation Network. (n.d.). *Job accommodation network.* Retrieved January 27, 2023, from https://askjan.org/

Lives in the Balance. (n.d.). *Different lenses, different practices, different outcomes.* Retrieved January 27, 2023, from http://www.livesinthebalance.org/Our-solution

20 Our Photo Gallery of Hope

Although children with ADHD may struggle during their school years, rest assured they *can* achieve happiness and success in life. The key is to help them find their special niche where they will excel. We're honored to feature several successful young adults who have tenaciously pursued their talents in spite of the occasional "speed bumps" of life. Nothing deterred them from finding their true passion in life.

Over the course of the last 30 years, Chris has followed these young people from their teen and preteen years to adulthood. All of them have been featured in her books and videos, during panel discussions, as conference speakers and in individual interviews with her. After all, these young adults are the true experts on their own ADHD. They've provided excellent insightful advice based upon the lessons they've learned from living with ADHD.

Thirty-Year Follow-Up from School Struggles to Present: Adults Living Successfully with ADHD

Alex Zeigler and wife Haley
(Coauthor Chris Dendy's son Alex)
Author, publisher, webmaster
Property management
Alabama

Christopher Hughes
(Coauthor Ruth Hughes's Son)
Park ranger
Anne Arundel County
Maryland

DOI: 10.4324/9781003364092-20

Lewis Alston
Emcee for Atlanta Gladiators
Events emcee, Polaris RZR & Red Bull
Patriots Auto Wash, general manager
Georgia

Chad McMurray (Marcia)
Electrician, PLC technician
HSN, maintenance III
Tennessee

Shawn Clippinger
US Marine
Director of business development
Kenco Logistics
Georgia

Khris Royal
Musician, producer
Dark Matter Band, founder
Louisiana

Amelia Hart
World history teacher
County Teacher of the Year
Specialty cake baker
Florida

Kati Schmidt
Artist, instructor
New mom
Tennessee

Erik Robertson (Carolyn)
Senior project manager
The Spur Group
Washington

Perry Green III
Nonprofit and political consultant
California

Nathan Grabowski
Dendy's grandson
Tennessee State Sales Manager
Monday Night Brewing
Tennessee

Hunter Dendy
Dendy's grandson
Outside sales representative
Rierson Corporation
North Carolina

Max Fennell
Professional triathlete
Fenn Coffee, owner
California

Tyler Howell
Director of Development
Our Generation for the Next
Red Bank City Commissioner
Tennessee

Alyssa Rock
Quality assurance engineer
AMD
Florida

Robert Green
Youth specialist
Missouri Department of Social
Services
Missouri

Samie Robertson
Customer service representative
Weed Man Lawn Care
Kentucky

Appendix 1
ADHD Iceberg Form

The ADD/ADHD Iceberg Chart

The Tip of the Iceberg—the obvious ADD/ADHD behaviors:

HYPERACTIVITY	IMPULSIVITY	INATTENTION

3 YEAR BRAIN MATURATION
30% DEVELOPMENTAL DELAY
Less mature
Less responsible
14 year old acts like 10

"Hidden Beneath the Surface"—
the not-so-obvious behaviors:

NEUROTRANSMITTER
DEFICITS IMPACT BEHAVIOR
Inefficient levels of neurotransmitters (norepinephrine, dopamine, and serotonin) result in reduced brain activity on thinking tasks

COEXISTING CONDITIONS
(2/3 have at least one other condition)

WEAK EXECUTIVE FUNCTIONING

SERIOUS LEARNING PROBLEMS (90%)
(Specific Learning Disability; 25-50%)

ADD/ADHD is often more complex than most people realize! Like icebergs, many problems related to ADD/ADHD are not visible. ADD/ADHD may be mild, moderate, or severe, is likely to co-exist with other conditions, and may be a disability for some students.

SLEEP DISTURBANCE (56%)

LOW FRUSTRATION TOLERANCE
(Difficulty Controlling Emotions)

IMPAIRED SENSE OF TIME

NOT LEARNING EASILY FROM REWARDS AND PUNISHMENT

Figure A.1 Blank ADHD Iceberg form.

Appendix 2
Academic and Behavioral Performance Rating Scale

Current Academic and Behavioral Performance
Teacher Rating

Student's Name:_____ Date & Class: _____

Completed by: _____ Time of Day Observed: _____

To identify current academic or behavior challenges, each teacher should answer several key questions. Please circle the answer that best describes the student's behavior and academic performance.

Academic Performance:

When the student is in my class, s/he	Strongly agree	Agree	Neutral	Disagree	Strongly disagree
1. Pays attention	1	2	3	4	5
2. Completes class and homework	1	2	3	4	5
3. Does work correctly	1	2	3	4	5
4. Complies with requests	1	2	3	4	5
5. Makes passing grades	1	2	3	4	5
6. Manages time well	1	2	3	4	5

Other Challenges: Are there any other behaviors that are interfering with the student's ability to succeed in school?

The student	Strongly agree	Agree	Neutral	Disagree	Strongly disagree
7. Organizes materials/information well	1	2	3	4	5
8. Gets started easily on work	1	2	3	4	5
9. Writes essays and reports easily	1	2	3	4	5
10. Does well in math/Algebra	1	2	3	4	5
11. Finishes long-term projects easily	1	2	3	4	5
12. Has good working memory	1	2	3	4	5
13. Memorizes information easily	1	2	3	4	5
14. Works more slowly than peers	1	2	3	4	5
15. Thinks carefully before acting or speaking	1	2	3	4	5
16. Is awake and alert in class	1	2	3	4	5
17. Stares into space, "zones out"	1	2	3	4	5
18. Is on time to class	1	2	3	4	5
19. Is on time to school	1	2	3	4	5

Comments:

_____

_____

Figure A.2 Academic and Behavioral Performance Rating Scale.

Appendix 3
College Readiness Survey

The College Readiness Survey for Parents: How Ready Is Your Teen?[*]

Will your teen be successful in college, or will your teen be one of the students who doesn't return for a second year or does not graduate? This survey was created from interviews with college students and what is known about what it takes to be successful in college. Think about your teen as you rate each item on a scale from 1 to 3, with 1 = My teen hardly ever does this, 2 = My teen does this sometimes, and 3 = My teen does this most of the time. Have your teen complete the teen's version of this survey[1] as well. Have a conversation about what areas are strengths and what areas are weaknesses, and make a plan to improve any areas you both rated as a 1 or a 2. Set one or two goals for each grading period throughout the year, and then retake the survey to chart progress and select new goals.

Self-Determination Skills

I.   **Self-Knowledge**
     My teen knows and is aware of his/her

____ Talents, interests, and dreams for the future.
____ Feelings and reactions when adjusting to new people, places, and situations and what helps during the adjustment process.
____ Strengths and weaknesses in academic and learning skills.

Self-knowledge score: ____/9 × 100 + ____%

II. **Self-Advocacy**
     My teen can

____ Easily introduce himself/herself to new people and hold conversations with others.
____ Clearly express his/her strengths and weaknesses to teachers or other people.
____ Admit when he/she doesn't understand something in class and comfortably ask for help.
____ Easily find the help or support he/she needs when any problem arises.

---

[*] Republished with permission of Magination Press, from *Ready for Take-Off: Preparing Your Teen with ADHD or LD for College*, by Theresa E. Laurie Maitland and Patricia O. Quinn, 2011; permission conveyed through Copyright Clearance Center, Inc.

____ Express his/her thoughts well, even when he/she has a different view or opinion, and stand firm when needed.

____ Talk with the other people involved when there is a conflict and problem solve to resolve the situation.

Self-advocacy score: ____/18 × 100 = ____%

III. Self-Management
My teen can

____ Listen and understand what his/her friends and family members are saying about him/her without becoming defensive.

____ Regularly set realistic goals in all areas of life.

____ Develop a plan to reach his/her goals and put them into action.

____ Periodically think about his/her progress in reaching these goals and make modifications as needed.

____ Persistently deal with any challenge without becoming frustrated until he/she finds an acceptable solution.

____ Observe his/her emotions and deal with them productively.

Self-management score: ____/18 × 100 = ____%
Your total Self-Determination Skills score: ____/45 × 100 = ____%

Daily Living Skills

I. Self-Care
My teen can

____ Wash and care for his/her own clothes.

____ Take any medication he/she needs with few or no reminders.

____ Make his/her own doctor appointments and call to refill prescription medications.

____ Prepare meals or choose healthy foods for daily meals.

____ Get adequate exercise to remain healthy.

____ Manage money well and be trusted with credit cards.

____ Use acceptable strategies to manage stress.

Self-care score: ____/21 × 100 = ____%

II. Organization
My teen can

____ Organize his/her room and possessions with few or no reminders.

____ Keep track of his/her important possessions and find them when needed.

Organization score: ____/6 × 100 = ____%

III. Time Management
My teen can

____ Awaken himself/herself each day and get out the door without any help from me.

____ Send himself/herself to bed each night at a reasonable time without any reminders from me.

____ Make good decisions and know how to balance his/her time between fun, chores, and schoolwork.

____ Get places on time with no problem.

Time-management score: ____/12 × 100 = ____%

Your total Daily Living Skills score: ____/39 × 100 = ____%

Academic Skills

I. **Self-Knowledge**
    My teen knows

____ His/her learning style and can find ways to help himself/herself learn and study best in different classes.
____ When and where he/she needs to study for the best results.
____ How to get motivated to face difficult assignments.

Self-knowledge score: ____/9 × 100 = ____%

II. **Study Skills**
    My teen knows how to

____ Take notes from reading assignments.
____ Take complete notes in class that are useful when he/she studies for exams.
____ Identify what's important when he/she is reading.
____ Organize his/her ideas and write and edit his/her papers.
____ Prepare for tests and final exams.
____ Review class notes, assigned reading, and other materials on a regular basis.
____ Use the help available in school when he/she doesn't understand something or wants to improve how he/she studies.

Study skills score: ____/21 × 100 = ____%

III. **Time Management**
     My teen can

____ Set up his/her own study schedule.
____ Consistently complete daily assigned homework.
____ Develop a system to keep track of due dates for all assignments.
____ Stay on top of his/her reading assignments and has ways to comprehend what he/she reads.
____ Write assigned papers, prepare for tests, and complete long-term projects in a timely manner.

Time-management score: ____/15 × 100 = ____%
Your total Academic Skills score: ____/45 × 100 = ____%

Now total the number of skills rated 2 or less: TOTAL = ____
You will use this score on the Skills Analysis Worksheet on the following page.

Skills Analysis Worksheet: Analyzing Your Survey Answers

1. Which skill area displays strengths (rated highest)? Add up the numbers and circle one of the skill areas listed below that corresponds to the highest score.

Self-determination Skills:	• Self-knowledge • Self-management	• Self-advocacy
Daily Living Skills:	• Self-care • Time management	• Organization
Academic Skills:	• Self-knowledge • Time management	• Study skills

2. Which skill area needs to improve the most? Add up the numbers and circle one that corresponds to the lowest score.

Self-determination Skills:	• Self-knowledge • Self-management	• Self-advocacy
Daily Living Skills:	• Self-care • Time management	• Organization
Academic Skills:	• Self-knowledge • Time management	• Study skills

3. Go back and look at the areas that you and your teen agreed were rated below 3. How many of the skills did you rate 2 or lower? ____ Total

4. Now count how many weeks until college begins: ____ weeks. Divide this number by the total number of skills rated 2 or lower. This will give an estimate of how many weeks remain to work on each skill before college begins.

    Total skills rated 2 or lower ____ / ____ number of weeks until college

Note

1 Only the parent's version is included in this book. Completing the parent's version will give you a good idea of your teen's readiness to enroll in college right after high school. For the teen's version, see *Ready for Take-Off* (publication information in the previous footnote on page 208).

Appendix 4
Sample Gap Year Plans

Sample Gap Year Plan with Action Goals

Amanda's Vocational Goals: Explore a Career in the Food Industry

1. Find a part-time job in a food-related business

Action Step 1: Make a list of local restaurants that she can easily get to without a car.
- June 15: Amanda will begin a list of local restaurants, including addresses, phone numbers, and websites.
- July 1: Amanda will have a list of 20 restaurants to call or apply online for a job.

Action Step 2: Ask people to provide a reference.
- June 22: Amanda and Mom will develop and practice a script for asking for a reference.
- June 23: Amanda will make calls to ask for references.
- June 30: Amanda will have completed all calls and gathered contact information for references.

Action Step 3: Develop a résumé that highlights her cooking experience. Have Dad look at it and make suggestions for improvements.
- July 2: Amanda will meet with Dad and look at examples of résumés.
- July 7: Amanda will have a draft résumé completed.
- July 8: Amanda will meet with Dad to review and refine.
- July 10: Amanda will edit the résumé and make clean copies.

Action Step 4: Prepare for an interview.
- July 8: Amanda will meet with Aunt Rose and make a list of interview questions.
- July 9: Get pointers from Aunt Rose on how to handle a phone interview vs. an in-person one.
- July 9–12: Amanda will practice answering interview questions one hour a day with Aunt Rose until she feels comfortable.

Action Step 5: Call restaurants to ask about a part-time job in the kitchen.
- July 12: Amanda will work with Dad to make notes on what to say on the call and write out a script asking if jobs are available.
- July 13: Amanda will practice what she will say when making the call.
- July 15 plus: Amanda will make 3 calls daily and make notes of the response from each restaurant.

Action Step 6: Apply for jobs online.
- July 15 plus: Amanda will apply online for each opening that she identifies from her phone calls. At least one application a day until she has a job.

Action Step 7: Go to interviews when scheduled.
- Two days before: figure out what to wear to the interview and make sure clothes are clean and ready to go.
- One day before: check directions to get to interview site and identify parking options. Practice the route if necessary.
- Day of interview: Amanda will check to make sure everything is ready (clothes, résumé, directions, etc.) and then concentrate on relaxing. Each interview is a practice for the next one.
- Day of interview: Leave for interview allowing for arrival 15 minutes before to be sure there are no problems.
- Day after interview: The day after her interview, Amanda will debrief with Aunt Rose identifying what went well and what she would like to change next time.
- Amanda will continue the above steps until she has a job

Action Step 8: When a job is offered, plan for starting new job.
- Family will celebrate! Dinner out at Amanda's choice of restaurant.
- Two days before starting: Again prepare clothes and gather documents (Social Security card, next-of-kin info, etc.).
- Day before starting job: Talk with Aunt Rose about any worries.
- Start job!

2. Take a baking class at the local community college.

Action Step 1: Submit application to college.
- July 15: Amanda will go online and explore the website of the community college, with special attention to baking classes offered in the fall, the application process, and information needed for accommodations for disability.
- July 18: Amanda will submit her application online.
- Application accepted! Another family celebration.

Action Step 2: Amanda will arrange an appointment with Disability Support Services on campus.
- August 1: Amanda will make an appointment with the Disability Services office on campus and send documentation of her disability.
- August 7: Amanda and Mom will attend the appointment with the disability support services counselor and develop her accommodations.

Action Step 3: Amanda will register for and start her class.
- August 10: Amanda will register for her baking class. Dad will pay the tuition.
- August 28: Amanda will start her class and share information about her accommodations with the instructor.

3. Visit the nearby Culinary Arts Institute.

Action Step 1: Amanda will arrange for a visit.
- Sept. 15: Amanda will explore the Culinary Art Institute website to learn more about the program and find out how to make an appointment to visit.

- Sept. 20: Amanda will check schedules with Mom and Dad and make an appointment to visit.

Action Step 2: Amanda and her parents will visit the Culinary Art Institute.
- Oct. 9: Amanda will visit the Institute with Mom and Dad.
- Oct. 10: Mom, Dad, and Amanda will talk about the visit and debrief over dinner.
- Jan 1: Amanda will decide if she wants to apply to the Institute for fall admission.

Amanda's Life Skill Goals

1. Amanda will learn to drive.

Action Step 1: Amanda will take the written test for her learner's permit.
- May 1: Amanda will download the study guide from the Motor Vehicle Administration to study.
- May 10: Amanda will make sure she has the documentation needed to present to the Motor Vehicle Administration (school form and birth certificate).
- May 12: Mom will take Amanda to the DMV to take her learner's test.

Action Step 2: Amanda will arrange for a driving school class.
- June 20: Amanda will explore what driving classes are available nearby.
- June 22: Amanda will present her two favorite choices and the costs to Mom and Dad. Make a choice with Mom and Dad.
- June 25: Amanda will apply to the driving school and Dad will pay the costs.
- July 1: Amanda will start driving school.

Action Step 3: Amanda will practice driving with Mom.
- July 1–Aug. 30: Amanda and Mom will spend 1 hour every day practicing driving and keep a log of the hours.

Action Step 4: Amanda will take her driving test once she has accumulated the number of hours required.
- Sept. 1: Amanda will check the DMV website and decide on some possible times to take the driving test.
- Sept. 1: Amanda will check with Mom and Dad to make sure she has transportation.
- Sept. 6: Amanda will take the test.
- Repeat as necessary
- Test Passed: Celebrate.

2. Amanda will manage her own finances.

Action Step 1: Amanda will set up a checking account and obtain a debit card.
- June 25: Amanda and Dad will go to the bank to set up a checking account in her name and get a debit card. Amanda will deposit $50 from her babysitting money and allowance saved.
- June 25: Dad will set up a transfer Amanda's allowance into her account until she has a job and can deposit her paycheck.

Action Step 2: Amanda will begin to manage her paycheck and some of her bills.
- First paycheck: Amanda will make arrangements to have her paycheck automatically deposited into her account.
- One month after first paycheck: Dad will stop depositing allowance into the account.

- One month after first paycheck: Amanda will become responsible for her part of her cell phone bill each month.
- Three months after first paycheck: Amanda will open a savings account and put in 10% of her paycheck to save spending money for the trip to Italy.

3. Amanda will reach out to make new friends.

Action Step 1: Amanda will identify and join new groups to increase the likelihood of making friends.
- Oct. 5: Amanda will join the culinary club at the community college.
- Nov. 1: Amanda will look for and join an online group interested in Italy.
- Dec. 1: Amanda will identify a volunteer opportunity that she thinks will be interesting and sign up for volunteering.

Amanda's Adventure and Fun Goals

1. Amanda and Mom will take a two-week culinary tour of Italy.

Action Step 1: Amanda will identify and choose the group tour.
- Oct. 1: Amanda and Mom will explore travel options to Italy with a focus on culinary interests.
- Oct. 15: Amanda and Mom will develop a budget for the trip.
- Nov. 1: Amanda and Mom will decide on a tour for the spring and make the arrangements. A travel agent may be useful to help.

Action Step 2: Amanda will prepare for the trip.
- Dec. 1: Amanda will find out what travel documents are necessary (passport, visa, etc.) and apply for these documents.
- Jan. 1: Amanda will begin to research information about the areas of Italy they will be visiting and share with Mom.
- April 1: Amanda will develop a list of items to take with her.
- April 15: Amanda will shop for new clothes and travel items needed for the trip.

Action Step 3: Amanda and Mom will go to Italy.
- May: The trip! Enjoy.

2. Amanda will buy a used car.

Action Step 1: Amanda and Dad will decide on a budget for purchasing a car.
- Nov.: Amanda and Dad will develop a budget, looking at her take-home pay from her part-time job and the projected cost of a car, gas, maintenance, and car insurance.
- Nov.: Mom and Dad will contribute $5,000 to purchasing a car.
- Nov.: Amanda and Dad will figure out how much she can spend on a car and be able to cover car payments, gas, maintenance, and car insurance.

Action Step 2: Amanda and Dad will shop for a used car with the intent of learning the costs and the types of cars that interest Amanda.
- Dec./Jan.: Amanda will explore used car sales on the internet.
- Dec.: Dad will teach Amanda how to look up a car's value via Blue Book and Consumer Reports.

- Jan.: Dad will help Amanda develop a list of questions to ask dealers and owners.
- Jan.,/Feb.: Amanda and Dad will make several visits to used car dealers to check out cars.

Action Step 3: Amanda will negotiate a loan for the remainder of the cost of the car.
- Feb.: Once Amanda has a firm grasp on her budget and her income from her part-time job, she and Dad will visit her bank to explore the possibility of a loan. Dad is willing to cosign, with the understanding she is responsible for all payments.
- Feb.: Amanda will fill out the loan application and all supporting documents. Dad will review before submitting to the bank.

Action Step 4: Amanda will buy a car.
- March: Amanda will choose and purchase a car with Dad's consultation.
- Celebrate purchase of car!

Action Step 5: Amanda will arrange for car insurance.
- Feb./March: Amanda will contact the family insurance agent and talk with him about the need for car insurance and costs.
- Purchase of car: Amanda will immediately purchase car insurance.

3. **Amanda will visit her friend Judy at Judy's college.**

Action Step 1: Amanda will talk with Judy to find a good time to visit during the winter.
- Thanksgiving: Amanda will get together with Judy over the Thanksgiving holiday and decide on a date for the visit in February.

Action Step 2: Amanda will make travel arrangements.
- Jan. 5: Amanda will check out options for traveling to Judy's college and discuss with Dad.
- Jan. 15: Amanda will make and pay for the arrangements to travel alone for the trip.

Action Step 3: Amanda will visit Judy at her college.
Feb.: Amanda will visit Judy. Enjoy!

Appendix 5
Gap Year Planning Form

Note: Include as many objectives and steps as you need. The level of detail can vary a lot depending on the individual's needs and goals, but do assign responsibility and beginning dates for each step. Dates can always be adjusted and will help keep participant(s) engaged and involved throughout the year.

Vocational Goals:

Objective 1:

    Action Step 1:

    Action Step 2:

    Action Step 3:

Objective 2:

    Action Step 1:

    Action Step 2:

    Action Step 3:

Objective 3:

    Action Step 1:

    Action Step 2:

    Action Step 3:

Life Skills Goals:

Objective 1:

    Action Step 1:

    Action Step 2:

    Action Step 3:

Objective 2:

    Action Step 1:

    Action Step 2:

    Action Step 3:

Objective 3:

    Action Step 1:

    Action Step 2:

    Action Step 3:

Adventure and Fun Goals:

Objective 1:

    Action Step 1:

    Action Step 2:

    Action Step 3:

Objective 2:

    Action Step 1:

    Action Step 2:

    Action Step 3:

Objective 3:

    Action Step 1:

    Action Step 2:

    Action Step 3:

Resources

Many students with ADHD may be overwhelmed with school and unlikely to use resources listed in this section. So the responsibility often falls on parents to review resources of interest, become familiar with their content, and then share helpful information with their children or teens, teachers, ADHD coaches or treatment professionals. Educational materials that were created specifically for young people with ADHD or parents who do not have a lot of time to read are noted with an asterisk. In addition to this book, the following resources may be helpful.

ADHD and Executive Function

Teenagers with ADD, ADHD, and Executive Function Deficits: A Guide for Parents and Professionals. Chris A. Zeigler Dendy. 3rd ed. Woodbine House, 2017. www.chrisdendy.com

A reference book appropriate for parents (and teachers) of preteens and teens that covers everything including the kitchen sink: diagnosis, executive functions, treatment, medications, home challenges, legal rights under the law, accommodations, etc.

Late, Lost, and Unprepared: A Parents' Guide to Helping Children with Executive Functioning. Joyce Cooper-Kahn and Laurie Dietzel. Woodbine House, 2008.

Discusses what executive functions are, symptoms of EF difficulties and the assessment process, then delves into practical suggestions for handling specific EF problems such as getting started, shifting gears, controlling impulses and planning and organizing. Strategies can be used both at home and at school.

Executive Functions: What They Are, How They Work, and Why They Evolved. Russell A. Barkley. Guilford Press, 2012.

Provides a comprehensive theory of executive functioning (EF) with important clinical implications. Barkley describes how abilities such as emotion regulation, self-motivation, planning, and working memory enable people to pursue both personal and collective goals that are critical to survival. Key stages of EF development are identified, and the far-reaching individual and social costs of EF deficits detailed.

Smart but Scattered Teens: The "Executive Skills" Program for Helping Teens Reach Their Potential. Richard Guare, Peg Dawson and Colin Guare. Guilford Press, 2013.

Guidance for helping a "smart but scattered" teen grow into a self-sufficient, responsible adult. The book gives parents a positive, science-based program for promoting independence by building executive skills needed to get organized, stay focused and control impulses and emotions.

Advice from People Who Are Living with ADHD

Over her 40-year career, Chris Dendy has developed books and videos with her family that feature the real experts on ADHD: teens and parents sharing the personal lessons they learned while living with ADHD.

A Bird's-Eye View of Life with ADD & ADHD: Ten Years Later. Chris A. Zeigler Dendy and Alex Zeigler. 3rd ed. CAZD Consulting, 2015. www.chrisdendy.com

A humorous, easy-to-read guide packed with cartoons, scientific facts and advice from 12 teenagers. The latest edition of this book provides a peek into the lives of 11 of these young adults some ten years later. A Spanish translation is available from TDAH Valles at info@tdahvalles.org.

Father to Father: Expert Advice on ADHD (DVD). Chris A. Zeigler Dendy and Alex Zeigler (with film clips from Clark R. Hill). CAZD Consulting, 2014. www.chrisdendy.com" www.chrisdendy.com

Four dads (two with ADHD and two with military backgrounds) talk about living day to day with children and teens with ADD and ADHD and speak candidly about the mistakes they made. The men describe their child's strengths; sources of conflict such as school problems, homework battles and conflicts between parents; the self-doubts that plague most parents; and benefits and concerns regarding medications. Tommy Dendy, a US Naval Academy graduate, gives a military dad's perspective on discipline.

Real Life ADHD! A Survival Guide for Children and Teens (DVD). Chris A. Zeigler Dendy and Alex Zeigler. CAZD Consulting, 2011. www.chrisdendy.com

A wonderful companion resource for *A Bird's-Eye View*, this DVD features advice on six ADHD challenges from real experts—a diverse group of 30 young people ranging in age from 12 to 21. Dr. Theodore Mandelkorn, MD, an ADHD specialist, also describes his experiences treating and personally living with ADHD. Chris's son Alex and his best friend, Lewis Alston, both of whom have ADHD, host the DVD. Lewis narrated the video, and Alex filmed and edited the video.

Anxiety and Depression

As discussed in Chapter 6, it's important for you to learn about anxiety and depression, their underlying causes and possible ways to reduce anxiety and feelings of depression. Parents may want to read the books below for key takeaways to share with their teen or young adult. Of course, some young people with ADHD will be interested in reviewing the books themselves and selecting helpful strategies.

The Anti-Test Anxiety Society. Julia Cook. National Center for Youth Issues, 2014.

This book, appropriate for younger students, tells the story of Bertha, a student who has test anxiety, and the teacher who helps her learn specific strategies for reducing her anxiety.

The Dialectical Behavior Therapy Skills Workbook: Practical DBT Exercises for Learning Mindfulness, Interpersonal Effectiveness, Emotion Regulation. Matthew McKay, Jeffrey Wood, and Jeff Brantley. New Harbinger Publications, 2019.

This book may be helpful for those who struggle with intense emotional reactions. It teaches the strategies and skills of dialectical behavior therapy, a branch of cognitive behavioral therapy that focuses on emotions. It explains how to manage emotional responses, tolerate negative feelings and communicate more effectively with others.

Conquer Anxiety Workbook for Teens: Find Peace from Worry, Panic, Fear, and Phobias. Tabatha Chansard. Althea Press, 2019.

This book arms teens with effective tools to tackle worrying—so that anxiety doesn't have to be overwhelming. Using the latest strategies from CBT (cognitive behavioral therapy) and mindfulness therapies, the author helps teens learn how to manage their thoughts, emotions and behaviors so that they don't trigger anxiety.

Control Your Depression. Peter Lewinsohn, Ricardo Munoz, Mary Ann Youngren, and Antonette Zeiss. Simon & Schuster, 1992.

The authors help guide you through understanding and taking control of your depression, pinpointing the specific areas that are problematic. They offer strategies to manage these feelings, whether due to social situations, troublesome thoughts, relationships, lack of motivation or other causes.

Feeling Great: The Revolutionary New Treatment for Depression and Anxiety. David Burns. PESI Publishing and Media, 2020.

Dr. Burns is one of the leading authors addressing anxiety and depression for both clinicians and people experiencing these disorders. In this book, he helps readers understand the dynamics of anxiety and depression and develop strategies to alleviate these feelings using techniques based on cognitive behavioral therapy and state-of-the-art research on depression and anxiety.

"I Know What to Do When I'm Feeling ..." Positive Parenting, 2018.

This illustrated flipbook, appropriate for elementary and middle school students, helps children recognize and respond appropriately to their emotions. The book helps children identify feelings such as anger, worry, fear, frustration, embarrassment and sadness. Available from https://thought-spot.com.

Raising Human Beings. Ross Greene. Harper Collins, 2017.

Written for parents of hard to reach children, this book explores ways to have a better relationship and be more effective parents.

The Explosive Child. Ross Greene. Harper Collins, 2014.

Dr. Greene focuses on helping parents reach children who are often frustrated, angry, and unresponsive to usual parenting strategies. He offers advice on reconnecting with children in a more productive way.

School Issues and Special Education (K-12)

*Know Your Rights: Students with ADHD. US Department of Education. July 2016. *www2.ed.gov/about/offices/list/ocr/docs/dcl-know-rights-201607-504.pdf.*

Explains that regardless of grades, trouble "concentrating, reading, thinking, organizing, or prioritizing projects," students in the United States may be protected under Section 504 of the Rehabilitation Act and must be evaluated.

Letter and Resource Guide on Students with ADHD. Department of Education (DOE), Office of Civil Rights (OCR). July 26, 2016. *www.ed.gov/about/offices/list/ocr/letters/colleague-201607-504-adhd.pdf.*

The letter, which gives policy guidance to states and school systems, states that ADHD students are underserved and clarifies the circumstances of eligibility for many more students for supports under Section 504 of the Rehabilitation Act.

Teaching Teens with ADD, ADHD, and Executive Function Deficits: A Quick Reference Guide for Teachers and Parents. Chris A. Zeigler Dendy. 2nd ed. www.chrisdendy.com

A one-stop resource for tips on academic challenges, executive function deficits, federal laws, helpful accommodations, developing an education plan (IEP or Section 504 plan), note taking, coping with disorganization, enhancing memory deficits, study strategies, medication issues time management, test taking, and problem-solving strategies.

Teenagers with ADD, ADHD, and Executive Function Deficits. Chris A. Zeigler Dendy. 3rd ed. Woodbine House, 2017. www.chrisdendy.com

Several chapters are devoted to school-related information—for example, homework battles, common learning challenges, effective interventions and accommodations, tips for communicating with the school and in-depth information on IEPs and 504 plans. The popular ADHD Iceberg plus helpful forms are included in the Appendix.

Wrightslaw.com. www.wrightslaw.com.

Attorneys Pete and Pam Wright are highly respected experts on education law and offer popular training programs throughout the United States. Their website offers a wealth of information that is helpful to parents and educators alike. Of particular interest are their many articles on ADHD and special education topics (www.wrightslaw.com/info/add.index.htm).

Succeeding in College

College: Continuing and Higher Education. Wrightslaw.com, November 25, 2019. www. wrightslaw.com/info/college.index.htm.
This article on the Wrightslaw website offers links and descriptions for dozens of online publications and organizations that can be helpful in understanding issues such as accommodations for the SAT/ACT, applying to college, accommodations at college, LD issues, legal rights and more.

*How to ADHD (YouTube videos). Jessica McCabe. https://www.youtube.com/c/HowtoADHD/videos.

McCabe, an actress with ADHD, has a YouTube channel devoted to ADHD and has recorded a series of videos, including on these topics: "How to Take Notes," "How to Study" and "How to Take a Test."

*How to Succeed in College Despite Being ADHD (YouTube video). Ben Glenn. 2013. https://www.youtube.com/watch?v=NhfG38pNkgc.

A five-minute pep talk for young people with ADHD about leaving home for a four-year college. Glenn, a motivational speaker with ADHD, stresses the need to be responsible and seek out accommodations.

*On Your Own: A College Readiness Guide for Teens with ADHD/LD. Patricia O. Quinn and Theresa E. Laurie Maitland. Magination Press, 2011.

As in their book for parents (listed next), Quinn and Maitland provide a checklist of specific independent living skills that enhance the likelihood of college success. The book also includes worksheets to help teens map out a plan and practice the skills needed for college success.

Ready for Take-Off: Preparing Your Teen with ADHD or LD for College. Theresa E. Laurie Maitland and Patricia O. Quinn. Magination Press, 2011.

Written by a college disability specialist and a developmental pediatrician, this book helps parents and teens create and implement a "Personalized College Readiness Program." Realistically, many high school graduates with ADHD will not have mastered all the skills needed for independent living, but the authors provide guidance so students with ADHD or LD acquire as many key skills as possible before entering college. The book includes a useful checklist of specific independent living skills that enhance the likelihood of college success.

Teenagers with ADD, ADHD, and Executive Function Deficits. Chris A. Zeigler Dendy. 3rd ed. Woodbine House, 2017. www.chrisdendy.com

Although this one-stop resource on ADHD and executive function focuses on the middle and high school years, it also includes detailed information on college, including admissions tests, choosing an appropriate college, medications, legal rights, eligibility for accommodations, and helpful strategies for success.

Getting and Keeping a Job

Americans with Disabilities Act: A Guide for People with Disabilities Seeking Employment. October 2000. https://www.ada.gov/workta.htm

Common questions and answers about rights and accommodations under the ADA.

Job Accommodation Network. www.askjan.org

The Job Accommodation Network is a good place to learn more about ADA and job accommodations for people with specific disabilities. A variety of helpful publications, including "Employees with Attention Deficit/Hyperactivity Disorder," can be downloaded.

O*NET Online. https://www.onetonline.org/

This Department of Labor site gives lots in information about every possible career including salaries, educational and licensing requirements, and predictions of future growth. It's a great resource when investigating career possibilities.

The Muse. www.themuse.com.

A job search and career counseling website that bills itself as "the go-to destination for the next gen workforce to research companies and careers." You can conduct job searches locally or nationwide and get advice on topics such as common interview questions: https://www.themuse.com/advice/interview-questions-and-answers.

Undergraduate Student Career Guide. Georgia State University Career Advancement Center. 2020. https://robinson.gsu.edu/files/2020/07/Undergraduate-Career-Guide.pdf.

Although developed for students at Georgia State, this online handbook also includes general information on what sorts of jobs you can obtain with various majors, conducting a job search, "branding" yourself, resume development and career advancement.

US Bureau of Labor Statistics. www.bls.gov.

As mentioned throughout the book, the US Bureau of Labor Statistics website is a wonderful source of information on salaries, occupations and careers that will be in demand in coming years. The site also includes a student-oriented section that is designed to help young people explore possible careers: www.bls.gov/k12/students/.

What Color Is Your Parachute? A Practical Manual for Job-Hunters and Career-Changers. Richard N. Bolles. Ten Speed Press, 2020.

The latest edition of the classic guide features resources, case studies and perspectives on today's job market, with advice on the most effective job-hunting strategies. The book includes a self-inventory to help users figure out what careers best fit their passions, skills and traits, as well as tips on writing résumés and cover letters, networking effectively, interviewing and negotiating a salary.

Index

Pages in *italics* refer to figures.

504 plans *see* Section 504 plans

Abney, B. 89
Academic and Behavioral Performance Rating
  Scale 36–39, 216
accommodations, college: applying for 149,
  152; common 151, 154; memos 154;
  notifying instructors of 152, 159–160; office
  that authorizes 148–149, 152
accommodations, job: disclosing need for 179,
  185–186; examples of 179–182, 184–185;
  requesting 185
accommodations, pre-college: Definition 28;
  examples of 26, 28; for ACT/SAT 151
accommodations, reasonable 184
ACT 150–151
activities; *see also* Talents/interests; School 85–86
ADDA-SR 36, 45, 52
ADDitude (magazine) 45
ADHD: age at diagnosis 26; books on 219–220;
  best treatment for 35; brain maturity 1–3,
  15; challenges 11–19; coexisting conditions
  14; disclosing to employer 179, 185–186;
  educating coworkers about 185–186; iceberg
  13, *14*, 27, 52, 87, 123, 207; review with
  teen 87; medication 35–39; NIMH study on
  36; notifying school about 84; racial
  disparities in diagnosis 31; reframing 3,
  45–46; support groups 47, 52; stigma of
  185–186; underdiagnosis 19, 31–32
ADHD, inattentive type: anxiety/depression 32,
  63; characteristics 19, 31–33, 104; in girls
  31–33; underdiagnosis 31
ADHD, young people with; *see also* Social skills;
  developmental delays 15–16; educating about
  ADHD 44–45; gifted 16, 19, 30, 34; girls
  31–33; overview of challenges 12–25; talents
  and interests of 42–53; traits to nurture 50
adulthood, age of 202
alarms 21, 23–24, 86, 119, 179–181
Aldrich, Jason F. 168
Alston, Lewis 46, 202

American Academy of Pediatrics 63
American Job Center 133, 171
Americans with Disabilities Act 28, 31, 123,
  152, 184–185, 224
anger *see* Emotions
anxiety; *see also* Stress; books on 220–221;
  counseling for 73; failure 59; impact on sleep
  19, 66; incidence of 63; in parents 76;
  medications for 73–74; more severe 69;
  self-help strategies 67–69; strategies to reduce
  64; symptoms of 66
apprenticeships: Examples 91–92; in high school
  81, 90–91; overview of 114
apps: as accommodation 155; for depression 72,
  73; for stress/anxiety 69–70; goal-setting
  171; reminder 27, 180; sleep 23
assessments: disagreements about 30; for special
  education 27, 29; for college 119–124
assistance, accepting 179, 189–190, 197
ASVAB 82, 99–100
Attention (magazine) 45
Auburn University 149, 159

Bandy, Judy 86
Barkley, Russell 2, 8–10, 12, 15–17, 19, 20, 32,
  45, 54, 56, 58–60, 74, 190, 219
Beacon College 136–137
behavior; *see also* Emotions; as communication
  43, 106; at college 192–193; discontinuing
  meds 198; executive function *14*; impulsive
  17, 46, 74, 126, 187, 192, 194, 195; laziness
  16, 18, 45, 164; rating scale 29, 36, 39, 217;
  reframing 3, 45–46; suicidal 63, 66, 70, 74–76
behavioral strategies 8, 67
bipolar disorder 13, 30, 198
Bird's Eye View of Life with ADHD 45, 220
bosses *see* Supervisors
brain: continued maturation 3–4, 12, 15–16, 87;
  delayed maturity of 15–16, 87, 110; impact
  of ADHD on 3–4, 12, 15–16; impact of
  sports on 47; impact of stress on 4
bullying 19, 62, 63, 65, 66, 70

calendars 71, 86, 180, 181
camps 92–93
career counseling 100, 172, 224
career exploration; *see also* Vocational interests;
    college/career academies 90; discussions
    about 94; engaging teen in 104–106;
    importance 94, 96, 134; interning/
    volunteering 90–92; STEM programs 89–90;
    summer classes/camps 93–94; summer jobs
    93; visiting workplaces 94
Career One Stop 171
career services office 149, 167–168
careers; *see also* Jobs; ADHD-friendly 97–98;
    ADHD unfriendly 103; construction 90, 98,
    112, 145; determining appropriate 101–103;
    discussions about 94; guidance at college
    162–163; high-tech 147; in demand 103,
    145–147; income potential 103, 146;
    interesting/unique 94; manufacturing 98, 138,
    143, 145; nursing 143; sample salaries 146;
    STEM 90; vocational testing 82–83, 99–101
cell phones 17, 23, 37, 64, 129, 132, 161, 180
certificate programs 136, 138, 141, 142
CHADD 7, 12, 36, 45, 52, 53, 186
classes: dropping/adding 110, 152, 166;
    extracurricular 85; online 150, 151;
    scheduling 84; selecting 80, 155; waiving 155
Clippinger, Shawn 202
coaches: ADHD 67, 129, 134, 189, 197;
    Academic 54, 158–159; executive function
    136–137; job search 171; sports 47–49, 98
coexisting conditions *see* ADHD
cognitive behavior therapy 59, 72, 73
college; *see also* Accommodations; College
    readiness; ProfessorsADHD- and LD-specific
    137; admission to 136; applying to 151–152;
    aptitude tests 99, 100, 150–151; career
    guidance office 149, 162, 167; community
    college 140–147; compared to high school
    122; degrees 135, 138, 145; difficulties caused
    by ADHD 117–118; disability services 144,
    148; expenses 144; failure 118, 140, 164–165,
    187–200; financial aid 152; four-year vs.
    university 135–136; guides 137; majors 148;
    medical services at 150; medication
    management at 160; parent involvement at
    157; placement tests 151; premature launch
    110; problems at 164–166; purpose of 116,
    161–162; reasons to delay 124–125;
    residential options 136, 150, 158, 191;
    resources on 222–223; roommate 150; safety
    net at 163–164; selecting 148–150; support
    needs at 157–158; switching to new 193
college alternatives; *see also* Gap year; Jobs;
    apprenticeships 90–93; GED 112, 114;
    income linked 112; military service 92, 102,
    113; transition to 117–118

college readiness: academic skills 119–124;
    delays in 108–109; disagreement about
    190–191; financial management 121,
    194–195; life skills 120–121; self-advocacy
    skills 123–124; social skills 121; vocational
    awareness 124
College Readiness Survey 120, 122, 124, 125,
    191, 208–211
communication: about emotions 64–65;
    important skills 55; parent-child 43, 189
community college: benefits of 137, 141–147;
    certificate programs 142; costs 138; examples
    of programs 142–143; examples of salaries
    146; need for highly-skilled 146; reasons to
    attend 140, 144; supports at 144; two-year
    degrees 142
computer; *see also* Apps; as accommodation
    154; skills 49, 147
consequences *see* Behavioral strategies
Consoli, Aidan 48, 68
construction work 90, 98, 112, 145
conversation skills 57
counseling: at college 100, 144; career 81, 100,
    101, 149; for parents 64; for young people
    64, 73, 158, 193, 196, 198–199
courses *see* Classes
crises 53, 63, 84, 158, 163, 166, 199
criticism, avoiding 8, 54
cyberbullying 65–66; *see also* Bullying

daydreaming 19, 31, 33, 36, 62
deadlines: flexible 154; missing 13, 151, 178,
    179; reminders of 69, 151
defiance 59–60
Denckla, Martha 2–4, 15, 78, 79
Dendy, Chris 5, 8, 36, 46, 125, 154, 208, 220
Dendy, Hunter 204
Dendy, Sandra 143
Dendy, Steven 143
Dendy, Tommy 220
depression: books on 220–221; counseling for
    64, 69–70, 73; incidence of 63; in parents
    76–77; self-help for 71–73; strategies to
    reduce 64–66; suicidal behavior and 74–76;
    symptoms of 70
developmental delays 15
dialectical behavior therapy 59, 73, 221
Didier, Jeremy 188
Didier, Sophie 188
disability support services 81, 144, 149
DISC assessment 100
disclosing ADHD 179, 184–186
discrimination, job 185
distractibility 183, 186
doctors *see* Physicians
Dodson, William 60
DOE letter on ADHD 222

Driving 52, 128, 133, 192, 198
dropping out 110, 118, 192
drug abuse 131, 160, 161
Duryea, Carly 55, 110, 111
Duryea, Kathleen 37
Duryea, Kendal 104

Edge Foundation 159
educational consultant 30, 40, 186
electronics, blue light from 23
emojis 64
emotional disturbance 30
emotions, parents: anger 43, 187, 189, 199;
    extreme 76; guilt 8; managing 187; self-
    doubt 187
emotions, teen's/young adult's: anger 59, 196;
    controlling 12, 59–60; guilt 191; increasing
    awareness of 65–66; job loss and 200;
    overreactive 60; unwillingness to discuss 201
employment *see* Careers, Jobs
employment projections 146
evaluation *see* Assessment
executive functions: academic challenges 16;
    books about 219; components of 17; delay in
    15, 79; educating about 45; external supports
    for 79–80, 86; function of 15–19; incidence
    of deficits 15; increased demands on 78;
    school performance and 15–19, 26–27
exercise 22, 39, 68, 71, 98
expectations: after dropping meds 198; as cause
    of stress 3, 65; changing 35; educational 78,
    79; realistic 3, 44

Facebook 52, 53, 65, 170
FAFSA 152
failure 39, 40, 52, 60, 63, 74; *see also* School
    failure
failure to launch 2
Father to Father 220
Fennell, Max 204
financial aid 152
financial management: Basic 194–195; job-
    related 175; skills needed for college 121,
    191–192; student loans 194–195
Focus 2, 102
forgetfulness 21, 34, 46, 165, 183, 185
Fortnite 58
Fox, Michael J. 117
friends; *see also* Social skills; difficulties making
    21, 60, 61; finding/bonding with 57–58, 62;
    importance of 55, 60; withdrawal from 61,
    75, 77

gap year programs: after leaving college 193;
    benefits of 110; developing 127–129; dos and
    don'ts of 126–127; examples of 129–134,
    212–216; formal vs. personalized 111–113;

goals 128; parent's role in 127; planning
    form 212–216; plus community college 110
GED 112, 113
Georgia State University 162, 168, 224
gifted students 19, 34, 37
girls with ADHD 19, 31–33, 58, 60–61, 74
goals: career 117; daily 171; gap year 128; IEP/
    Section 35; long-term 96; transition 81
Grabowski, Ashley 100, 162, 163
Grabowski, Nathan 204
grades, academic 33, 40, 42, 44, 70, 74, 78, 193
graduate programs 135
Green, Perry 85, 203
Green, Robert 205
Greene, Ross 190
Grounding 69
Guerin, Ryan 83
guided imagery 69

Harding, Sydney 167
Hart, Amelia 45, 203
health care; *see also* Medications; at college 150;
    insurance 175; privacy laws 121, 199
help, accepting 189–190, 196–197
high school: career academies 90; demands
    during 78, 79; future planning during 86;
    IEP/504 plans during 28–30; medication
    adjustments in 79; self-advocacy skills for
    86–87; STEM programs 89–90; transitioning
    to 2, 83–87
HIPAA 203
homework: difficulties completing 8, 15, 16, 26,
    29, 31, 35; medication and 36–37, 39;
    readiness for college 119, 193; taking breaks
    from 69
Howard Community College 123, 144
Howell, Tyler 204
Hughes, Christopher 6, 87, 105, 120, 134, 159,
    162, 189, 194, 198, 201
Hughes, Ruth 6, 144
human resources 187

Iceberg, ADHD *see* ADHD, iceberg
IDEA: Eligibility 29–30; Emotional Disturbance
    (ED) 30; mitigating measures 32; Other
    Health Impairment (OHI) 29; purpose of 28;
    transition services 80–82
IEPs 27–31, 34–36, 80, 87
impulsivity *see* Behavior
inattentive *see* ADHD, inattentive type
independence: and basic living skills 119; and
    residential options 125; expectations for 79;
    managing ADHD 121–122; time needed to
    develop 124–125
instructions, remembering 18, 179, 181, 184
insurance, health 175
internet safety 57

internships, high school 81, 90–93
interviews 162, 171–173
IQ 16, 29, 31

Jacksonville State University 155
Jennings, Bryan 114
Job Accommodation Network 182, 185, 186, 224
job accommodations *see* Accommodations
job boards/search engines 169–170
job clubs 171
Job Corps 112, 113, 114
job shadowing 81, 130
jobs; *see also* Careers; ADHD disclosure 173, 184; Accepting 173; Accommodations 179–182; assistance in keeping 174; being fired from 195–196; common challenges 179; during high school 93; finding good match 180, 168–169, 178; in demand 145–146; interpersonal problems 177–178; interviewing for 162–163, 171–172; plans for success 183–184; sampling 114; searching for 161, 167–171; soft skills 174; starting new 174; stigma and 185–186; vocational rehabilitation 81, 101, 171; work ethic 174
Jones, Jonathan 112
junior high *see* Middle school

Karlgaard, Rich 3

labor statistics 96, 145–146, 224
Landmark College 136
late bloomers 3–4
laziness *see* Behavior
learning disabilities: giftedness and 34; IDEA eligibility and 30; Incidence 13, 15; job accommodations for 184
Learning Disabilities Association (LDA) 52
Letter, Policyfrom DOE 222
Liebel, Spencer 63
life skills 120–122, 126, 138
light: blue 22; waking to 23; for SAD 72
likeability 55–57
LinkedIn 93, 169, 170
Lives in the Balance 190
loans, student 195
lockbox 163
losing things 33, 181
Lynn University 137

Maitland, Theresa 124, 208, 223
majors, college 102, 117, 135, 136, 144, 148, 149, 155, 162, 163
manufacturing careers 90, 92, 98, 103, 138, 145–146
MAPP 82, 100
Massey, Tamara 160

McMurray, Chad 202
Mediation 31
medical care *see* Health care
medications, ADHD: Adderall 36–38; abuse of 160; Concerta 36, 38; effects of 36, 56; managing at college 121, 160–161, 193; on the job 179; refusing 198; Ritalin 36, 37, 39; safeguarding 161, 193; sharing 193–194; tolerance 79; Vyvance 36, 38
medications, anxiety/depression 73–74
meditation, mindfulness 71
melatonin 20, 22, 23
memory, working: definition of 16; difficulties with 16, 17, 39, 151; reducing demands on 17
mentors 17
middle school: increasing demands in 78–79; medication adjustments in 79; medication fine-tuning 79; monitoring performance in 80; self-advocacy skills for 86; transitioning to 2, 79–81
Mike Rowe Works 145
military service 83, 99, 103, 113
mitigating measures 31
Moore, Tatum 143
Mt. Saint Joseph University 137
MTA study 36, 63
Murphy, Jill 86, 87
Muse, the 172, 224
Music 23, 67, 68, 93, 98

names, forgetting 182
National Resource Center on ADHD 186
negative thinking, reframe 72
Nelson, Jason 63
Northwest Georgia College and Career Academy 89
note taking 155
nursing 140, 142, 145

online classes 150
oppositional defiant disorder 60
organization 118, 119, 158, 159, 210
other health impairment (OHI) *see* IDEA

PACER Center 82
parent survey 2
parents; *see also* Emotions; ADHD education for 44–45; attitudes of 4; criticism of 8–9, 87; developmentally appropriate support 87; guilt trips 8; helicopter 8–9; involvement of 9, 40, 87–88, 163–164; limit setting and 43; nurture self 52; parenting ups and downs 7, 76; relationship with child 43, 187–189, 199; role in monitoring school progress 34–35; role in troubleshooting work issues 177–178; support for 52–53

passions *see* Talents/interests
Paxon, Marie 7
personality tests 100–101
physicians: finding new 175; medication plans and 198–199; prescribing drugs at college 121, 160–161
pinterest 65
Pittsburgh Inst. of Aeronautics 141
priorities, setting 180
privileges, earning 129
problem-solving 123, 190, 196–197
problems, hiding 189
processing speed 16, 17, 29, 33, 39, 66, 154
procrastination 118, 180
professions *see* Careers
professors: no parent contact with 157; notifying of accommodations 123, 159; selecting 150, 155
psychologists 101
punishment 8, 39

Quinn, Patricia 31, 32, 124, 209, 223

reading problems 15, 16, 18, 19, 40, 144, 155, 182
reading software 155
Ready for Take-Off 124, 208, 223
Real Life ADHD 220
rejection, sensitivity to 57
relationships *see* Friends, Social skills
relaxation strategies 23, 69, 71
reminders: camouflaged 164; medication 161–162; need for 10, 17, 151
resilience 50
résumés 149, 162, 168, 169
rewards 170
Robertson, Erik 203
Robertson, Sammie 212
Rock, Alyssa 211
role-playing 57–58
Rowe, Mike 145
Rowland, Tina 158
Royal, Kendrick 109
Royal, Khris 44, 202

Salaries 145, 146, 169
SAT 136, 144, 150–151
Schmidt, Kati 203
Seasonal Affective Disorder 72
school; *see also* Middle school; High school; Homeworkaddressing problems at 27; documenting ADHD with 27, 29, 30, 84; executive function deficits and 16–18; failure 26, 40, 192–193; learning challenges at 16–17; medication use at 38; monitoring progress at 36–39; parent support and 39;

readiness 1, 85–86; resources on 222; suspension 84
Section 504; and college supports 123; purpose 28–29, 152; scope of 222–223; transition planning 80
Section 504 plans 27, 29, 34–35, 80, 84
self-advocacy 81, 82, 86, 123
self-esteem 26, 40, 42–53, 57
shyness 19, 60
sleep disturbances 19–23
sleep stages 20
small businesses 185
smart speakers 23
SOAR 112
social emotional learning 65
social media 62, 63, 65, 170
social networking sites 169, 170
social skills: controlling emotions 59–60; difficulties with 19, 54, 59; enhancing 56–58; gender differences 60–61; lagging skills 12–24; likeability and 55–56; needed at collegenm 121
soft skills 124, 174
sports 47, 49
STEM programs 89–90
Stigma 185–186
stress; *see also* Anxiety; reducing 65–69; sources of 62–63, 124; vs. anxiety 66
Strong Vocational Interest Inventory 99
suicidal risk 63; warning signs 74–76
sunlight 67
supervision, appropriate 9
supervisors: discussing problems with 179; getting along with 174, 178; supportive 173
support, appropriate 87
supports *see* Accommodations
suspension 84

talents/interests 43–53, 108, 110, 124, 174, 201; Promoting 84–86
teachers; *see also* Professors; as mentors 47; communicating with 34, 35, 80; harmful attitudes of 26; meeting with 83–84; requesting specific 84; views on EFD 18
Teaching Teens with ADD, ADHD, & Executive Function Deficits 40, 80, 123, 165, 222
technical colleges *see* Private technical/career colleges
technology 155; *see also* Apps; Computers
Teenagers with ADD, ADHD, and Executive Function Deficits 36, 84, 125, 154, 165, 219
tests: college entrance 144, 150–151; vocational interest 82–83, 99–100, 162

Thomas, Dave 114
time: management 158, 181, 210; sense of 45
time-out 189
timers 181
transition planning 81–82; Pre-employment
    training services 81
transitions, major 1–2, 4–5, 119, 174; middle
    and high school 78, 79
tutoring 123, 137, 144, 155, 158, 191

ultimatums 190
University of the Ozarks 137
US Bureau of Labor Statistics 97, 145, 146, 224

video games 61, 71, 85, 127, 197
videos 220, 223
virtual learning *see* Online classes
vitamin D 72
vocational interests; *see also* Career exploration;
    exploring at school 80; inventories/tests
    82–83, 99–100, 162

vocational rehabilitation 81, 101, 171
volunteering 91, 111–112, 128

waivers, class 155
waking up 19
West Georgia College 155
WIOA 81
work environment 173
work *see* Careers, Jobs
working memory deficits *see* executive
    functions; "Cognitive Counter Space," 17;
    Impact on academics 17–18; Limited
    capacity 17
Wright, Pete and Pam 222
Wurtzel, Claire 17

Year Up 113

Zeigler, Alex 5, 13, 21, 22, 46–47, 49–50, 52,
    64, 78, 164, 201, 220
Zoom 172

For Product Safety Concerns and Information please contact our
EU representative GPSR@taylorandfrancis.com Taylor & Francis
Verlag GmbH, Kaufingerstraße 24, 80331 München, Germany